Social Science Concepts

Social Science Concepts

A User's Guide

∗

GARY GOERTZ

PRINCETON UNIVERSITY PRESS

PRINCETON AND OXFORD

Published by Princeton University Press, 41 William Street, Princeton, New Jersey 08540

In the United Kingdom: Princeton University Press, 3 Market Place, Woodstock, Oxfordshire OX20 1SY

Library of Congress Cataloging-in-Publication Data

Goertz, Gary, 1953–
Social science concepts : a user's guide / Gary Goertz.
p. cm.
Includes bibliographical references and index.
ISBN-13: 978-0-691-12410-0 (cloth : alk. paper)
ISBN-10: 0-691-12410-8 (cloth : alk. paper)
ISBN-13: 978-0-691-12411-7 (pbk. : alk. paper)
ISBN-10: 0-691-12411-6 (pbk. : alk. paper)
1. Social sciences–Research. 2. Qualitative research.
3. Political science–Research.
I. Title.

H62.G575 2006
300′.72–dc22   2005043930

British Library Cataloging-in-Publication Data is available

This book has been composed in Utopia

Printed on acid-free paper. ∞

pup.princeton.edu

Printed in the United States of America

10 9 8 7 6 5 4 3 2 1

✳ *Contents* ✳

* List of Tables *

vii

* List of Figures *

✳ *Acknowledgments* ✳

First, I must thank my coauthors of various chapters. Bill Dixon, Joe Hewitt, and Jim Mahoney contributed extensively to making this a better work and it has been a pleasure to work with them. In more general terms, Andy Bennett, David Collier, Colin Elman, and John Gerring have been supportive throughout and have provided many useful comments on earlier versions of the manuscript. The creation of the Qualitative Methods Section of the American Political Science Association and the annual Training Institute on Qualitative Methods (at Arizona State University) provided an intellectual community receptive and interested in the issues of concepts and their methodology. A couple of the chapters have been presented at the Qualitative Methods Institute and the feedback from the participants has been of great value. Over the years I have had many interesting conversations with Bear Braumoeller and these have contributed significantly to my thinking on many of the topics covered in this volume.

Special thanks must go to Charles Ragin. Charles joined the faculty of the University of Arizona when this book was half done. His input, his books, and his insights have been invaluable. The overall approach taken in this book complements those that he has promoted and defended over the years. In many respects this volume can be seen as a companion work to his *Fuzzy-Set Social Science.*

Finally, I would like to acknowledge my undergraduate mathematics professor and mentor Arnold Wedel, who taught me how mathematics and social sciences can be fruitfully integrated.

Social Science Concepts

Introduction

To define a thing, is to select from among the whole of its
properties those which shall be understood to be designated
and declared by its name; the properties must be very well
known to us before we can be competent to determine which
of them are fittest to be chosen for this purpose.

Every proposition consists of two names [concepts]: and
every proposition affirms or denies one of these names, of the
other.... Here, therefore, we find a new reason why the
signification of names, and the relation generally, between
names and the things signified by them, must occupy the
preliminary stage of the inquiry we are engaged in.

J. S. Mill

JOHN STUART MILL BEGAN his *System of Logic* with a "book" devoted
to concepts. Starting with concepts was a logical choice since they are
some of the main building blocks for constructing theoretical propositions. Propositional logic involves the proper manipulation of symbols. For this to have usefulness in science these symbols need to
be given substantive content. In this book I show how one can construct substantive concepts and discuss the implications for empirical
(qualitative and quantitative) research of different concept structures.

In spite of the primordial importance of concepts, they have received relatively little attention over the years by social scientists.[1]
Giovanni Sartori and David Collier stand out as the dominating figures
in the work on concepts. Yet the contrast with the massive literature
on quantitative measures, indicators, scales, and the like cannot be
more extreme. Hence we have a paradox: as Mill noted, concepts are
a central part of our theories, yet researchers, apart from Sartori and

---

[1]One might inquire about the definition of a concept. Instead of giving a definition
(see Adcock 1998 for a survey), I prefer to define them implicitly through a discussion
of how to construct them. This is roughly analogous to geometric primitives like point
and line which are defined via theorems about them.

Collier, have focused very little attention on social science concepts per se (though see Ragin 2000).

This paradox has arisen in part from the deep differences between quantitative and qualitative scholars. As a matter of the sociology of social science (at least in political science and sociology), qualitative scholars have been most concerned with concepts—which are generally seen as nonmathematical and deal with substantive issues—while quantitative researchers have focused on scaling, indicators, reliability, and other issues dealing with producing good quantitative measures.

In this book I straddle this gap (or chasm if you prefer) between the qualitative scholars' concern for substantively valid concepts and the quantitative scholars' interest in good numerical measures. As the title of this volume indicates, it will not be a balanced treatment: it will focus on concepts. However, I develop the methodological and mathematical implications of concepts for the design and building of quantitative measures. As Lazarsfeld and Barton said decades ago:

> [B]efore we can investigate the presence or absence of some attribute . . . or before we can rank objects or measure them in terms of some variable, *we must form the concept of that variable.* (1951, 155, my emphasis)

While we all pay lip service to the mantra that theory should guide methodology, it is often the case that the cart is leading the horse. Symptomatic of this is the Jaggers and Gurr discussion of the polity concept of democracy (1995).[2] Their analysis of the concept of democracy is in fact located in the section entitled "Operationalizing Democracy": clearly the focus is on the quantitative measure, not on the concept. In contrast, I shall spend a lot of time on the various conceptualizations of democracy, and only afterward will I analyze the downstream consequences for quantitative measures.

Given the division between quantitative and qualitative scholars it is hard for anyone to keep her attention focused on both at the same time. Goertz's Second Law[3] says:

> The amount of attention devoted to a concept is inversely related to the attention devoted to the quantitative measure.

---

[2]This article is by far the most cited of those published by the *Journal of Peace Research* (Gleditsch, Metelits, and Strand 2003).

[3]Goertz's First Law is that necessary condition hypotheses can be found for all important social and political phenomena (Goertz 2003).

The contrast between Collier and Bollen on democracy illustrates this law in action. Collier and Mahon (1993) provide an insightful analysis of the concept(s) of democracy, but give little guidance on how one might put these ideas into quantitative action. Bollen has made major contributions to the literature on the quantitative measures of democracy, but his discussions of the concept of democracy rarely exceed a few sentences.

This book thus tries to violate Goertz's Second Law. I analyze in detail the major ways one can build concepts, but I do not stop there. I continue the analysis by examining how different concept structures have important methodological implications for the construction of quantitative measures. For example, as chapter 4 on democracy shows, to be faithful to one's concepts implies measures quite different from those that one finds in the quantitative literature on democracy indicators, scales, etc.

The publication of the book by King, Keohane, and Verba (1994) relaunched the debate about the distinctiveness, or lack thereof, of qualitative methods. The formation in 2003 of the Qualitative Methods section of the American Political Science Association was one response to the King et al. challenge. This new section has created three awards, one of which is the Giovanni Sartori Book Award. Going back to Sartori's famous 1970 article, one finds that much of it is an attack on quantitative methods. In contrast, I shall take concepts very seriously, but at the same time I shall develop formal and mathematical models of how most qualitative theorists construct concepts. My analysis thus cuts both ways: it finds that some of Sartori's claims must be seriously qualified; it also finds that many quantitative measures do not fit well with the concepts they are supposed to reflect.

*

Much of the literature on concepts takes what I call a semantic approach (Sartori 1970, 1984; Gerring 1997). Sartori typifies this way of thinking about concepts. For example, the first half of his essay (1984) deals with a semantic analysis of words such as "state" or "état." From a more philosophical perspective, concepts are related to definitions; in fact there is no real difference between defining a word and providing an analysis of a concept (Robinson 1950). To ask questions like "what do you mean by democracy?" is to invite the interlocutor to provide a definition. The answer does not really differ from the response to the question "what is your concept of democracy?"

In contrast, this volumes argues that a concept involves a theoretical and empirical analysis of the object or phenomenon referred to by the word. A good concept draws distinctions that are important in the behavior of the object. The central attributes that a definition refers to are those that prove relevant for hypotheses, explanations, and causal mechanisms. In a theoretical and empirical view of scientific concepts their semantics change as our understanding of the phenomenon changes. Take the example of "copper": the very definition or concept of copper has changed, reflecting new knowledge generated by chemists.

Indicative of a more literary and philosophical approach, Sartori (1984) starts with the classic problem of translation. Should *état* in French be translated as "state" or "government" in English?[4] Another classic chestnut is the translation of the Italian Renaissance concept of *virtú*. Notice that my standard examples are not problematic in this sense: the concept of copper in English does not differ from *cuivre* in French. This is because English and French chemists have the same atomic theory of copper. The debate over the definition of corporatism, for example, is not about its definition per se, but about the phenomenon (real life) of corporatism.

Lurking in the background is the issue of nominalism versus realism. At the level of semantic signs, there is no debate; the words, signs, or symbols we use to designate phenomena are arbitrary. For example, Babbie in his popular textbook on social research (2001) expounds an extreme nominalist view regarding concepts. He puts himself in the Red Queen's camp on the issue of meaning and what determines it. More generally, all those who focus purely on semantic issues are liable to end up seeing definitions as arbitrary. If the concept is not intimately related to the empirical analysis of a phenomenon then there is nothing to which one can anchor the concept, and everything becomes a matter of who is in charge of the definition. For example, communist countries were often called people's "democratic" republics; this usage was an abuse of political and semantic power. If we were to change our definition of democracy to accommodate these countries then our hypotheses about democracy would have to change as well. Likewise, we cannot divorce our concept of corporatism from how corporatism fits into theories, as either an independent or dependent variable.

[4]One should note that *gouvernement* is a French word as well.

The alternative to the nominalist view of concepts can be called, not surprisingly, the realist perspective on concepts and definitions. This distinction goes back at least to Locke, but probably all the way to Aristotle. Both philosophers distinguished between "essential" and "superficial" characteristics of an object. Change in essential characteristics constituted a change in kind, while changes in superficial traits—"nominal" in Locke's terminology—did not result in a change in kind. For example, a change in a democratic regime from presidential to parliamentary does not entail a change from a democratic to authoritarian regime. However, take away essential properties, say, civil rights, and the regime changes its fundamental character. To go back to chemistry, a change in temperature of an element does not mean a change in its classification in the chemical table, while a change in the number of electrons does.

Concepts are theories about ontology: they are theories about the fundamental constitutive elements of a phenomenon. While many quantitative scholars may find the term "ontological" provocative and many interpretativists may object to my usage, I use the term in a straightforward way to designate the core characteristics of a phenomenon and their interrelationships. For example, we can ask about what constitutes a welfare state. Typically, these are states that provide goods and services like unemployment insurance, medical services, retirement benefits, and the like. To *be* a welfare state *is* to provide these goods and services.

In short, I propose a causal, ontological, and realist view of concepts. It is an ontological view because it focuses on what constitutes a phenomenon. It is causal because it identifies ontological attributes that play a key role in causal hypotheses, explanations, and mechanisms. It is realist because it involves an empirical analysis of the phenomenon. My approach stresses that concept analysis involves ascertaining the constitutive characteristics of a phenomenon that have central causal powers. These causal powers and their related causal mechanisms play a role in our theories. A purely semantic analysis of concepts, words, and their definitions is never adequate by itself

*

A core theme running throughout this volume is that the structure of concepts is crucial. As the literature on scales, indicators, and the like illustrates, there are many ways to construct a quantitative measure.

Apart from the few key articles by Collier and his colleagues there is little or no discussion on the different ways one can construct concepts.

I stress that most important concepts we use are *multidimensional* and *multilevel* in nature. For example, Sartori's (1970) article talks about high-, medium-, and low-level categories while Collier and Mahon (1993) use the terminology of primary and secondary categories. I prefer to use the framework of "three-level" concepts.

The most important level theoretically is usually the concept as used in theoretical propositions, such as "corporatism," "democracy," or "welfare state." This I refer to as the *basic level*. It is "basic" in the sense of Eleanor Rosch and her colleagues; it is cognitively central. It is the noun to which we attach adjectives (Collier and Levitsky 1997) such as parliamentary *democracy* or democratic *corporatism*. The basic level is what we use in theoretical propositions.

The next level down from the basic level is what I call the *secondary level*. For example, when we say that democracy consists of civil rights, competitive elections, and so forth, we are descending to the secondary level to give the constitutive dimensions of the basic-level democracy concept. It is when we move down to the secondary level that the multidimensional character of concepts appears. The secondary-level dimensions form much of the ontological analysis of concepts. They also play a central role in causal mechanisms of various sorts.

The next level down I call the *indicator/data level*. Alternatively, it could be called the operationalization level. At this level we get specific enough that data can be gathered, which permits us to categorize—either dichotomously or on a more fine-grained scale—whether or not a specific phenomenon, individual, or event falls under the concept.

In summary, we can dissect and analyze concepts by (1) how many levels they have, (2) how many dimensions each level has, and (3) what is the substantive content of each of the dimensions at each level.

Table 1.1 illustrates that most of the prominent efforts to conceptualize democracy have a three-level character. With the partial exception of Coppedge and Reinicke, all see democracy as a multidimensional, multilevel concept. Because democracy is a complex concept it is important to analyze its component parts. Typically, one includes secondary-level dimensions like "competition" (i.e., for office) and "participation" (i.e., voting) in what it means to be a democracy. The secondary-level dimensions remain part of the theoretical edifice, but they are concrete enough to be operationalized by the indicator/data

6

level. The third indicator/data level is where we get down to actual empirical data. For example, typically there are multiple indicators of secondary-level factors like participation and competition. These indicators are the variables that are actually coded for and form the bases of quantitative measures.

The second aspect of concept structure that I explore is how components at one level are combined or structured to produce dimensions at the next higher level. The basic-level concept of democracy is constituted by multiple secondary-level dimensions: how are these dimensions "combined" to arrive at the basic-level concept?

Throughout this book I continually contrast two different structural principles for constructing multidimensional and multilevel concepts. The first goes back to Aristotle and builds concepts using the structure of necessary and sufficient conditions. In classic philosophical logic to define a concept is to give the conditions necessary and sufficient for something to fit into the category. Each of these necessary conditions is a secondary-level dimension: the structural glue that binds the secondary-level dimensions together to form the basic level is the mathematics of necessary and sufficient conditions.

The necessary and sufficient condition view of concepts was so standard that Sartori (1970) just assumes it. However, developments in philosophy, logic, and cognitive psychology have shown that there are other ways to construct concepts. I shall focus on the "family resemblance" concept structure which is in many ways the polar opposite of the necessary and sufficient condition one. In their groundbreaking article Collier and Mahon (1993) introduced the idea of family resemblance concepts into the political science literature. The family resemblance structure can be seen as the opposite of the necessary and sufficient condition one because it contains no necessary conditions. All one needs is enough resemblance on secondary-level dimensions to be part of the family. For example, in chapter 6 I discuss two concepts used in the study of international conflict. The concept of a "crisis" according the the International Crisis Behavior group (Brecher, Wilkenfeld, and Moser 1988) uses the classic necessary and sufficient condition approach to concepts, while the idea of a "militarized interstate dispute" (Jones, Bremer, and Singer 1995) uses a family resemblance–like approach.

The qualitative literature on concepts is best formalized mathematically by set theory or logic. For example, to construct concepts with necessary and sufficient conditions or family resemblance means that

TABLE 1.1
Some Concepts and Measures of Democracy

Creator	Secondary Level	Indicator/Data Level	Method of Aggregation
Alvarez et al. 1996	Contestation	Multiple parties	Multiplicative
		Executive turnover	
	Offices	Election executive	
		Election legislature	
Arat 1991	Participation	Executive selection	Multiplicative at secondary
		Legislative selection	Additive at indicator
		Legislative effectiveness	
		Competitiveness of nominations	
	Competitiveness	Party legitimacy	
		Party competition	
	Coerciveness		
Bollen and Grandjean 1981	Political liberties	Press freedom	Additive at secondary
		Freedom of group opposition	Factor analysis at indicator
		Government sanctions	
	Popular sovereignty	Fairness of elections	
		Executive selection	
		Legislative selection	

Coppedge & Reinicke 1991	Contestation	Free and fair elections Freedom of expression Freedom of organization Pluralism in media	Guttman scale
Gastil 1978–	Political rights Civil rights	9 components 13 components	Additive
Hadenius 1992	Elections Political freedoms	Suffrage Elected offices Meaningful elections Freedom of organization Freedom of expression Freedom from coercion	Additive at secondary Additive/multiplicative at indicator
Jaggers and Gurr 1995	Constraints on executive Competitiveness participation Executive recruitment	Constraints on chief executive Competitiveness of participation Regulation of participation Competitiveness of recruitment Openness of executive recruitment	Additive
Vanhanen 1990	Competition Participation	Election results Voters/total population	Multiplicative

one is implicitly using the mathematics of logic. I will argue that these formal tools are the natural way to model my two core concept structures. We shall see that the logical AND typifies the necessary and sufficient condition structure while the logical OR is the natural way to model the family resemblance structure. Fuzzy logic will also play a key role in this volume in extending the traditional view of logic as dichotomous to the domain of continuous variables.

Chapter 2 in many ways forms the core of this volume. I lay out the basic three-level view of concepts and discuss the main issues surrounding how multidimensional and multilevel concepts can and have been constructed, focusing on the necessary and sufficient condition and family resemblance concept structures. I suggest that most complex and abstract concepts have in fact this three-level structure. The basic and secondary levels are really the theory of the concept, while the indicator/data level is the connection to measures and data collection.

Central to the Sartori and Collier literature on concepts is a concern with "conceptual stretching." Conceptual stretching occurs when concepts are loosened up so that they apply to additional cases. In the philosophical literature this is the contrast between *extension* and *intension*. The classic principle was that as we loosen the concept (i.e., decrease intension) we increase its extension (number of empirical cases). One aspect then to concept structure is its coverage or permissiveness. Chapter 3 treats Sartori and Collier's concern about how the structure of the concept relates to its empirical coverage.

Sartori (1970) borrowed from philosophical logic the basic principle that as intension decreases extension increases: as concepts become more permissive by requiring fewer attributes, they cover more cases. What Satori assumed without discussion was that concepts were constructed with necessary and sufficient conditions. However, what chapter 3 shows is that if one adopts the family resemblance framework then in fact increasing intension (adding more attributes) can *increase* extension. The key point is that concept structure has important downstream consequences on the empirical coverage of the concept.

Ideal type concepts are most distinguishable by their extension of zero: normally "ideal" means in practice that empirical examples are extremely rare or nonexistent. Here again we see the concern with the relationship between intension and extension. The ideal type concept focuses attention on the extreme end of the concept continuum. How do we define the extreme end point? How useful is it to have an end point with no empirical observations? In spite of the widespread use of ideal types, it is almost impossible to find a methodological discussion of them. The theoretical and methodological tools developed in chapter 2 allow me to systematically analyze the ideal type concept in chapter 3.

Chapter 2 provides the mathematical tools to formalize the necessary and sufficient condition and family resemblance concept structures. With this methodology in hand, one can ask about quantitative measures (I consider dichotomous codings as quantitative). Chapter 4 on democracy illustrates the consequences of clarity about concept structure for the building of quantitative measures. There I show that almost everyone, which is a large number of people, conceptualizes democracy in terms of necessary and sufficient conditions, but at the same time almost no quantitative measures use the mathematics of logic appropriate to the concept. Instead the inappropriate mathematics of addition, average, and correlation are almost universally adopted (e.g., see table 1.1). I take the popular polity data on democracy (Jaggers and Gurr 1995) and show that if one constructs a quantitative measure that reflects the polity scholars' own concept of democracy then one arrives at a quantitative measure that is quite different from the one developed by Gurr and his colleagues. I use the example of democracy to stress that theory, that is, concepts, should drive methodology: we must first think clearly about the substance and structure of our concepts and then we can begin to think about how to validly operationalize that theory into a quantitative measure.

Since most complex concepts are three level, we need to ask about the degree to which the quantitative measure reflects the concept structure. In fact there are two structural questions: (1) how to combine indicators to form the secondary-level dimensions and (2) how to combine secondary-level dimensions to get the basic-level concept. The key issue in the context of this introduction is that almost all scholars use the necessary and sufficient condition structure to combine secondary-level dimensions into the final democracy concept. All of the quantitative measures use either addition or correlation. *However, none of these is the appropriate mathematical formalization of the necessary and sufficient condition structure.*

Chapter 2 proposes that the necessary and sufficient condition and family resemblance conceptual approaches represent two poles of a continuum. As with all complex concepts themselves, we can ask if

11

there is some underlying unidimensional continuum which lies between these two anchor points.

Chapter 5 shows that one can think of different concept structures in terms of *substitutability* (Most and Starr 1989). Necessary conditions can be defined as those that do not permit substitutes. In contrast, the family resemblance approach is characterized by the fact that the absence of one characteristic can be substituted for by the presence of others. The continuum that connects the necessary and sufficient condition and family resemblance poles is thus the degree to which substitutability is possible.

Chapter 5 examines a field where scholars have claimed that one concept structure is most appropriate. The literature on the democratic or liberal peace has focused on the hypothesis that democracies do not fight wars with each other. This literature—along with the international conflict literature in general—must deal with the problem of concept structure because international conflicts have two or more parties. The question arises about what should be the concept of say, democracy, for a dyad. We have democracy scores for each party to the conflict, but it is not clear how to aggregate the democracy scores of the two parties to construct a measure for the dyad as a whole. Hence we have the same problem as in structuring the secondary-level dimensions to form the basic-level concept.

After Dixon first proposed the weakest-link idea in 1993, scholars quickly arrived at a consensus that it was the appropriate measure of dyadic democracy. The argument is that the constraints on waging war between two countries are determined by the less democratic of the pair, i.e., the weakest link. The weakest-link measure uses the necessary and sufficient condition concept structure. Each link of the chain is necessary: the strength of one link cannot substitute for the weakness of another. Thus the weakest-link claim can be translated into one concerning substitutability and concept structure. If the weakest-link hypothesis is correct then the more substitutable the dyadic measure of democracy the less it should be correlated with international military conflict. Chapter 5 employs measures of dyadic democracy that vary in their degree of substitutability. It examines whether in statistical fact the weakest link is better than other alternative concept structures that involve more substitutability, such as the maximum or the mean.

Chapter 5 provides a concrete extended example of how concepts have causal theories embedded in them. The weakest-link measure was a concrete expression of a theory about the interaction between democratic countries. This embedded hypothesis is assumed when the measure is used to test the democratic peace with basic-level variables. The standard basic-level hypothesis is between a military conflict dependent variable (e.g., militarized disputes or crises) and a dyadic democracy independent variable. The weakest link is used to make up that basic-level, dyadic democracy independent variable which is then correlated with the dependent conflict variable.

More generally, a survey of the conflict literature shows that about one-third of the typical conflict variables have embedded hypotheses in them. This survey also shows that for some other variables scholars have preferred, implicitly, the family resemblance concept structure which allows for complete substitutability. For example, when coding multiple alliance commitments between two states, one takes the strongest one. In terms of substitutability, the strongest commitment compensates completely for the weaker ones. In summary, causal hypotheses embedded in concepts are pervasive in the quantitative conflict literature.

Part I of this volume examines the theoretical, structural, formal, and empirical aspects of concept building. Chapter 2 discusses the three-level framework and the prototypical family resemblance and necessary and sufficient condition concept structures. Chapter 3 deals with how structure relates to empirical coverage (i.e., extension). Chapter 4 illustrates the downstream consequences of concept structure and theory for quantitative measures. Chapter 5 shows how important theoretical propositions are embedded in concepts and how they can be empirically tested. These chapters illustrate with many concrete examples the causal, ontological, and empirical nature of concept building.

*

I stress the central role of causal theory throughout my analysis of concepts. This is not novel in and of itself, but the kind of theorizing I discuss is hard to find. In particular, to understand how my analysis differs from the quantitative standard it is useful to consider the theoretical and substantive context within which theories of measurement have developed. This is particularly important for political scientists and sociologists since the early history of the measurement of concepts occurs in psychology and educational testing.

The problem in psychology was to get some numerical means of capturing some very abstract—and unmeasured—concept like "intelligence" or "authoritarian personality." In terms of my three-level framework "unmeasured" refers to the basic and secondary levels of the concept, while "measured" refers to the indicator/data level. Typically the indicators in the psychological literature are responses to items on pencil and paper tests. Factor analytic techniques responded to the need for ways to make inferences about unmeasured concepts like intelligence based on its external manifestations such as responses to problems.

Lazarsfeld and Blalock were among the key players in importing the factor analytic approach to concepts into political science and sociology. For example, Blalock's 1982 volume *Conceptualization and Measurement in the Social Sciences* expresses very well the factor analytic approach to concepts and measurement (see also Bollen 1989). Lazarsfeld (1966) provides a nice history of how he and others took the basic insights of psychological methodologies and applied them to social and political phenomena.

My approach to concepts differs in a number of fundamental ways, partially because of my focus on concepts and partially because of my interest in substantive concepts like corporatism, democracy, crisis, militarized disputes, and so on. My point is not to say that the factor analytic approach is wrong, but that there are issues it overlooks, that there are other approaches to concepts, and that one should and can vary the approach according to the substantive phenomenon under study.

First, the factor analytic approach argues that there is a *causal* relationship between the basic or secondary level and the indicator level: the latent variable causes the indicator. This is basically the disease-symptom model of phenomena: the disease causes the symptoms, not vice versa. In the factor analytic approach one is concerned that the indicators may have different causes, some of which may not be the one that the researcher is focusing on. So one cannot think of the factor analytic approach as just being about correlations; it implies a real causal model between the latent, unmeasured variables and the indicators: "The position taken . . . is that indicator variables can usually be linked to underlying or unmeasured concepts by postulating causal models in which one's assumptions are made explicit. In some simple causal situations, as where correlations among indicators are assumed to be produced by a single underlying variable, operational procedures such as factor analysis can be used to obtain empirical estimates of the unmeasured variable" (Blalock 1968, 6).[5]

Second, in contrast, I discuss the *ontological*—noncausal—view of concepts. Here the basic- and secondary-level dimensions are not causes but *constitute* what the phenomenon *is*. For example, to have competitive elections is not a symptom of democracy, it is not caused by democracy, but rather it constitutes what democracy is. I do not think that the factor analytic approach is problematic in that intelligence causes one to score higher on IQ tests. Clearly, symptoms are caused by diseases; however, what the disease *is* differs from what the symptoms are. I suggest that for many concepts that political scientists and sociologists are interested in the ontological view makes more sense.

Third, the ontological view makes more sense when one basically has a functionalist view of the phenomenon. Many feel that democracy cannot function correctly unless basic civil liberties are present. The secondary-level dimensions are really a *theory* about the *interrelationships* of the parts of the conceptual whole. Hence, when the theoretical language, implicitly or explicitly, is functionalist in nature, one probably will want to take an ontological approach to the concept.

Fourth, often scholars argue at the indicator level that there is *functional equivalence*, i.e., various phenomena that satisfy the secondary-level dimension. Within the factor analytic school, it is important that indicators of the same unmeasured, latent variable be highly correlated with each other. However, a theory of functional equivalence does not require high correlation; in fact the opposite is often a good sign. Functional equivalence, by definition, means that the occurrence of an attribute A can substitute for the occurrence of attribute B; hence a secondary-level dimension can be present when there is little or no correlation between the indicators.

---

[5] Good methodologists have always been conscious of the issue of causal direction in concepts and measures: "Nearly all measurement in psychology and the other social sciences assumes effect indicators. Factor analysis, reliability tests, and latent class analysis are examples of techniques that assume effect indicators. However, there are situations in which indicators are more realistically thought of as causes of the latent variable rather than the reverse. Tests for causal versus effect indicators have recently become available (Bollen and Ting 2000), but most empirical research implicitly assumes effect indicators. Incorrectly specifying indicators as causal or effect indicators leads to a misspecified model and holds the potential for inconsistent parameter estimates and misleading conclusions (Bollen and Lennox 1991)" (Bollen 2002, 616–17; see also Blalock 1964, 162–69, who uses the name "cause" indicators).

Fifth, Blalock and the psychologists were concerned with abstract concepts and phenomena with no easily measurable manifestation. A measure of "sex" or "gender" was not the kind of concept that the factor analytic school was concerned about. For these concepts the link between measurement and the concept—between measured and unmeasured—was so clear and direct that it was not seen as problematic. The concepts that I shall focus on as core examples are those that are complex and multidimensional, but which often have quite direct links between the secondary-level dimensions and the data-level indicators. Unlike the huge gap between the concept of intelligence and the response to questions on a test, the difference between a secondary-level concept of democracy such as competitive elections and the actual data level is not large.

These five differences constitute a fundamentally different perspective on concepts. To focus on concepts is to think about the nature of the phenomenon being conceptualized. Factor analysis correctly emphasizes that the effects of the phenomenon are important. However, just as important, if not more, are the causes of the effects. It is worth examining the disease just as much as its symptoms.

*

[T]o be a man, or of the species man, and have the *essence* of a
man, is the same thing.
John Locke

I would like to use Martha Nussbaum's concept of "human well-being"—based on Sen's (1985) work—as an example of a three-level concept in action. She presents a complex, multilevel, multidimensional view of human well-being. This example provides a brief introduction to many of the topics covered in this volume, and illustrates what a complex three-level concept looks like in practice. It is an interesting case because, given that she is working within a very different intellectual context (political philosophy), it reinforces the point that one needs to develop concepts appropriate to the substance of the phenomenon as well as the theory.

Embedded in her concept we shall see causal hypotheses about how human beings function in biological, psychological, and sociological terms. It is not a definitional debate, but one about the reality of human lives in various cultures around the world. It is ontological

because it is about human nature. In short, in terms of its content and
structure Nussbaum's concept of human well-being provides a good
introduction to three-level concepts as causal, ontological, and realist.

She clearly sees the concept of human well-being in ontological
terms: "Here, then, is a sketch of an internal-essentialist proposal,
an account of the most important functions of the human being, in
terms of which human life is defined" (1992, 214). She is "defining"
or conceptualizing what it means to be human. She wants to know
empirically how human beings and their lives are constituted. She
does not want a series of indicators or symptoms of what it is to be
human, but rather a description of the essence of human well-being.

She describes many functions and capabilities, aspects of what it
means to live a good human life. Here are a few to give a flavor of her
analysis:

> Basic Human Functional Capabilities:
> 1. Being able to live to the end of a complete human life, as far as is
> possible: not dying prematurely, or before one's life is so reduced as to be
> not worth living.
> 2. Being able to have good health; to be adequately nourished; to have
> adequate shelter; having opportunities for sexual satisfaction; being able
> to move from place to place.
> ...
> 7. Being able to live for and with others, to recognize and show concern
> for other human beings, to engage in various forms of familial and social
> interaction.
> ...
> 10. Being able to live one's own life and nobody else's; being able to live
> one's own life in one's very own surroundings and context. (1992, 222)

These functions are her secondary-level dimensions.

Her subtitle—"In Defense of Aristotelian Essentialism"—suggests
that she is using the standard approach to concepts, necessary and
sufficient conditions. An intimate bond links the necessary and sufficient condition structure to essentialism. If some characteristic is
essential for an animal to be a human being, then that characteristic
is a necessary condition for being human. She is quite clear that the
various dimensions she discusses are necessary:

> As far as [secondary-level] capabilities go, to call them part of humanness
> is to make a very basic sort of evaluation. It is to say that a life without this

item would be too lacking, too impoverished, to be human at all. (1992, 220)

At the secondary level she denies substitutability between dimensions:

> The Aristotelian essentialist claims that a life that lacks any one of these [capabilities], no matter what else it has, will be lacking humanness....
> The list is, emphatically, a list of separate components. We cannot satisfy the need for one of them by giving a larger amount of another one. (1992, 222)

Her conceptualization of a human being uses the basic three-level framework common in complex, multidimensional concepts. The necessary factors like those listed above lie at the secondary level of the human well-being concept. At the third level we find a sensitivity to historical and cultural differences. In terms of chapter 5, we have substitutability in the ways, for example, a human being can be nourished, sheltered, have sex, and so forth:

> The political plan [secondary level], while using a determinate [necessary condition] conception of the good at a high level of generality, leaves a great deal of latitude for citizens to specify each of the components more concretely and with much variety, in accordance with local traditions or individual tastes. (1992, 224)

At the third level, we allow for culture variation in the filling of the requirements at the secondary level. Hence we have a structure with necessary and sufficient conditions at the secondary level and substitutability at the indicator/data level. I think that this particular structure is quite common and I will use it myself in reformulating the polity measure of democracy in chapter 4.

The theory of what it means to be human is quite explicitly a functionalist one. She proclaims this in the title of her article "Human Functioning and Social Justice." Some of the essential characteristics deal with the physiological aspects of being human, such as shelter, clothing, food, and sex. Some deal with the psychological aspects of being human, like the possibility to make choices. Others deal with the social character of human beings, like being able to live with and for others.

The Sen-Nussbaum approach to human well-being or quality of life thus typifies the ways scholars build complex multidimensional and multilevel concepts. It also illustrates the distinction between an ontological view of concepts and a factor analytic one. Nussbaum is not asking what are the indicators or effects of human well-being but what human well-being is. It is causal because she is making claims about what happens biologically, psychologically, and socially to people who fail to attend to secondary-level functions. It is a realist approach to human well-being, based on her reading of anthropology, sociology, and biology.

*

Part II focuses on a key use of concepts, the selection of cases. The conceptualization of both the independent and dependent variables has enormous implications for empirical analyses and causal inference. Almost without exception the population under analysis is defined with concepts. All the chapters in part II show the strong impact of concepts on case selection and then on causal inference.

Figure 1.1 illustrates how concepts and case selection interact. Absolutely core in research design, particularly in qualitative analysis, is the concept that drives the selection of positive cases. The positive case concept is almost always what the researcher is trying to explain. The choice of these positive cases is absolutely central in the qualitative context. Often one or two cases are central to the *general* theory (e.g., the Netherlands for Lijphardt). Hence there is a risk that these positive core examples do not fit well with the concept. If one is basing the general theory more or less explicitly on these positive, but marginal, cases then one runs the risk of having a general theory that does not fit well the set of positive cases. In terms of figure 1.1 one is choosing examples from the gray zone instead of cases of the nongray, positive set.

One can see this issue arise in the literature on corporatism. Katzenstein's very influential analysis (1985) of corporatism was driven by his two core cases of Austria and Switzerland. Hicks in his review (1988) of Katzenstein stresses that Switzerland is not a good example of corporatism. Siaroff's (1999) meta-analysis of corporatism measures brings this out very clearly; Switzerland does not fit well into the core set of corporatist countries, it belongs in the gray zone. Hence any theory of corporatism driven implicitly or explicitly by marginal cases is likely to prove problematic.

Chapter 6 shows that variation in the concept of international crisis induces selection effects. As chapter 3 discusses in detail, concept

Scope conditions

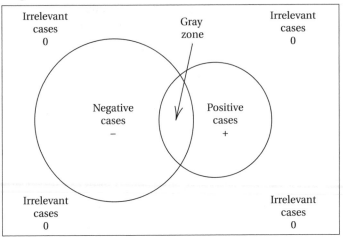

FIGURE 1.1
Case selection: Positive, negative, and irrelevant cases

structure has a large impact on the inclusivity or permissiveness of a concept in terms of empirical coverage and extension. In the context of international crisis, a looser concept allows in more lower-level crises. In terms of figure 1.1, depending on the concept of crisis used, cases move from the gray zone to the positive set (looser concept) or to the negative set (stricter concept).

As is well known, any selection criterion (e.g., variation in concept) that correlates with the dependent variable is likely to produce selection effects. Chapter 6 shows this phenomenon in action for international crisis concepts. There are very strong correlations between the concept of crisis applied and the dependent variables commonly used in the literature.

Much trickier are the issues surrounding how concepts are used to select the negative cases. Skocpol (1979) is quite clear about what social revolution is, but it is not at all clear what the universe of non–social revolutions consists of. Here we see a very significant problem linking concepts to research design, the nature of "non" concepts, which typically define the negative cases needed to test hypotheses and theories.

The negative case problem is exacerbated for Skocpol by the fact that the non–social revolution cases are divided into the negative ones and those that are "irrelevant" to a test of Skocpol's theory. The United States in 1900 is certainly a case of non–social revolution; should it be included in a test of her theory? Chapter 7 introduces the Possibility Principle as a solution to this problem of dividing the negative cases from the irrelevant ones. In short, one uses the theory of the positive cases to determine which of the negative ones are those where the outcome "was possible." The Possibility Principle expresses a widely held intuition—for both quantitative as well as qualitative scholars—about what constitutes relevant control cases. For example, Skocpol chooses as her control cases events such as Russia 1905 or Prussia 1848 where it seems that social revolution "might have occurred." Chapter 7 uses the Possibility Principle to construct the complete set of negative cases within the scope of Skocpol's theory of social revolution. The purpose of the Possibility Principle is to solve the problem of "non" concepts in terms of selecting negative cases.

In the case of Skocpol we use the Possibility Principle only to select the negative cases. However, one can use the Possibility Principle to select entire populations. Here the focus is on eliminating the irrelevant observations, not on choosing the negative ones. When the Possibility Principle is used only to select negative cases the issue of the boundary between the positive and irrelevant cases (see figure 1.1) does not arise, but when the Possibility Principle is first used to select the population and then another concept is used to select the positive cases, boundary issues arise. This is when the "impossible can happen." In summary, one can use the Possibility Principle to (1) select the negative cases only or (2) eliminate the irrelevant cases independently of the determination of the positive and negative cases. Chapter 8 examines this latter application of the Possibility Principle.

Chapter 8 looks at the concept of "politically relevant dyads" to see how the Possibility Principle informs population selection in the context of large-N studies. In particular, I shall use the literature on militarized interstate conflict. Scholars have used the specific concept of "politically relevant dyads" to choose the population of cases. We shall see that the boundary line between the positive and irrelevant cases plays a large role in choosing the population.

The Possibility Principle underlies this discussion as well, as one can see from the following discussion where the word "possible" or its synonyms like "might have" appear frequently:

> In addition to the time-saving device [politically] relevant dyads represent, many proponents of their use argue there are fundamental reasons

for restricting analysis to relevant dyads. Weede (1976, 396) claims we should restrict analysis to relevant dyads because "only in this relatively small subset of dyads is there a possibility for irreconcilable conflicts of interest to arise and create a substantial risk of war." Similarly, Maoz and Russett (1993, 627) suggest analysis of all dyads is inappropriate because "the vast majority are nearly irrelevant. The countries comprising them were too far apart and too weak militarily, with few serious interests potentially in conflict, for them plausibly to engage in any militarized diplomatic dispute." The strongest statement along these lines is Lemke's (1995, 29) claim that relevant dyads matter because they comprise the correct referent group, and thus function as a true control group, against which war dyads are compared. The reason the set of relevant dyads is the correct referent group for war dyads is that it is only the relevant dyads that might have had a war. (Lemke and Reed 2001, 128)

It is worth noting that the concept of "political relevance" has the typical three-level concept structure. At the secondary level one says that states have the possibility of having a military conflict if they have either the opportunity OR the willingness. These secondary-level dimensions must receive operationalization at the data/indicator level. For example, opportunity is normally operationalized as either major power status OR geographical contiguity. One can see these substantive factors mentioned in the long quote just above, for example when Maoz and Russett say that countries "too far apart" (i.e., no opportunity) AND with no "irreconcilable conflicts of interest" (i.e., no willingness) constitute the set of irrelevant observations.[6]

One can think of the research chain discussed in part II as concepts ——> case selection ——> causal inference. Perhaps the most dramatic effects of concepts are at the end of the chain. Chapters 6–8 illustrate in different ways the impact of concepts on causal inference. In chapter 6 we see that those factors that conflict scholars have typically seen as key in selection effects—particularly power variables—are those where the variation in concepts produces the greatest variation in causal inference. Chapter 7 shows that the variable relatively ignored by most readers of Skocpol—peasant revolt—is empirically more important than the state crisis variable that has received far more attention. Chapter 8 illustrates how the common practice of including in the statistical analyses the variables used to define the population (i.e., politically relevant dyads) has a major impact on the

[6]The negation of (A OR B) is (not-A AND not-B).

22

causal evaluation of the population-defining variables. So while concepts typically are used at the beginning in terms of research design, their downstream impacts on causal inference cannot be ignored.

*

J. S. Mill started his *System of Logic* with a book on concepts because they are used as components of scientific propositions. Part III looks at how multilevel concepts appear in theories. In chapter 9 I analyze Skocpol's theory of social revolutions, Hick's study of the causes of the welfare state, Ostrom's work on common pool resource institutions, and Downing's analysis of democracy in early modern Europe. With these various examples we shall see a variety of different ways to build concepts, on both the independent as well as the dependent variable side of the equation. We shall see necessary and sufficient condition and family resemblance concepts in real-life theoretical contexts.

Three-level concepts have two theoretical levels, the basic level and the secondary level. If we ignore measurement issues (i.e., the indicator/data level) we can focus on the theory which uses basic-level independent and dependent variables, which themselves include causal hypotheses from the secondary level. These are then what I refer to as two-level theories. All the examples discussed in chapter 9 involve causal relationships at the basic and secondary levels.

We must structure variables at the basic level to form theories just as one needs to structure secondary-level dimensions to form concepts. Not surprisingly, in the concluding chapter I use for theories the same structural principles of necessary and sufficient conditions and substitutability that earlier chapters discuss for concepts. We shall see the (fuzzy) logic of AND and OR used in the logic of theoretical propositions just as I have used that logic in the analysis of concepts. The "aggregation" problem is theoretically different since we are combining the independent variables to explain the dependent, but we can use the same formal principles and mathematics to make this move. Of course, this is what Mill was really referring to in his system of logic, the logic of causal propositions.

This similarity between the explanatory theory at the basic level and the theory of concepts should not be surprising, but reassuring. Both are theories about phenomena. Nussbaum claims her theory is an empirical one; it describes something about the reality of human life. The theories described in chapter 9 are causal analyses of important phenomena.

In summary, there is an underlying theoretical logic used in this book that cuts across the analysis of concepts as well as the causal explanations of outcomes. I suggest that this logic provides a powerful set of tools for understanding social phenomena and that it underlies a great deal of theorizing about phenomena and concepts. Two theories described in chapter 9 belong to recent presidents, Elinor Ostrom and Theda Skocpol, of the American Political Science Association; perhaps there is something to these theoretical structures.

PART ONE

THEORETICAL, STRUCTURAL, AND
EMPIRICAL ANALYSIS OF CONCEPTS

*

Structuring and Theorizing Concepts

On those remote pages [of an ancient Chinese encyclopedia]
it is written that animals are divided into (1) those that belong
to the emperor, (2) embalmed ones, (3) those that are trained,
(4) suckling pigs, (5) mermaids, (6) fabulous ones, (7) stray
dogs, (8) those that are included in this classification,
(9) innumerable ones, (10) those drawn with a very fine
camel's hair brush, (11) others, (12) those that have just broken
a flower vase, (13) those that resemble flies from a distance.
Jorge-Luis Borges

SARTORI DEVELOPED A SEMANTIC and definitional approach to concepts. In contrast, my approach is ontological, realist, and causal. The
core attributes of a concept constitute a *theory* of the *ontology* of the
phenomenon under consideration. *Concepts are about ontology.* To
develop a concept is more than providing a definition: it is deciding
what is important about an entity. The arguments about why attribute
X is important form part of the ontological theory of the object.

For example, we can ask what "copper" *is*. One property of copper
is its reddish color. However, we would not consider a definition of
copper based on its color very adequate; much better would be a
conceptualization of copper based on its atomic structure. The atomic
structure of copper is a better and more useful basis for thinking about
copper than an approach based on qualities like its redness. One way
to think of this is via the disease-symptom metaphor. The ontological
theory of an object, event, phenomenon ideally focuses on the disease
and only secondarily on its symptoms. We consider the redness of
copper an effect (symptom) of more basic aspects of copper's defining
characteristics.[1]

[1]The choice of important characteristics of a phenomenon depends on theoretical
context. Sometimes the theory focuses on transient characteristics of the object, e.g.,
its velocity. Sometimes superficial characteristics are important, e.g., the redness of
copper matters to an interior designer.

The theoretical ontology of concepts is important because we attribute *causal powers* to the secondary-level dimensions that constitute the concept. Harré and Madden define causal powers as " 'X has the power to A' means 'X will/can do A,' in the appropriate conditions, *in virtue of its intrinsic nature*" (1975, 86). Notice that these causal powers are ontological because they refer to X's "intrinsic nature." Like Locke before them and me in the present volume, the standard analogy is the chemical elements. In short, secondary-level dimensions play key roles in causal mechanisms. Redness does not play a role in most causal explanations using copper; in contrast, the atomic structure of copper is used in many hypotheses and theories about copper.

The ontological theory expounded by the concept focuses on the concept's internal structure and its constituent parts, but that analysis is intimately related to how the object as a whole interacts, usually in a causal way, with its environment. We tend to identify as core dimensions those that have causal powers when the object interacts with the outside world. We use the atomic structure of copper to explain why it is a good conductor of electricity.

We often attribute causal powers to secondary-level dimensions when we make hypotheses using the basic-level concept. For example, I shall analyze the democratic and liberal peace in chapter 5. The basic hypothesis is that democracies do not fight wars. Causal mechanisms by which democracies do not fight wars involve attributes of democracy, for example, the ability to replace leaders via election. How we conceptualize democracy must be consistent with the causal mechanisms of theories that use the democracy concept. Because the constituent parts of the concept play a role in causal hypotheses, my approach to concepts is a realist one. One cannot neatly separate the ontology of a concept from the role it plays in causal theories and explanations.

Because I focus on multidimensional and multilevel concepts the question of concept structure must (and should) arise. How are the dimensions and levels combined to build a concept? Throughout this book I discuss two archetypical structures, necessary and sufficient condition and family resemblance. The necessary and sufficient condition structure is the default option. It has a history that goes back to Aristotle, and philosophical links to essentialist views of objects and phenomena, along with mathematical ties to two-valued logic. Until the middle of the twentieth century it faced no competition as the way

28

to define and conceptualize phenomena (e.g., Cohen and Nagel 1934). Even today it remains the standard approach to concepts and definitions in philosophical logic textbooks (e.g., Copi and Cohen 1990).

The attack on essentialism, and hence the necessary and sufficient condition view of concepts, in philosophy was spearheaded by Ludwig Wittgenstein (1953), who proposed that concepts can have no essential, necessary, characteristics, but that nevertheless there is a family resemblance that allows one to group together many objects under one rubric. The classic example is the concept of a game. Various games have many characteristics in common when they are compared, say, pairwise. However, there are no characteristics that all games share; hence no properties necessary for an activity to be considered a game. In other words, for any attribute proposed as necessary for something to be a game we can find activities that we all consider to be games, but which do not possess that attribute.

Another sustained attack on the classic necessary and sufficient condition framework has come from cognitive psychologists who have studied how individuals (i.e., nonscientists) categorize phenomena. To categorize is to implicitly or explicitly have a concept. Conversely, to have a concept permits categorization. A key idea in the cognitive psychology literature is that individuals categorize based on the similarity to prototypes. Whether a certain animal is considered a "bird" depends on how similar it is to prototypical birds like robins, sparrows, etc. (see Murphy 2002 for a nice survey of the cognitive literature).

Both family resemblance and prototype theories of concepts are crucial because they stress that categories generated by concepts may not have clear boundaries. I believe this to be a ubiquitous problem and I will refer to the "gray zone" to give it a name.

The necessary and sufficient condition structure suggests a crisp— i.e., dichotomous—view of categories where membership is all or nothing. A common claim is that a concept is really dichotomous, for example, many feel democracy has this characteristic. These two positions frequently go together, a necessary and sufficient condition *and* a dichotomous view of the object (e.g., Przeworski et al. 2000 on democracy). However, since I am not using a classic, Aristotelian logic, but a fuzzy one, I shall separate the issue of dichotomous concepts from their structure, which may or may not invoke the necessary and sufficient condition principle. Throughout this volume I shall assume that dimensions are continuous, and that a dichotomous dimension is just a special case.

In summary, we can take my continuing example of the chemical elements as an excellent metaphor for what this chapter proposes in the realm of social science concepts. There are two issues in discussing chemical elements. The first is the substantive component parts, such as electrons, protons, neutrons, etc. The second is the geometric structure of these elements. The same is true of most important social science concepts. We need a good analysis of the substantive dimensions of the concept along with how these secondary-level dimensions are structured.

A theory of a chemical element elaborates its ontology (e.g., what it is to be copper). A bad ontology focuses on substances like, earth, fire, air, and water which are not in fact part of copper at all. Less egregious is to focus on superficial or accidental properties which are not important, such as the redness of copper. Much of what good ontology entails is an analysis of those properties which have causal powers and which are used in causal explanations and mechanisms. The atomic structure of copper explains how it acts in many situations, e.g., its conductivity, reactivity with other chemical agents, reaction to heat, and so on. Social science concepts are no different.

THE BASIC LEVEL

While I have stressed the multilevel and multidimensional character of many key social science concepts, almost always *one* concept lies at the top of the pyramid. It is this concept that appears in theoretical models, propositions, and theories. At the basic level there are three important separate, but related, issues: (1) the negative pole, (2) the substantive content of the continuum between the two poles, and (3) the continuity that exists or not (i.e., dichotomous versus continuous) between the poles.

Frequently the goal of the research project is to explain the positive pole, be it democracy, crisis, war, or militarized dispute. The basic-level concept is often controversial *because* it is the dependent variable under scrutiny. Much research thus begins not with a conceptual range, but rather with one end—almost always the positive one—of the continuum. Hence part of concept-building is to think not only about the positive, but also about the negative end of the spectrum.

We can take as an example Schmitter's widely cited conceptualization of corporatism. It is a good example of how one can start with a complex idea about a particular phenomenon. Schmitter's definition of corporatism runs as follows:

> Corporatism can be defined as a system of interest representation in which the constituent units are organized into a limited number of singular, compulsory, noncompetitive, hierarchically ordered and functionally differentiated categories, recognized or licensed (if not created) by the state and granted a deliberate representational monopoly within their respective categories in exchange for observing certain controls on their selection of leaders and articulation of demands and supports. (Schmitter 1979, 13)

There is clearly a lot going on in this definition. It is obviously multidimensional and multilevel; not surprisingly the literature on the concept of corporatism is large (e.g., Lehmbruch 1977; Katzenstein 1985; Panitch 1980; Cameron 1984; see Siaroff 1999 and Collier 1995 for surveys).

While one often has a pretty good feel for the phenomenon referred to by the positive concept—often because it is tied to concrete empirical examples—there is often a radical asymmetry between the positive and the negative poles. For example, the concept of "war" is clear when juxtaposed with the vagueness of the negative pole. What is this negative concept? Peace? Nonwar? The negative pole in the corporatism literature is most often taken to be pluralism.[2]

Schmitter defines pluralism as follows:

> Pluralism can be defined as a system of interest representation in which the constituent units are organized into an unspecified number of multiple, voluntary, competitive, nonhierarchically ordered and self-determined (as to type or scope of interest) categories which are not specifically licensed, recognized, subsidized, created or otherwise controlled in leadership selection or interest articulation by the state and which do not exercise a monopoly of representational activity within their respective categories. (Schmitter 1979, 15)

One can see that much in this concept of pluralism is the negation of what appeared in the concept of corporatism, e.g., compulsory/voluntary, singular/multiple, hierarchical/nonhierarchical, and so

---

[2] It is not at all clear that Schmitter thinks that the opposite of corporatism is pluralism since he also has "monist" (e.g., USSR) and "syndicalist" types. Nevertheless, these other two types have not found much echo in the literature, and it is fair to say that for most scholars the negative pole of corporatism is pluralism.

forth. Good concept-building makes these contrasts explicit and systematic.

The difficulty of conceptualizing the negative pole can appear in various ways. One good test is to take the negative pole as the positive and ask about its negative. If we look at the (American) literature on pluralism it is not obvious that the negative pole is corporatism. Similar indications of difficulty surface when the negative pole has various possible labels. For example, the negative pole of democracy might be dictatorship or authoritarianism; historically it was monarchy. Alvarez et al. (1996) have three dimensions for "dictatorship" (1) mobilizing or exclusionary, (2) how many formal centers of power (executive, legislative, parties), (3) framework of law or more arbitrary system. This is clearly not just the opposite of their concept of democracy.

Lijphart's analysis of democracy illustrates how one can have two separate concepts at ends of the democracy spectrum with a continuum between them. He (1984) contrasts the "Westminster Model" with "Consensus Model" of democracy on the basis of eight secondary-level dimensions.[3] He then links these two via a continuum: "It is also possible, however, to derive all the characteristics of the majoritarian [Westminster] model logically from the principle of concentrating as much political power as possible in the hands of the majority. Conversely, all of the characteristics of the consensus model logically follow from the premise that political power should be dispersed and shared in a variety of ways" (1984, 207–8).

Mechanically and numerically the negative pole can be operationalized as zero on all of the secondary-level dimensions that characterize the positive extremes. For example, non–social revolution occurs when one or more of the positive attributes of a social revolution is absent. As a broad generalization of social science practice, the negative pole is often the negation of the positive: it has no independent theoretical existence. But it is always useful to ask about the negative pole and the degree to which it is different from "not" the positive pole. Asking this question can often result in a sharpening of the analysis of

---

[3]They are (1) concentration of executive power, one-party and bare-majority cabinets/executive power-sharing, (2) fusion of power and cabinet dominance/separation of powers, (3) asymmetric bicameralism/balanced bicameralism or minority representation, (4) two-party system/multiparty system, (5) one-dimensional party system/multidimensional party system, (6) plurality system of elections/proportional representation, (7) unitary and centralized government/federalism and decentralization, (8) exclusively representative democracy/written constitution and minority veto.

the positive pole. If the negative pole is taken to be the negative of the positive then this should at least be a conscious decision.

After considering the nature of the positive and negative poles one needs to be clear about the substantive character of the continuum linking the two. Confusion on this point can lead to serious problems down the road. A good example of how this can be problematic is the concept of an (enduring) rivalry (see Diehl and Goertz 2000 and Thompson 2001 for the two most prominent views on the concept of rivalry). The literature on enduring rivalries started in the early 1990s from a concern about the positive pole, long-lasting conflicts like U.S.-USSR, India-Pakistan, France-Germany, and the like. Indicating instability in the concept and the underlying continuum was that different terms were being used. For example, the literature started with "enduring rivalry"; Goertz and Diehl (2000) when talking about the concept preferred "rivalry"[4]; Thompson (1995) used the term "principal rivalries"; Thompson (2001) adopted the term "strategic rivalries."

Diehl and Goertz (2000; see Klein, Goertz, and Diehl 2004 for an updated discussion) explicitly discussed the negative pole of "isolated conflict" while Thompson never explicitly addressed the negative pole question. Underlying much of the debate about the concept of rivalry were conflicting views about the underlying continuum between the positive pole of enduring/strategic rivalry and the negative. The adjective "enduring" made it seem that temporal duration was core. In practice severity was also very important, because many looked at rivalries as the source of much war. One of the ongoing debates in the literature is the nature of low-level, long-term conflict. The Diehl and Goertz concept of rivalry allows this. In contrast, Thompson's view is that rivalries consist of "enemies"; they are severe and very hostile relationships.

As this brief overview implies, these issues are not resolved. In the context of this chapter, the key issue is that one should address explicitly the underlying continuum between the positive and negative poles. This can add tremendous coherence to the overall research project. We will see the same issue arise below when I contrast the necessary and sufficient condition and family resemblance concept structures as two extremes of a substitutability continuum. Instead of seeing these two structures as free-floating alternatives it is possible

---

[4]The second part of the book focused in particular on enduring rivalries, which are a subset of all rivalries.

to move along the continuum to points in between them. By explicitly conceptualizing the two poles and the continuum in between, the coherence of the whole concept-building enterprise is dramatically increased.

Once there is a clear view—at least at the basic level—of the positive and negative ends of the spectrum, one can begin the analysis of whether it is really a continuum or not. For example, Sartori has vigorously spoken out against "degreeism" (1984). The most prominent debate over this issue is whether or not democracy is dichotomous or not (see Alvarez et al. 1996 for a dichotomous view and Elkins 2000 for a critique).

My strategy is to treat all concepts as continuous, including dichotomous concepts as a special case. There are strong arguments for building continuous concepts. One of the biggest advantages is that it directly confronts the problem of the gray zone. If one's ontology specifically allows for the existence of borderline cases then one is ready to see them in reality. If one starts with dichotomous concepts then the tendency is to downplay, if not ignore, the problems— theoretical and empirical—of the gray zone.

Often, to dichotomize is to introduce measurement error. A dichotomous view of corporatism implies that all countries with value 1 are basically equivalent. This may be far from true. For example, Katzenstein (1985) includes Switzerland as a corporatist system, even though he concedes it lies at the weak end of the corporatism scale. However, one could easily put Switzerland into the category of noncorporatist countries (see Siaroff 1999 for a survey of corporatism measures). A continuous view of the concept of corporatism puts Switzerland where it belongs, in the gray zone.

Democracy provides another important example where the gray zone can matter a lot. There exists a huge literature on democratic transitions, which are virtually by definition in the gray zone. It is hard to imagine how one could develop a theory of democratic transitions without a gray zone view of democracy, since every country must pass through it on its way to becoming (or not) a stable democracy. In a different context, democracy plays a large role in the international conflict literature via the democratic peace. Yet there are important cases—Germany and the United Kingdom—where the country was democratic in terms of its domestic politics, but where the king had a very important, if not dominant, role in foreign policy.

One trap in this area is to confuse the empirical distribution of cases with the conceptual continuum. It may be a fact of life that half-democratic, half-authoritarian regimes are unstable and short lived (just as some chemical and physical states are unstable), but that empirical fact calls for a theoretical and causal explanation, not for a change in the concept itself. The actual distribution of cases along the basic-level continuum should not play a very strong role in concept-building. It is the job of causal theory to explain the empirical distribution of cases.

At the basic level the concept builder should do the following.

- Explicitly analyze the negative pole.
- Theorize the underlying continuum between the negative and positive poles.
- Theorize the gray zone; then determine whether or not the concept should be considered continuous or dichotomous.
- Do not let the empirical distribution of cases influence many decisions. Usually the empirical distribution of cases should be explained, not presumed in concepts.[5]

Even for contested concepts, these issues are often not directly faced. However, since much theory, methodology, and case selection hinges on these decisions, a conscious, explicit, and theoretically informed choice can start the scholar down the yellow-brick research road.

Two Prototypical Concept Structures: Necessary and Sufficient Condition and Family Resemblance

Once a preliminary idea has been formed about the concept at the basic level one can begin to construct a multidimensional and multilevel concept. The secondary-level dimensions will almost always refer to the positive concept; many of the same issues that arise at the basic level will reappear at lower levels. For each secondary-level dimension, the question of the negative pole will arise. In each case it is important that, in addition to the positive dimension linking up with the positive basic-level concept, the negative ends of the secondary-level

---

[5] I will address this issue again in chapter 3 in the context of ideal type concepts, which usually have no empirical cases at one or both poles; see p. 83.

dimensions make sense as well. Nevertheless, I, and most scholars, focus attention on the positive end of the basic level when constructing
lower-level dimensions.

In this section I begin my analysis of the prototypical ways to build
multilevel and multidimensional concepts. While it is certainly possible to construct hybrid structures, or even radically different ones,
most concepts can be seen as variants on the necessary and sufficient
condition structure or the family resemblance one.

Since the necessary and sufficient condition structure is standard it
is not uncommon to see it explicitly used. For example, the concept of
crisis that I examine in chapter 6 is very explicit about the dimensions
and their structure:

> [A] crisis is a situation with three necessary and sufficient conditions
> deriving from a change in its external environment. All three conditions
> are perceptions held by the highest-level decision-makers: (1) *a threat to
> basic values*, with a simultaneous subsequent awareness of (2) *finite time
> for response*, and of the (3) *high probability of involvement in military
> hostilities*. (Brecher, Wilkenfeld, and Moser 1988, 2)

But for rare exceptions (e.g., Collier's work), the family resemblance
approach to concepts does not appear openly as an alternative to the
necessary and sufficient condition one. A good way to think about
the family resemblance structure is as a rule about sufficiency with
no necessary condition requirements. In a dichotomous setting the
family resemblance rule almost always takes the form of "*m* of *n*."
The phenomenon falls into the concept category if the number of
secondary-level dimensions present exceeds a certain threshold (m).
If one takes the necessary and sufficient condition approach to be expressed as "*if and only if n* characteristics are present" then the family
resemblance takes the sufficiency-only form of "*if m* of *n* characteristics are present."

A problem in the analysis of the structure of concepts is that the
author often does not provide any structure at all. Discovering the
structure then becomes a matter of textual exegesis, or at worst guess-
work. For example, here is Karl on the concept of democracy:

> [D]emocracy is a political concept involving several dimensions: (1) con-
> testation over policy and political competition for office; (2) participation
> of the citizenry through partisan, associational, and other forms of collec-
> tive action; (3) accountability of rulers to the ruled through mechanism

of representation and the rule of law; and (4) civilian control over the
military. (Karl 1990, 2)

She is quite clear on the substance of her secondary-level dimensions
but she provides no guidance on how these combine to form the basic-
level democracy concept.

A useful trick in text exegesis is to see if the discussion of the dimensions makes claims that the absence of the dimension excludes the
case from the category. These claims express the basic characteristic
of the necessary condition structure that the absence of a necessary
condition eliminates the object. For example, Lipset describes two
dimensions to the concept of democracy:

> Democracy in a complex society may be defined as a political system
> which supplies regular constitutional opportunities for changing the gov-
> erning officials, and a social mechanism which permits the largest pos-
> sible part of the population to influence major decisions by choosing
> among contenders for political office. (Lipset 1960, 27)

We do not know how these two dimensions combine. But if one examines the text that follows this quote he goes on to imply that these
are necessary by looking at cases where one condition is absent and
explaining why that does not constitute a democracy.

If the necessary condition part of the structure has to be inferred
from discussions, then the situation is worse for the sufficiency part of
the structure. While scholars are relatively comfortable with the idea of
saying something is a necessary condition component of the concept,
they are much more hesitant to say what is sufficient for democracy.
For example, Collier and Levitsky (1997) propose that the "procedu-
ral minimum" for democracy "presumes fully contested elections with
full suffrage and the absence of massive fraud, combined with effective guarantees of civil liberties, including freedom of speech, assem-
bly, and association" (1997, 434). So while they are quite clear about
the necessary condition part of the concept of democracy they make
no statement about sufficiency (Sartori 1984 explicitly avoids the sufficiency question; see the discussion of Dahl's view of democracy in
chapter 3 for another example).

One of the advantages of having to construct a quantitative measure
(be it dichotomous or continuous) is that, like death, it focuses attention on key issues. We can use the absence of the necessary condition
dimensions to code the zero (nondemocracy) cases, but to count a

given country as a democracy implies some sort of sufficiency criterion. Depending on the (con)text it may be reasonable to assume that,
in the absence of any specific claims about sufficiency, all the necessary conditions are jointly sufficient. It must be stressed that giving
"minimum" sets of dimensions is theoretically and methodologically
incomplete. A complete concept structure must include sufficient criteria. If we are to say anything positive about cases we must have
sufficient conditions.

In short, it is quite common for an analysis of the secondary-level
dimensions of a concept to be given, but quite often this list has no
structure. That the necessary and sufficient condition structure has
been the standard for over 2000 years could lead to the reasonable
view that in the absence of discussion the necessary and sufficient
condition structure is the default structure. However, as we shall see,
things are not so simple.

One possible interpretative technique would be to infer the concept
structure from the structure of the quantitative measure. Unfortunately, this does not work in general because the question of how
concept structure matches (or not) with quantitative measures has
not really been posed (this is the topic of chapter 4).

Nevertheless, on occasion, looking at quantitative measures can
be a good way to see the family resemblance concept structure—but
almost never the necessary and sufficient condition one. The concept
of the "welfare state" illustrates how this can work. We typically think
of the welfare state as providing certain kinds of goods and services,
such as unemployment insurance, health care, retirement income, etc.
Underlying this notion of the welfare state is a family resemblance
structure. The secondary-level dimensions are the various kinds of
goods and services provided by the state.

There is no one service that a state *must* (necessarily) provide to
be a welfare state, but if the state produces "enough" of these services
we classify it in the welfare state category. Operationally, Hicks (1999)
defines a welfare state circa 1930 as one that provides at least three of
the four following services: (1) unemployment compensation, (2) old
age pensions, (3) health insurance, or (4) workman's compensation.
In sum, if the basic measure of the concept applies the m of n rule to
classify objects, then it is using a family resemblance structure.

One goal of this book is to encourage people to be more conscious
and explicit about how they build multidimensional and multilevel
concepts. While the necessary and sufficient condition structure is

sometimes explicitly used, the family resemblance one almost never lies on the surface; one must look at the theoretical framework, quantitative measures, and other indirect evidence for concept structure.

The concept builder should do the following.

- Do not just list dimensions of the concept.
- Be explicit about the necessary conditions, if any.
- Give sufficiency criteria. This is true for both necessary and sufficient condition and family resemblance structures.
- Do not force the reader to guess at structure from the discussion of examples or the mathematics of a quantitative measure.

THE MATHEMATICS OF CONCEPT STRUCTURES

If we are to validly translate concepts into quantitative measures then we need some way—or ways—of formalizing concept structures. This has multiple advantages. It permits us to directly link concept structures with eventual quantitative measures. It also makes explicit the theory and hypotheses that lie in the ontology of the concept. Finally, it makes clear some of the options for concept-building. Instead of taking the default structure or even ignoring the problem altogether formalization can mean better theory and better methodology.

I will explore two kinds of mathematics. The first is (fuzzy) logic and set theory. This fits more naturally with the necessary and sufficient condition structure since it receives direct expression via logic. Once we understand the fuzzy logic mathematics of necessary and sufficient conditions along with family resemblance structures we can then explore how these modeling options contrast with statistical procedures.

The necessary and sufficient condition structure poses no real problems if one applies two-valued Aristotelian logic with dichotomous variables. Table 2.1 illustrates this with a two-dimensional concept. X_1 and X_2 are the secondary-level dimensions each of which is necessary. So if X_1 or X_2 equals zero then so does X (I will use boldface capital characters for basic-level concepts, roman letters for secondary-level dimensions, and italic characters for the indicator/data level). We see sufficiency because when X_1 and X_2 are present then X has value 1. For example, Przeworski et al. (2000) have a necessary and sufficient condition view of democracy along with dichotomous variables, and everything works as it should.

TABLE 2.1

Necessary and Sufficient Condition Concept Structure: Logical AND

X_1	X_2	X
1	1	1
1	0	0
0	1	0
0	0	0

One can think of table 2.1 as a truth table in logic. The logical operator which produces this particular truth table is the logical AND (I will use the upper-case "AND" to refer to the logical AND, and likewise for the logical OR). In terms of set theory, AND is equivalent to the intersection operator. This leads us to the first important mathematical principle of concept structure:

The necessary and sufficient condition concept structure is mathematically modeled by AND or the intersection in set theory.

The family resemblance structure in the two-dimensional case is the idea that we categorize the object into the family if X_1 or X_2 or both are present. Recall that the family resemblance approach has sufficiency without necessity so X_1 can substitute for X_2, and vice versa. Here we have the *m* of *n* rule in action: if at least one of the two dimensions is present then it belongs to the concept.[6]

[6]Tversky (1977) defines family resemblance as $FR(a, b) = a * b - (a - b) - (b - a)$ where a,b are attributes of two items a and b. The basic idea is that family resemblance is the common attributes (i.e., $a * b$) minus the uncommon attributes [i.e., $(a - b)$ and $(b-a)$]. See Smith and Osherson (1984) for a very similar approach to concepts. Beckner defines "polythetic" in exactly family resemblance terms: "A class is ordinarily defined by reference to a set of properties which are both necessary and sufficient (by stipulation) for membership in the class. It is possible, however, to define a group K in terms of a set G of properties $f_1, f_2, \ldots, f_n$ in a different manner. Suppose we have an aggregation

40

TABLE 2.2
Family Resemblance Concept Structure: Logical OR

X₁	X₂	X
1	1	1
1	0	1
0	1	1
0	0	0

If we ask what logical operator generates the pattern in table 2.2, the answer is OR. Of course, the set theoretic partner to OR is the union. Hence we have the following mathematical principle for the family resemblance concept structure:

The family resemblance concept structure is mathematically modeled by OR or the union in set theory.

Since I want to be able to deal with continuous variables one needs a logic or set theory that uses continuous instead of two-valued logic. It turns out that fuzzy logic fits the bill perfectly, since it is an infinite-valued logic. By convention fuzzy logic variables range from zero to one, which for our immediate purposes is merely a matter of calibration.

The question then arises as to the fuzzy logic equivalents to the dichotomous AND and OR (or in set theoretic terms the intersection and the union). While there are various possible options for AND and OR within fuzzy logic (see Smithson 1987 or any fuzzy logic textbook)

---

of individuals ... such that (1) each one possesses a large (but unspecified) number of the properties in G; (2) each f in G is possessed by every individual in the aggregate; and (3) no f in G is possessed by every individual in the aggregate. By the terms of (3), no f is necessary for membership in this aggregate, and nothing has been said to either warrant or rule out the possibility that some f in G is sufficient for membership in the aggregate" (1959, 22; see also Bailey 1973).

the most common and prominent operator is the minimum for AND while the maximum serves as the continuous homologue to OR.

Notice that the minimum and maximum work perfectly in the dichotomous case. In tables 2.1 and 2.2 the minimum of the X_1 and X_2 columns gives the X value for necessary and sufficient conditions, while the maximum does the right thing for OR. Hence fuzzy logic will generate the results we expect in the dichotomous case. There are thus no particular mathematical problems with a necessary and sufficient condition concept structure with continuous dimensions. There are, of course, potential substantive concerns which may remain, but there are no formal reasons opposing continuous dimensions for either the necessary and sufficient condition or the family resemblance concept structures.

One can visualize the necessary and sufficient condition or family resemblance structure with two dimensions in terms of the "fuzzy logic cube" (Kosko 1993). Figures 2.1a and 2.1c illustrate AND and OR with continuous fuzzy logic mathematics. If you reduce the figures from three to two dimensions you get upper and lower triangles. As Ragin (2000) repeatedly shows, upper-triangular data configurations typify sufficiency while lower-triangular configurations represent necessary conditions and the logical AND.[7]

Table 2.3 summarizes the basic principles that formalize our two basic concept structures. The family resemblance structure uses the Aristotelian logical OR, the fuzzy logic maximum, or the set theoretic union. In contrast, the necessary and sufficient condition structure uses the Aristotelian logical AND, the fuzzy logic minimum, or the set theoretic intersection.

So how then do the standard quantitative, statistical measures and their structures fit into this framework? First, we can note from the outset that the mathematics used in virtually all methods textbooks do not mention the minimum or the maximum as structural principles.[8] In the literature on statistical measures the two dominant operators are the mean or correlation. If we add these to the list we have a number of possibilities for building concepts and their corresponding quantitative measures. The key point in the context of this chapter is that they are not the same things. The minimum is not the maximum,

---

[7]Hermann (1969) uses a cube to conceptualize "crisis." At one end of the continuum are crisis decisions and at the other end are routinized decisions.

[8]In practice, the minimum and maximum are quite common; see chapter 5 for examples.

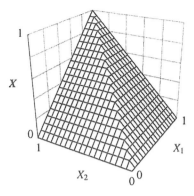

Figure 2.1a: AND/Minimum

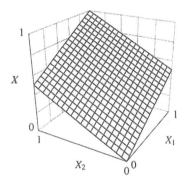

Figure 2.1b: Mean

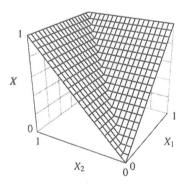

Figure 2.1c: OR/Maximum

FIGURE 2.1
Mathematics of concept structure: AND, mean, and OR

TABLE 2.3
The Logic of Concept Structures

Mathematics	Family Resemblance	Necessary and Sufficient Condition
Classic logic	OR	AND
Fuzzy logic	Maximum	Minimum
Set theory	Union	Intersection

and neither is the mean or a correlation. One can take the data in tables 2.1 and 2.2 and calculate the mean, which is clearly not the same as what one finds in the X column. Similarly, the mean or a correlation will not produce surfaces like those found in figures 2.1a and 2.1c.

Figure 2.1b illustrates what the mean looks with two secondary-level dimensions. Comparing this figure with the maximum and the minimum, i.e., figures 2.1a and 2.1c, respectively, shows that these are not similar concept structures. All three are equal if all secondary-level dimensions are equal: in other words along the (0,0,0) to (1,1,1) diagonal all measures are the same. The differences get larger and larger the more the values of X_1 and X_2 diverge. One can see that the mean surface really cuts between the maximum and the minimum by touching the top edge of the minimum and the lower edge of the maximum.

The key point is not that the logic of family resemblance or necessary and sufficient conditions is necessarily better or worse than statistical measures, but that they are *different*. The choice of concept structure—and thus implicitly quantitative measures—should be driven by the theory of the ontology of the phenomena concerned. But it is useful to analyze the theoretical, methodological, and mathematical implications of the choice of a given concept structure.

THE SUBSTITUTABILITY CONTINUUM BETWEEN NECESSARY AND SUFFICIENT CONDITION AND FAMILY RESEMBLANCE STRUCTURES

In addition to being prototypical concept structures the necessary and sufficient condition and family resemblance structures lie at the ends of a concept structure continuum. In the previous section I stressed how fundamental it is to think about the continuum between positive and negative poles. A continuum lies between my two standard concept structures: the substitutability continuum.

In the last list of guidelines for the concept-builder I stressed that one always needs sufficiency criteria. This is true for both necessary and sufficient condition and family resemblance concepts. A key difference between the two then is that one has necessary conditions while the other has none. By definition a necessary condition cannot be substituted for. In contrast, the family resemblance approach allows for the absence of a given characteristic to be compensated by the presence of another. The substitutability continuum (its mathematics and methodological issues) is the central topic of chapter 5 so I need not go into detail here.

The substitutability contrast between the necessary and sufficient condition and family resemblance approaches provides good reason to view these two structures themselves as two poles of a continuum of concept-building strategies. As chapter 3 shows, this continuum can be seen in terms of how liberal or conservative the concept structure is in terms of the number of observations it includes. All things equal, the family resemblance structure is more liberal than the necessary and sufficient condition one. This comes out clearly in the formalization of the necessary condition structure as "*if and only if n* characteristics" which must have fewer than, or an equal number of cases as, "*if m of n* characteristics."

Notice the key role of substitutability in the family resemblance approach. The absence of one dimension can be compensated by the presence of other dimensions. So one can ask the substitutability question in cases of doubt about concept structure. If the discussion seems to suggest no substitutability then the inference is that the necessary and sufficient condition structure is probably best; if there seems to be significant substitutability between dimensions then the family resemblance structure is likely to fit better.

The necessary and sufficient condition structure lies at the nonsubstitutability end of the spectrum while the family resemblance lies at the other, complete substitutability pole. We can ask how the average (and by analogy correlation, which is a central tendency technique) fits into the substitutability continuum. It would be correct to say that it falls somewhere in the middle. As chapter 5 discusses in detail, one can find the mean in the middle of the substitutability continuum. This can be visualized by comparing figure 2.1a, which is the minimum (i.e., substitutability zero), to figure 2.1b, which is the mean, to figure 2.1c, which is the maximum (i.e., maximal substitutability). You will see that the mean surface lies between the minimum and the maximum (they are all equal on the diagonal).

Much of this volume is a working out of this basic tension between the "logic" of concepts, which is frequently of a necessary and sufficient condition or family resemblance sort, and the "statistics" of quantitative measures. Fuzzy logic plays a key role in permitting us to give mathematical and formal representation of the ways in which most scholars have thought about concepts. Using the concept of substitutability permits us to contrast the mathematics of fuzzy logic with the mathematics of statistical measures. The substitutability continuum provides a method for comparing and contrasting different concept structures, be they drawn from logic or statistics.

In short, the concept-builder should do the following.

- Theorize the substitutability between dimensions. There are various ways to change the substitutability between dimensions (see below and chapter 5 for some options). One can choose anything from no substitutability to complete substitutability.

Salience and Essentiality: Weighting Dimensions

Once there are multiple dimensions or indicators then the question of weighting arises—or should arise. Within an additive or statistical approach to measures this is not problematic per se. A statistical approach almost by definition gives different weights to different indicators. In contrast, it is not obvious what weighting would mean in a necessary and sufficient condition context or when one is using fuzzy logic to model the concept. For example, what does it mean to say that dimension 1 is "more necessary" than dimension 2?

The issue of substitutability is closely connected to the relative importance of dimensions. Almost by definition a necessary condition is more important than one that can be substituted for. Thus, to make a decision about substitutability is also to make a decision about weighting. Nevertheless, within a necessary condition or family resemblance framework one can vary the individual weights of the substitutable or necessary dimensions.

Obviously weighting can, and probably should, be done based on some (ontological) theory of the object, or it can be based on empirical correlations. In this section I look at the general issues surrounding weighting in my two prototypical concept structures, necessary and sufficient condition and family resemblance. I will not address the often tricky problem of how to actually assign weights, but rather I address the issue of assigning weights to begin with. This is particularly important using the logic or set theory approach to concepts where how weighting might be done is generally unknown, and where often the idea of weighting never even arises.

It seems reasonable to assume that for most phenomena some secondary-level dimensions are more important than others. Particularly if one takes a functionalist ontology, some parts of the whole are more crucial (e.g., necessary) than others. Some might be essential while others only facilitate. In any concept-building enterprise one must directly address at the theoretical level the question of weighting. The advantage of the correlational approach is that statistical techniques along with the data automatically generate weights. The key point is that when constructing a concept the question of weighting needs to be specifically addressed.

As an observation on the practice of social science one can make the following generalizations about weighting in concepts and numeric measures.

1. The necessary and sufficient condition structure inevitably assumes equal weighting of dimensions.

2. A nonstatistical, arithmetical approach to measures usually applies unweighted averages.

3. Weighting is automatic if statistical (e.g., correlational, factor analytic) techniques are employed.

Measures of the democracy (for example, those listed in table 1.1) illustrate these empirical observations on the practice of weighting for one concept for which there are many measures. For example, Alvarez et al. (1996), who most clearly take a necessary and sufficient condition view of democracy, use no weighting, which is directly related to their use of dichotomous variables. Almost by definition dichotomous variables cannot be weighted (an argument against them); hence the use of dichotomous variables directly leads to unweighted dimensions. Most of the measures in table 1.1 are unweighted sums or averages. For example, the Freedom House measure is the average of 22 indicators. Bollen and Grandjean (1981) provide a good example of a statistical approach, where clearly the latent variable dimensions are determined by the factor analysis, data, and specific measurement model used.

There is at least one important exception, the polity measure of democracy. As I will discuss in detail in chapter 4, this family resemblance measure is a weighted sum. Here we have a case where each of the five indicators receives its own a priori weight. However, it is hard to find any justification of the weights given (see Munck and Verkuilen 2002 for more on this point).

Within a statistical or arithmetic approach to measures weighting poses no particular conceptual problems. While it may be hard to assign specific weights for a particular concept, the idea of weighting is not problematic.

However, when moving to fuzzy logic ways of modeling concepts, along with necessary and sufficient condition concepts, such is no longer the case. Some might dispute that it makes any sense at all to say that one necessary condition is more important than another. Also, it is not clear mathematically what weighting means when using the AND (necessary and sufficient condition) or OR (family resemblance) concept structures.

It might seem contradictory to say that X_1 is more necessary than X_2. But we do have some intuitions that imply weighting for necessary conditions. If some necessary conditions are "trivial" then others must be "important." Hence we have the beginnings of a weighting system. As a first cut (see Goertz 2004 for an extensive analysis in terms of set theory and fuzzy logic) we can propose a weighting system with sufficiency at the one end and trivialness at the other. Clearly, a necessary condition that is also sufficient is important, while a trivial necessary condition is not.

The intuition behind the idea of a trivial necessary condition is that those factors which are easy to obtain or which are almost always present are trivial, but real, necessary conditions. We can take Nussbaum's view of human functioning. Clearly, air is necessary to function well as a human being, but since it is usually (though less so these days) not hard to get air it is a less important necessary condition than food, whose acquisition is problematic for millions, if not billions, of people.

Part of the conceptual difficulty with weighting necessary and sufficient conditions lies with their frequently associated dichotomous variables. Once one moves to continuous (e.g., fuzzy) logic then there

48

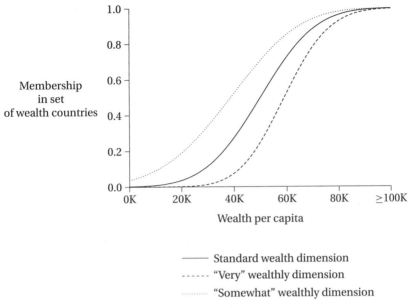

FIGURE 2.2
Weighting dimensions: Fuzzy logic hedges

are no conceptual barriers to weighting variables. In fact, fuzzy logic has an extensive array of methods for doing this. Most of these fall under the category of "hedges" (e.g., Lakoff 1973) which are used to indicate relative importance.

Figure 2.2 illustrates how this typically works for the hypothetical dimension of "wealth." The solid curve represents the scale that could be used for an unweighted wealth dimension. The dashed line portrays a dimension that is "very" important. The most common mathematical way to model this weighting is via the square root operator. Notice that for "very" wealthy the square root is below the standard, solid line. The same X-value thus receives a lower score on the dimension weighted by "very" than it does on the standard one. We can also have dimensions that are "somewhat" important, shown in the figure by the dotted line. The canonical "somewhat" weight in fuzzy logic uses the square operator to get this line (see Goertz 2003 for more extended examples in an international relations context; any fuzzy logic textbook, e.g., Cox 1999, will give a complete presentation). In summary, weighting does not prove problematic when one uses fuzzy logic to formalize concepts.

The ability to weight dimensions thus exists for the mathematics commonly used to structure concepts. The point I stress is that one can do this for both necessary and sufficient conditions and family resemblance concept structures. Of course, this does not solve the pragmatic problem of how to assign weights. This problem hinges on both the specific substance of the ontological concept as well as its three-level structure. The practical advice for the concept-builder is to explicitly address the weighting question. If one adopts the unweighted option then it should be a conscious choice; if one weights based on theoretical and/or empirical considerations then that too needs explicit defense (*pace* the polity procedure of unjustified weights). It is particularly easy to avoid the weighting question when using necessary and sufficient condition structures or dichotomous variables. Hence posing explicitly the question of the salience and relative importance of dimensions becomes all the more important.

For the concept-builder, it is important to consider the following issues.

- Explicitly ask the weighting question.
- Justify the weighting scheme used.

THREE-LEVEL CONCEPTS

OR and AND thus represent in short the basic structural principles of the necessary and sufficient condition and family resemblance concept structures. These two structures within a three-level framework generate a variety of alternatives for building concepts. One can use AND and OR at either the secondary and the indicator level. Table 2.4 describes the four possibilities produced by crossing the AND and OR structures with the secondary and indicator levels.

In the Introduction we saw that Nussbaum's view of a human being utilized AND at the secondary level of the essential functions of human well-being, while using OR at the indicator level to incorporate cultural diversity into her concept. I suspect that this particular three-level structure is quite common. In fact, I shall use it in chapter 4 when I reformulate the polity measure of democracy.[9]

---

[9]In formal terms we can convert a structure of OR at the indicator level and AND at the secondary to the converse because $(x_1 + x_2 + x_3) * (y_1 + y_2 + y_3) = (x_1 * y_1) + (x_1 * y_2) + \cdots + (x_3 * y_3)$, but this rarely makes any theoretical sense.

TABLE 2.4

Three-Level Concepts and Concept Structures

	Concept Structures	
Example	Secondary Level	Indicator Level
Nussbaum (1992)	AND	OR
Alvarez et al. (1996)	AND	AND
Schmitter (1982)	OR	OR
??	OR	AND

If we make some assumptions about how quantitative measures reflect concept structures, notably that additive measures translate back into family resemblance concepts, then we can easily discover examples of the use of OR at both levels. We can take Schmitter's three-level concept of corporatism as an example of how the basic family resemblance structure can be used at both levels. Figure 2.3 interprets how Schmitter has structured his corporatism concept (see the next section for a discussion of the various arrows and symbols).[10]

Alvarez et al. (see also Przeworski et al. 2000) conceive of democracy as a three-level concept with AND at both levels. They propose two secondary-level dimensions for democracy of "contestation" and "offices" where contestation has indicator-level variables of multiple parties and executive turnover, while offices involves the election of the executive and the election of the legislature. If any of the indicator-level variables has value zero then its secondary-level dimension is zero, which then implies a basic-level democracy value of zero.

The fourth alternative in table 2.4 uses AND at the indicator level with OR at the secondary level. This appears to be a relatively uncommon concept structure. Perhaps the popularity of its converse—OR at the indicator level with AND at the secondary level—partially explains this rarity. In chapter 9 on concepts in theories we shall see that the AND/indicator-level, OR/secondary-level structure is very common

---

[10]Chapter 8 provides another very important example, the concept of "politically relevant dyads" which plays a major role in research design in large-N studies of international conflict; see figure 8.1.

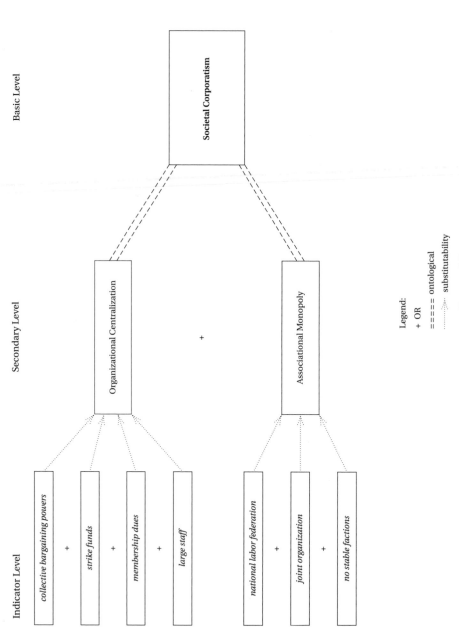

Basic Level

Secondary Level

Indicator Level

Societal Corporatism

Organizational Centralization

Associational Monopoly

collective bargaining powers

+

strike funds

+

membership dues

+

large staff

national labor federation

+

joint organization

+

no stable factions

+

Legend:
+ OR
= = = = ontological
.... substitutability

FIGURE 2.3
Three-level concepts: Societal corporatism

for theories. In fact, Ragin's Boolean (1987) and fuzzy set (2000) methods generate this structure by default. It does seem paradoxical that a structure common in theories is rare for concepts. This is a topic for future research.

Figure 2.3 is the first of many three-level figures that will appear in this volume. Three-level concepts are complex beasts and figures are by far the best way to understand the complex set of issues and decisions involved. As table 2.4 summarizes one, can use AND or OR for either level. This is one set of important design decisions.

When reading about concepts in practice the appropriate structure of the concept is often not clear. It then often becomes a matter of interpreting examples in the text, looking at quantitative measures, and looking at causal hypotheses involving the concept. Nevertheless, it is rare to find a complex or abstract concept that does not implicitly have a three-level structure. Usually the basic level is too abstract and complex to be directly converted into the indicator/data level. The secondary level provides theoretical linkage between the abstract basic level and the concrete indicator/data level. For example, the basic-level concept of "intelligence" usually receives the secondary-level formulation "verbal ability," "analytic ability," or "mathematical ability," which then allows the actual creation of test questions.

The last sections have examined the formal, mathematical expression of the necessary and sufficient condition and family resemblance concept structures. Qualitative theorists tend to prefer the use of necessary and sufficient conditions, but have not made the ties to logic and set theory. These two prototypical concept structures can be contrasted with the mean and correlation typical of statistical approaches to measurement and conceptualization. The concept-builder should do the following.

- Be explicit about the formal relationships between secondary- or indicator-level dimensions. The three canonical possibilities are (1) minimum/AND, (2) mean, and (3) maximum/OR.

Theoretical Relationships between Levels: Ontology, Causality, and Substitutability

The previous sections have focused on the formal, structural relationships between indicators or secondary-level dimensions. In this section and its subsections, I examine the theoretical relationships

TABLE 2.5
Theoretical and Formal Relationships

Theoretical Relationship	AND	OR	Symbol	Temporal Priority
Ontological	Yes	Yes	=====	No
Causal	Yes	Yes	——→	Yes
Conjunction of necessary causes	Yes	No	——✕——	Yes
Noncausal conjunction of necessary conditions	Yes	No	·······⫶ɪᴏ⫶·········	No
Substitutability	No	Yes	·······⫶ɪᴏ··	No

between and within levels. I have stressed that concepts are fundamentally about ontology. At the same time concepts interact with causal hypotheses in complex ways. Ontology and causality are intimately related to the realist approach to concepts. Table 2.5 lists the theoretical relationships between levels that I include in my analysis (i.e., column one). The AND and OR columns show how the theoretical relationships interact with formal, mathematical principles. Chapter 9 provides some examples of how these relationships appear in some prominent work dealing with the welfare state, social revolution, and other important phenomena.

The issue of causal analysis *in* concepts has rarely received the attention it is due. Within a three-level concept one must confront the problem of causal analysis. Causal analysis in concepts is uncommon in part because we expend most causal effort at the basic level in analyzing the relationships between independent and dependent variables. I have referred throughout this chapter to the ontology of concepts. The relationship between ontology and causal analysis can vary, as we will see, but most of the time hypotheses about causal effects play a role. Above, I have stressed that we choose many secondary-level dimensions because of their role in causal explanations.

One might object that by introducing causal analysis into the concept itself I am muddying the waters. One might suppose that the causal claims in concepts should be testable, so now the researcher must examine not only her hypotheses at the basic level, but also those contained in the concept. I believe, however, that it is not possible to easily separate the causal hypotheses within the concept and the causal hypotheses at the basic level that use the concept. In fact, a major goal of chapter 5 is to examine empirically and statistically the causal hypotheses embedded in some core concepts in the liberal peace literature.

The causal ontological analysis of concepts cannot be divorced from the causal propositions at the basic level. The causal powers of an object or its causal liabilities (i.e., things that can happen to an object; Harré and Madden 1975) at the basic level have intimate links to the object's ontology. To take the liberal peace which I analyze in chapter 5, if a regime changes its nature from authoritarian to democratic then its causal powers change. To use a prosaic example, if you change the number of electrons in a copper atom you get another element with different causal powers and liabilities.

Basic-Level Dimensions as Causes: Statistical Models

> In short, we expect an association between indicators that depend on or "reflect" a variable, that is, if they are the "effects" of the variable. But if the variable depends on the indicators—if the indicators are the "causes"—those indicators may be either positively or negatively correlated, or even unrelated. Therefore, we should decide whether indicators are causes or effects of a variable before using their intercorrelations to assess their validity.
> *Kenneth Bollen*

The dominant statistical approach to concepts has essentially two levels, basic-level concepts and indicators. One can ask about the relationship between the indicator and the concept: is it causal in nature? If so, what is the nature of this causal relationship? There are at least three possibilities worth exploring: (1) concept causes indicator, (2) indicator causes concept, and (3) a noncausal relationship.

It is quite common to just ignore the whole question of causal analysis in the relationship between concept and indicator. However, the factor analytic approach does assume a causal connection:

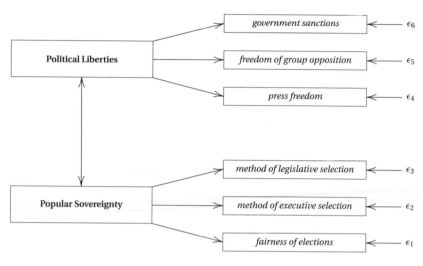

FIGURE 2.4

Latent variable model of democracy. *Source*: Bollen and Grandjean 1981

In factor analytic, latent variable, LISREL approaches the basic-level factors—latent variables—cause the indicators.

Blalock's 1979 American Sociological Association presidential address illustrates nicely the statistical view of the concept-indicator problem: it is almost all about cause running from unmeasured variables to indicators. We can use Bollen's analysis of democracy as an example of this way of thinking about concepts. Figure 2.4 shows a typical latent variable model with its unmeasured latent variables, its indicators, and error terms. Bollen and Grandjean (1981) explicitly examine the multidimensionality of the democracy concept. Formally, the indicators are the effect of the latent causes:

$$x_i = \beta_1 \mathbf{X}_1 + \beta_2 \mathbf{X}_2 + \epsilon_i \tag{2.1}$$

Here $\mathbf{X}_1$ and $\mathbf{X}_2$ are *unmeasured* basic-level concepts which produce indicators x_i (this notation is unconventional in the latent variable context, but keeps with my notation for three-level concepts). The latent variables usually work theoretically at the basic level (hence the boldface characters) while the indicators are at the indicator/data level. As a result, normally the secondary level is absent from these factor analytic models. With extremely rare exceptions, statistical models of concepts are two level, (1) variables and (2) indicators. The "variables" typically are the basic-level factors that appear in the major theoretical hypotheses and models.

In particular, Bollen and Grandjean want to know if the two theoretical (latent) dimensions of democracy (1) popular sovereignty and (2) political liberty can be found in a confirmatory factor analysis. Their analysis finds that in fact the two latent variables are not distinct and that democracy is best represented by a single latent factor model.

Typically, distinct latent variables will be included as individual variables in the structural (basic level) equation. Because a good latent variable requires high correlations among it indicators, good distinct latent variables should not be too highly correlated.[11] If we interpret the causal arrows in their usual sense then the latent variables have two causal roles: (1) they are causes of the dependent variable (structural equation) and (2) causes of the indicators.

As Bollen notes in the epigraph to this subsection, one must distinguish between indicators as cause or effect. The latent variable approach takes the indicators as effect, but principal component analysis takes them as cause:

$$X = \beta_1 x_1 + \beta_2 x_2 + \cdots + \beta_n x_n + \epsilon. \tag{2.2}$$

Since the unmeasured, basic-level X now stands on the dependent variable side of the equation it is normally considered the effect of the indicators x_i.[12] While this causal option does exist, it is not currently popular among political scientists and sociologists.

The LISREL approach thus typifies what I have called the disease-symptom model. For example, the symptoms of AIDS were known before the virus itself was discovered. The cognitive psychology literature uses the idea of cue validity to distinguish how effective certain

[11]There is some debate about what the ideal correlation should be among indicators; some argue that medium to low correlations are good. See Bollen and Lennox (1991) for a review.

[12]For example Velicer and Jackson describe the difference: "Some investigators distinguish between factor analysis and component analysis by referring to the former as a latent variable procedure and the latter as a manifest variable procedure. A latent variable is an unobserved, underlying error-free variable that, with the addition of sampling error, accounts for the observed or manifest variables. Component analysis can be described as a weighted linear composite of a p observed variables, and is therefore described as a manifest variable procedure" (1990, 17–18).

cues are in identifying or categorizing objects. One can quite reasonably look for clues, cues, and indicators that reveal the presence of a phenomenon. Part of the ontological theory will then be a causal analysis of how the phenomenon produces these cues and clues.[13]

It is the nature of cues and other "identification procedures" (Osherson and Smith 1981) that they produce false positives and negatives. For example, Keil and Batterman (1984) have performed interesting experiments with children that illustrate these points. They investigated the concept "robbers" via two scenarios: (1) a very friendly and cheerful woman who gives you a hug but then disconnects your toilet bowl and takes it away without permission and with no intention to return it; and (2) a smelly mean old man with a gun in his pocket who comes to your house and takes your TV set because your parents didn't want it any more and told him he could have it. Clearly they are juxtaposing typical cues for identifying a robber against the definition of a robber as one who "takes without permission." They found that smaller children used the typical features to categorize robbers while older children used the rules (see Hampton 1995 for a similar sort of experiment with adults; Smith, Patalano, and Jonides 1995 discuss experimental evidence that people start with rule-based categorization and then add features that are "characteristic" of the category). These kinds of examples suggest that we want to distinguish between ontological properties and indicators that are effects or typical of the phenomenon.

Concept-builders should

- Clearly examine the causal relationships between indicators and secondary- and basic-level factors. Identify clearly those indicators which are the *effects* of the phenomenon or *cues* that signal the presence of the phenomenon.

---

[13]"*Cue validity* is the conditional probability that an object is in a particular category given its possession of some feature (or 'cue')" (Lakoff 1987, 52, emphasis in original); Rosch suggested that "category cue validity" is the sum of the cue validities of the individual attributes. Similarly, Miller and Johnson-Laird (1976) talk about a concept having a *core* and an *identification procedure*. For example, "woman" might have a core (e.g., reproductive system), but the identification procedure might be things like voice, hair, body shape. This is exactly how paleontologists proceed with extinct species.

Ontology and Concepts

I propose that the basic difference between a qualitative and a quantitative scholar's thinking about concepts lies in the (implicit) use of the disease-symptom model for concepts by the latter group and the use of ontological approaches by the former. In other words, qualitative scholars tend to think of concepts (when they are not distracted by the problem of developing indicators or quantitative measures) in terms of their ontological properties.

The ontological approach does not in the first instance see causal relationships between levels. Because secondary-level dimensions *constitute* what the phenomenon *is* the relationship is one of identity, not causation. To have elections is not an indicator of democracy, but to have elections is what it means to be a democracy. Hence, there is a close connection between semantic approaches to concepts and ontological ones. The key point in the context of this chapter is that there is a noncausal relationship between the secondary-level dimensions and the basic-level concept. Of the five relationships listed in table 2.5, three are noncausal in nature.[14]

The concept of a welfare state illustrates quite nicely the combination of an ontological approach to concepts with a family resemblance structure. By definition a welfare state provides basically two kinds of services, income security via programs like old age pensions, unemployment insurance, and support for poor people, and medical programs or insurance. If you want to measure how extensive the welfare state is you examine to what degree the state provides these services. For example, many use the International Labor Organization data which cover spending on these kinds of public or semipublic programs. To be a welfare state is to provide or pay for these kinds of services. I do not think it makes much sense to talk about an unmeasured or latent variable that "causes" this kind of spending. It makes more sense to say that those kinds of programs *constitute* a welfare state.

Figure 2.5 shows how Hicks (1999) conceives of the circa 1930 welfare state, an example I will analyze in more detail in chapters 3 and 9. He includes four of the major programs that constitute a welfare state: (1) workman's compensation, (2) health insurance, (3) old age

---

[14]Because there are no conventions about how to visually represent noncausal relationships I have invented my own.

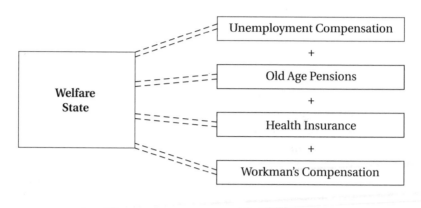

Legend:

===== ontological

+ OR

FIGURE 2.5
Ontological concepts and family resemblance structures: "Welfare state"

pensions, and (4) unemployment compensation. If any three of these four are present he considers, dichotomously, that a welfare state exists. In figure 2.5 the series of equal signs goes from each secondary-level dimension to the basic-level concept. I do this to emphasize the relative independence of the dimensions vis-à-vis the whole. In contrast, with the necessary and sufficient condition structure there is a tighter interdependence because of the necessity of each component.

The welfare state example also illustrates how closely arithmetic addition is tied to OR. An obvious way to implement the family resemblance structure is to add up the expenditures of all the welfare state–related programs. This makes much more sense than using the maximum of the fuzzy logic OR. When Hicks uses dichotomous data he naturally adopts a family resemblance m-of-n rule. In other analyses of later time periods he uses total expenditure data. In both instances he uses family resemblance structures; the particular choice of family resemblance measure depends on data issues, not on a change in the conceptualization of the welfare state.

Skocpol clearly sees "social revolution" in necessary and sufficient condition terms (see chapter 9 for details), so we can graphically illustrate the ontological, necessary and sufficient condition concept as in figure 2.6.

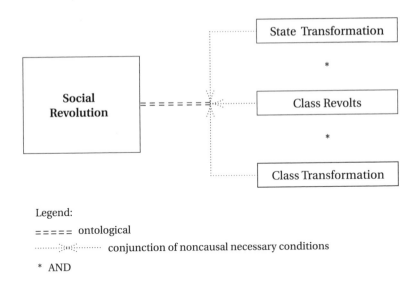

Legend:

===== ontological

············⋮⋮⋮············ conjunction of noncausal necessary conditions

* AND

FIGURE 2.6
Ontological concepts with necessary and sufficient condition structures:
"Social revolution"

To stress the interdependence of the dimensions in the necessary and sufficient framework I use dotted arrows that connect together before going to the basic-level concept. Unlike the family resemblance structure, each of these dimensions must be present for the event to be considered a social revolution. Also, note that I have used dotted arrows in this figure. Unlike solid arrows that traditionally indicate causation, the joined dotted arrows symbolize noncausal necessary conditions. Adcock and Collier refer exactly to the interdependence typical of the necessary and sufficient condition structure in the case of democracy: "In cases where the elected government lacks effective power to rule, it is not valid to treat the other defining attributes of democracy (e.g. competitive elections) as meaningfully measuring the presence of democracy. The absence of effective power to rule does not merely make countries somewhat less democratic; it undermines the meaningfulness of the other defining attributes of democracy" (Adcock and Collier 2001, 559).

Table 2.5 includes a column entitled "Temporal Priority." Temporal priority is intimately related to the concept of a cause: normally causes can only precede (or be simultaneous) with their effects. A key rule is that normally only noncausal relationships can exist between levels on the dependent variable side. Presumably, the basic-level independent variables, not the outcome's secondary-level variables, are the causes of the basic-level dependent variable. This can most clearly be seen in the distinction between causal and noncausal conjunctions of necessary condition factors. Causal conjunctions will normally appear on the independent variable side, while noncausal conjunctions along with ontology constitute the dependent variable concept (see figure 9.1 in chapter 9 for Skocpol's complete theory, which nicely contrasts the causal and noncausal conjunctions of necessary conditions).

The ontological view of concepts makes sense of how many qualitative scholars think about social and political phenomena. For example, Wendt (1998) has argued for this kind of relationship: "Constitutive theories have a different objective, which is to account for the properties of things by reference to the structures in virtue of which they exist." I suggest that this is less mysterious than it usually sounds in the social constructivist literature. Part of the problem is that we have simultaneously an ontological theory of the phenomenon and we choose the secondary-level dimensions in part because of their causal powers at the basic level. There is no escaping this duality, since a good conceptualization is in the final analysis in large part determined by its usefulness in basic-level causal theories.

Indicator/Data Level Relationships: Substitutable or Causal

In a three-level concept structure the indicator level links the more theoretical analysis in the basic and secondary levels to the more practical requirements of converting these ideas into empirical practice. In this subsection I discuss the ontology of the indicator level. As with this chapter in general, I argue that often a noncausal view of indicators as part of concept structures makes more sense in many political and social contexts.

The indicator level contrasts with higher levels in the degree of theoretical abstraction used. Basically, secondary- and basic-level dimensions are too abstract to give guidance in actual data gathering; hence the indicator/data level is where the concept gets specific enough to guide the acquisition of empirical data. Much of the literature on the welfare state stresses the central role played by "worker mobilization." For example, in Hicks's analysis of the formation of the 1920s and 1930s welfare state (see figure 9.2 in chapter 9 for the complete model) the worker mobilization variable is clearly the most important cause. However, to actually code data—even dichotomously—Hicks must decide what "worker mobilization" means in concrete terms. Quite clearly, workers have used two organizational forms to aggregate their interests. They have formed unions and/or become driving forces in political parties (e.g., the Social Democratic parties in many European countries). The size of unions and the importance of worker political parties are specific enough so that data acquisition is possible.

I suggest that at the indicator/data level one often uses the substitutability relationship as the central organizing and conceptual tool. While exceptions can be found (e.g., Alvarez et al. 1996; see also table 2.4) I think in comparative cross-national or cross-temporal research there are powerful reasons that push the researcher to adopt substitutability (with its corresponding family resemblance theoretical foundations) as the dominant framework for building concepts at the indicator level (Locke and Thelen 1995).

The labor mobilization example shows how *within* a given society there are often alternative means to achieve a certain end. Workers can mobilize via the creation of unions, the creation of political parties, or both. This ubiquitous phenomenon I refer to as substitutability; an alternative term is equifinality. Both substitutability and equifinality stress that there are multiple paths to a given goal.

Substitutability becomes crucial in another way in comparative work. Frequently one must make decisions about functional equivalence across countries, cultures, or historical periods. Part of Nussbaum's model of human functioning allows for cultural differences in the performance of core functions, such as housing, food, and so on. Hicks in his coding of the welfare state variable considered that the private Ghent system of welfare provision was functionally equivalent to the more common public, state-run systems.

In summary, both the availability of alternative means within countries and differences between states push the researcher to choose the substitutability relationship for the indicator/data level. In my figures I use the dotted arrow to symbolize the noncausal nature of this relationship. In many contexts the dotted arrow serves as well to emphasize that equifinality is the process.

Substitutability is the natural way to incorporate historical and cultural diversity into the larger theoretical framework. Basically, the secondary and basic levels stress the commonalities *across* diverse contexts. Since they are used in basic-level general theories and

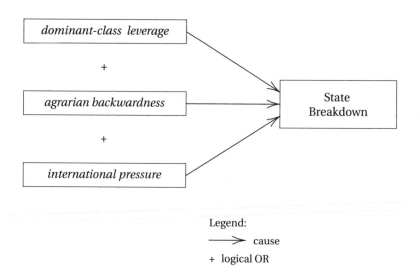

FIGURE 2.7

Causal relationship between indicator and secondary level: *States and Social Revolutions*

propositions they must be abstract enough to fit many situations. It is then at the indicator level that the concept structure must take into account diversity across nations and time. Thus the three-level conceptual structure I propose in this book provides a nice compromise of theoretical generality at the secondary and basic levels, while the historical and cross-national sensitivity of the indicator level provides a solid empirical foundation for the theoretical superstructure.

Sometimes the relationship between the indicator level and the secondary level is really a causal one. In this scenario the "indicator" level factors typically propose a finer-grained causal analysis of the secondary-level dimensions. A good example of this is Skocpol's explanatory model of social revolution (see chapter 9 for more detail; see also Mahoney 1999). Figure 2.7 provides part of Skocpol's model focusing on the core "State Breakdown" secondary-level independent variable.

Here we see that there are different causal mechanisms by which state breakdown can occur. Because there are multiple mechanisms we use the family resemblance OR to model the relationship.[15] Again,

[15]The OR should be interpreted as meaning that some combination of the three causal factors is sufficient, not necessarily that each one is sufficient on its own.

one must consider whether one is using the disease-symptom model where the indicators are effects, or whether one is turning the causal arrow in the other direction.

The three-level framework implies two core questions when building a concept.

- What is the theoretical relationship that links the indicator/data level to the secondary level?
- What is the theoretical relationship that links the secondary level to the basic level?

CAUSAL HYPOTHESES EMBEDDED IN CONCEPTS

I have stressed throughout that secondary-level dimensions are often chosen because they play key roles in causal explanations and mechanisms. Often these hypotheses are taken for granted. For example, chapter 5 looks at how dyadic concepts in the conflict literature have used the necessary and sufficient condition structure (i.e., weakest link) to conceptualize dyadic democracy. As discussed in that chapter, there are good theoretical reasons for this choice, but nevertheless it remains a hypothesis. It has become very common practice to use weakest-link measures for a variety of variables in the conflict literature so the implications of the choice are extensive. Chapter 5 provides some techniques for evaluating empirically the hypotheses built into such measures.

Since one cannot avoid causal hypotheses when building concepts one should be as conscious as possible about them. As chapter 5 suggests, one could go so far as to empirically test them, but at the very least one should be as explicit as possible about them. When Dixon first proposed the weakest-link measure in 1993, he quickly convinced most scholars. This was because he clearly tied a theory of the democratic peace to a quantitative measure. Since the theory was convincing, the measure was quickly and uncontroversially adopted.

There are, however, other situations where one might not want to build hypotheses into the concept itself. The debate over rivalry concepts (see above, p. 33) provides an example where one should not include an empirical hypothesis in the concept. Here the debate is over whether a rivalry can exist between two countries of radically different size. According to the logic of power politics it would be impossible for a significantly weaker country to maintain a long-term hostile and militarized relationship with a much larger one. The stronger side should prevail relatively quickly, ending the conflict.

When analyzing "strategic rivalry" Thompson (2001) spends most of the concept theory section discussing exactly this problem. The question is whether we should conceptualize rivalries as only between relatively equal powers or leave the question open. Diehl and Goertz (2000; Klein, Goertz, and Diehl 2004) have shown that this is problematic because in fact one can easily find long-term asymmetric rivalries. Thompson himself realizes that there is a problem because when he gets to data collection he has to decide what to do with these cases (normally he includes them). Here is a case where one would not want to build power symmetry into the rivalry concept, but leave the issue open for further empirical and causal examination.

As general rules for concept-builders, we have the following.

- Think hard before hardwiring hypotheses into concepts. Often hardwiring makes it difficult to test hypotheses down the road and often will raise problems when gathering data.
- Avoid hypotheses that involve factors not a part of the secondary level (e.g., rivalry can easily be conceived of without invoking power variables).
- Avoid in particular hypotheses that come into play when using the concept on the dependent variable side of the equation. Potential causes of the phenomenon should almost always be left out of the concept itself.

Conclusion

One can trace the origins of the statistical, factor analytic, disease-symptom view of concepts to basic causal views of the world common among quantitative scholars. Correlational views of causation take a billiard ball universe as their fundamental metaphor. J. S. Mill took physics as his prototypical and canonical science and most quantitative scholars have followed him.

I have quite systematically used chemistry and the chemical elements as devices to explain the ontological view of concepts. The example of chemical elements is a nice one in the context of Mill, since he recognized that chemistry did not really fit his model of science.

It is perhaps not surprising that quantitative scholars have a view of causation that draws on the "constant conjunction" of correlation. I think qualitative scholars draw on the analogy of chemistry where an analysis of the chemical elements is more about the substantive nature of the parts of a chemical element and how they are structured.

Just as there are sciences of physics and chemistry so I think that there can be different, but equally legitimate, approaches to psychological, sociological, and political concepts. Particularly when dealing with institutions or other typically sociological or political phenomena I think that the chemical model of concepts is more appropriate. As I have shown in this chapter the ontological view can be formalized and mathematically modeled. There is nothing inherently unscientific or sloppy about theorizing concepts in ontological terms. Chapter 4 provides a concrete application of many of the ideas outlined in this chapter in the context of concepts and measures of democracy. I show that most comparative scholars conceptualize democracy in terms of necessary and sufficient conditions. I use the mathematical machinery introduced here to generate a quantitative measure of democracy that fits much better the concept of democracy than those typically used in the literature.

Concept Intension and Extension

> While I proposed to myself nothing more than to improve the
> chemical language, my work transformed itself by degrees,
> without my being able to prevent it, into a treatise on the
> Elements of Chemistry.
> *Antoine Lavoisier*

T HERE ARE FEW ARTICLES in political science that deserve the predicate "classic," but certainly Sartori's "Concept Misformation in Comparative Politics" merits the label. Thirty-plus years since its appearance in the *American Political Science Review* (1970) it shows up regularly on qualitative and research methods syllabi.[1] As I stated in the Introduction, Sartori and Collier form a league of their own when it comes to the literature on concepts. In many ways Collier's work is a natural extension of Sartori's and as such will receive substantial attention in this chapter.

Sartori's major contribution to the literature on concepts is perhaps his idea of the ladder of generality.[2] He was concerned with how the extension (i.e., empirical coverage) of a concept varied with its intension (i.e., the concept itself). Loosening the concept results in "conceptual stretching" whereby a concept would become applicable to more cases, but would be potentially stretched beyond recognition. In my terms, Sartori was thinking about what happens when one adds or subtracts secondary-level dimensions, and the impact of that on the empirical coverage of the concept. Often this addition or subtraction is done via adjectives; as a result I will talk about "concepts +/− adjectives" as a shorthand for what happens when one changes intension by changing the number of secondary-level dimensions, and the downstream consequences of this on the number of observations in the category (i.e., extension).

---

[1]A sample the syllabi on the qualitative methods site http://www.asu.edu/clas/polisci/cqrm/ would reveal this.

[2]Sartori's term was "ladder of abstraction" but following Collier I use "ladder of generality" since that is a more accurate term.

Ideal types fit into this discussion because in general they have zero extension, i.e., there are no actual examples of the ideal type. When ideal types of this sort are used it raises a set of issues regarding the underlying basic-level dimension and how to structure the secondary-level ones. It is quite surprising, given the frequency with which scholars refer to ideal types, that there exists little methodological analysis of them.

Finally, I end with a brief analysis of the gendered welfare state. Typically, with concepts +/− adjectives the adjective points to a new or underappreciated secondary-level dimension, e.g., gender. Over the last ten to fifteen years scholars have investigated this previously unexplored facet of the welfare state (see Pierson 2000 or Orloff 1996 for reviews). Because scholars have looked at a new dimension to the welfare state they have produced a new series of analyses. To add gender dimensions to the classic welfare state concept means examining new hypotheses about it. Gender is an important new dimension because it is closely linked to causal hypotheses about the causes and effects of the welfare state.

THE LADDER OF GENERALITY AND CONCEPT EXTENSION

Sartori is probably best known for his discussion of conceptual stretching and the ladder of generality. These related topics deal directly with the multidimensional concepts that concern me in this volume. Sartori never really makes explicit his view on concept structure, probably because it was not considered problematic when he wrote. Since Aristotle's time, concepts are defined via necessary and sufficient conditions. Of course, we now know that it ain't necessarily so. In this section I explore concept structures and their relationship to Sartori's claims about conceptual stretching and the ladder of generality. First, I analyze the basic principle of the ladder of generality in terms of extension, intension, and concept structures. I then proceed to illustrate how the basic mathematical and logical principles work themselves out using the literature and quantitative data on concepts such as peasant, (social) revolution, and welfare state.

While Sartori did not hide the source of the basic ideas he used in his classic *American Political Science Review* (1970) article, he did not really elaborate on their origins either. His view on concepts comes quite directly from philosophical logic (the use of philosophical logic is quite overt in Sartori, Riggs, and Teune 1975). It would be hard to find a philosophical logic textbook (starting with J. S. Mill) that does not have a chapter on definition and concepts. All these textbooks see concepts as defined via necessary and sufficient conditions. Sartori does not really say this explicitly, but one can go to a classic philosophical logic textbook of the 1930s and 1940s by Cohen and Nagel, who are more explicit about it[3]:

> "A 'definition,'" according to Aristotle, "is a phrase signifying a thing's essence." By the essence of a thing he understood the set of fundamental attributes which are the necessary and sufficient conditions for any concrete thing to be a thing of that type. It approximates to what we have called the conventional intension of a term. (Cohen and Nagel 1934, 235)

Gerring in his book on concepts gives a brief genealogy which ends with Sartori (see also Adcock and Collier 2001):

> The classical approach to concept formation [necessary and sufficient conditions] may be traced back to Aristotle and the scholastic philosophers of the Middle Ages. For later variants, see Chapin (1939), Cohen and Nagel (1934), DiRenzo (1966), Dumont and Wilson (1967), Hempel (1952, 1963, 1965, 1966), Landau (1972), Lasswell and Kaplan (1950), Lazarsfeld (1966), Meehan (1971), Stinchcombe (1968, 1978), Zannoni (1978) and most important Sartori (1970, 1984), and Sartori et al. (1975). (Gerring 2001, 66)

The methodological problem that motivated Sartori was one of comparative politics. If we have a fine-grained, multidimensional concept that applies well to one or two cases, then it might not "travel" well when applied to other cultures, countries, or time periods. Sartori suggests that in order to make the concept more general—i.e., applicable to more observations—one can "stretch" the concept by reducing its attributes (i.e., number of dimensions).

Sartori thus refers to the relationship between *intension* and *extension.* Basically, the intension is the concept while the extension are the cases that fall under the concept. For example, for Skocpol "Social revolutions are rapid, basic transformations of a society's state and class structures; and they are accompanied and in part carried through by

---

[3] One can find the same basic presentation in contemporary philosophical logic textbooks, e.g., Copi and Cohen (1990).

class-based revolts from below" (1979, 4–5). The extension, within her scope conditions, consists of Russia 1917, China 1950, and France 1789. Within larger scope conditions Foran (1997) has added other cases such as Iran 1979 and Mexico 1910.

In principle, it is the intension that determines the extension. In good social science, theory should drive the choice of cases. It is the theory of social revolution that should determine which cases are selected, not necessarily the everyday use of the term "revolution," or informal ideas about which cases fit. However, in practice, scholars often generate general concepts based on one or two cases (e.g., the Netherlands for Lijphart or Austria and Switzerland for Katzenstein) and then generalize to other countries that seem similar.

If one increases the number of secondary-level attributes in the intension *and if*—this is the big if that Sartori does not mention—one uses the necessary and sufficient condition structure then there is an inverse relationship between intension and extension:

> The law of inverse variation must, therefore, be stated as follows: *If a series of terms is arranged in order of increasing intension, the denotation of the terms [extension] will either remain the same or diminish.* (Cohen and Nagel 1934, 33)

In short, we can increase the coverage (i.e., extension) of a concept by reducing its intension (i.e., number of attributes). More specifically, and more accurately, we can increase the extension by reducing the number of necessary attributes in the intension. "Conceptual stretching" thus means in operational terms eliminating necessary dimensions. This makes the concept more general and simultaneously increases the distance it can travel.

Table 3.1 illustrates Sartori's conceptual stretching principle. Here the concept under discussion is "peasant" where there are five potential characteristics or dimensions that have been applied to define a peasant. Notice that as the number of characteristics increases the extension decreases. Kurtz says that "Obviously[!], the more properties in the definition (the more specific it is), the fewer real-world 'peasants' it would tend to cover" (2000, 98). He then links this claim in a footnote to Sartori's idea that extension is inversely related to intension.

The fly in the ointment is that this all depends on the necessary and sufficient condition structure. As we shall shortly see, if one uses the family resemblance structure one can get the opposite relationship: extension *increases* with intension.

TABLE 3.1

The Ladder of Abstraction: Dimensions Underlying Various Concepts of "Peasant"

Intension	Minimalist	Anthropological	Moral Economy	Marxian	Weberian
Rural cultivators	Yes	Yes	Yes	Yes	Yes
Peasant villages characterized by distinct cultural practices		Yes	Yes		Yes
High levels of rural social subordination			Yes	Yes	Yes
Peasants control/own land				Yes	Yes
Extension	Very Large	Large	Moderate	Moderate	Very Small
Examples	Popkin (1979) Lichbach (1995) Bates (1988)	Redfield (1960) Kroeber (1948) Banfield (1958)	Scott (1976) Magagna (1991)	Wolf (1969) Paige (1975)	Moore (1966) Shanin (1971)

Source: Kurtz (2000)

This becomes pretty clear once one begins to think about the mathematical operations that typify the necessary and sufficient condition structure in contrast with the family resemblance one (see table 2.4). Since Sartori uses logic as his preferred mathematics we can contrast the necessary and sufficient condition AND with the family resemblance OR. Clearly, if we add attributes with AND the extension can only go down (or remain the same in exceptional circumstances). However, if we use OR to add dimensions then the extension almost certainly goes up. This is visible if one imagines Venn diagrams; the intersection of two sets (representing two attributes) is almost always smaller than either set individually. In contrast, the union is almost always larger than the individual sets. In practice, the family resemblance approach does not use the union per se. Typically, two observations are considered members of the same family if they share *enough* characteristics in common, an application of the *m*-of-*n* rule.

To show that the ladder of generality does not work for family resemblance concepts we can revert to what is called an existence proof: give an example where intension increases extension. Suppose that the family resemblance rule is "if more than two of four dimensions are present then the country is a welfare state." We can contrast that situation with an increase in intension to six dimensions while keeping the rule that a country is a welfare state if it has more than half the total number of dimensions. Assume that the cases follow the binomial theorem, e.g., one can toss four or six coins to decide if the country has a welfare state or not.

According to the binomial formula the percentage of welfare states increases from 31 percent of the total with four dimensions to 34 percent with six. This calculation assumes that each dimension occurs with probability .5. The more likely a country is to code positively on each dimension the bigger the difference becomes, although modestly. For example, with a probability of each dimension occurring of .75 we now get 83 percent of the cases as welfare states on the more-than-half rule with six dimensions, with 74 percent on the four-dimension concept. In summary, the claim about the inverse relationship between extension and intension does not hold for concepts in general. In fact, for the family resemblance school of concepts there can be a positive relationship between intension and extension.

To see how this can work in a modest way with real data I use Hick's data on the formation of welfare states in developed countries in the early twentieth century. I discuss his overall theory at some length in chapter 9 and I shall return again to the welfare state later in this chapter. In his analysis of welfare state formation Hicks considered that a welfare state had formed in 1920 if it provided at least three of four classic services of welfare states: (1) old age pensions, (2) workers accident compensation, (3) health care, and (4) unemployment insurance. To examine how the ladder of generality can work in the opposite direction we can contrast two family resemblance rules: (1) a welfare state exists if it has at least one of two services or (2) a welfare state exists if it has at least two of four services. In short, I use the *m*-of-*n* rule of one-half: in one case it is "at least one of two" and in the second it is "at least two of four."

Using Hick's data (1999, 51) for when his 15 developed countries established these various programs we find the following results.[4] Using only two dimensions to conceptualize the welfare state means that we have six possible ways to define a welfare state from a total of four dimensions. So for two dimensions we get the following number of welfare states:

- Workers compensation, Unemployment compensation = 14 welfare states
- Pensions, Workers compensation = 14 welfare states
- Pensions, Health = 13 welfare states
- Health, Unemployment compensation = 11 welfare states
- Pensions, Unemployment compensation = 10 welfare states
- Health, Workers compensation = 10 welfare states

For four dimensions the result is

- At least two of four dimensions present = 13 welfare states

So with real data we can see that by increasing intension from two dimensions to four we increase extension half the time from 10 or 11 welfare states to the 13 welfare states that result from the application of the "at least 2 out of 4" rule.

CONCEPTS+/ADJECTIVES

The ladder of generality focuses on what happens in terms of extension when the dimensions of the concept are added or removed. Perhaps the most common way to add and subtract dimensions is by attaching adjectives to the concept. More generally we have the linguistic and

---

[4]I use Hick's "binding or extensive" data.

semantic fact that we often attach adjectives to concepts. For example, a bewildering array of adjectives has been used to modify the basic-level concept of democracy. Corporatism has been modified by "liberal," "societal," or "democratic," among others. What is not clear is how adding an adjective modifies the three-level structure of concepts. I suggest that the adjective is usually a secondary-level dimension. What I call the "classical" operation (following Collier and Levitsky) means that the adjective is a new dimension that is "added" to the existing ones, i.e., "concepts+/adjectives," increasing the number of secondary-level dimensions by one. A second, less common, nonstandard use is for the adjective to refer a concept with *fewer* secondary-level dimensions, i.e., "concepts/−adjectives," what Collier and Levitsky call a "diminished subtype." I use the term "concepts+/−adjectives" to suggest that we need to consider that in some cases the adjective means we are subtracting a secondary-level dimension while in others we are adding one.

The classical approach to concepts as we have seen, is a necessary and sufficient condition one. Concept+/adjective then means we are adding a new dimension to the existing one. For example, "presidential" when modifying democracy adds a new attribute to those already existing for democracy. Since classical concepts use the necessary condition operation as their structural principle we use AND to conjoin the attribute presidential to the concept democracy. The basic principle is that "all noun modifiers are to be treated via conjunction" (Lakoff 1987, 14). For example, I can cite Stepan and Skach on parliamentary and presidential democracy:

> A pure parliamentary regime in a democracy is a system of mutual dependence: (1) The chief executive power must be supported by a majority in the legislature and can fall if it receives a vote of no confidence. (2) The executive power (normally in conjunction with the head of state) has the capacity to dissolve the legislature and call for elections. A pure presidential regime in a democracy is a system of mutual independence: (1) The legislative power has a fixed electoral mandate that is its own source of legitimacy. (2) The chief executive power has a fixed electoral mandate that is its own source of legitimacy. These necessary and sufficient characteristics are more than classificatory. (1993, 3–4)

Notice that the intension of both definitions is limited by democracy, e.g., "A pure parliamentary regime *in a democracy*." At the end the authors explicitly see the "parliamentary" adjective as adding two necessary conditions which are jointly sufficient (for example, see figure 3.1 below).

As we have seen, the fuzzy logic of necessary and sufficient conditions uses the minimum. So a fuzzy logic concept+/adjective would be interpreted in that fashion:

> They [Osherson and Smith 1982, a classic article] now consider three concepts: *apple, striped,* and *striped apple.* They correctly observe that within classical fuzzy set theory there is only one way to derive the complex category *striped apple* from the categories *apple* and *striped,* namely, by intersection of fuzzy sets—which is defined by taking the minimum of the membership values in the two component fuzzy sets. (Lakoff 1987, 140)

In the classic sense concept+/adjective invokes the subsetting operation. Notice in particular that within the classic conception adjectives do not take away characteristics but can only add dimensions; hence within the classic theory the extension of a concept+/adjective must always be smaller.

As we have seen in the previous section, the ladder of generality is all about adding and subtracting dimensions. Since we have a classic necessary and sufficient condition concept the ladder of generality says that by adding an adjective we then reduce the extension of the concept. When students of comparative politics compare parliamentary to presidential democracies they are contrasting *within* the population of democracies.

It is important to understand that this serves as the baseline, default interpretation of a concept+/adjective. However, actual semantic, linguistic practice does not always conform to the canons of logic.[5] I would like to examine some ways in which this can happen. I will leave the most obvious variation until the next section, where the adjective signals one is removing attributes, hence concepts/−adjectives. But first I would like to briefly discuss another problem that can arise when the basic-level concept is not fixed. Since it is not fixed, adjectives become necessary to assign a certain interpretation to the concept. The example I shall use is the concept of revolution.

---

[5]There is a huge cognitive psychology literature on concepts+/−adjectives. It is clear that the ordinary person's manipulation of concepts and adjectives does not conform to classic necessary and sufficient condition logic. For a good review see Murphy 2002.

Table 3.2 gives a modified survey of the concept of revolution taken from the anthology edited by Sartori on concepts (Kotowski 1984). The names that appear on this list constitute many of the key contributors to the literature on revolution over the years before 1984. Kotowski is quite explicit about the fact that the characteristics listed in the table are necessary conditions for a revolution.[6]

Clearly, Moore and Skocpol have the most restrictive concept of revolution since theirs contains the most necessary conditions. By the ladder of generality principle their concepts will have the least extension of any of those in the table. The first thing that any knowledgeable reader of Skocpol will exclaim is that her book is not about revolutions per se but about *social* revolutions. Voilà. We see that an adjective "social" has been added to the concept of revolution.

If we subtract two attributes, (1) changes in systems of stratification and (2) major political structural change, we arrive at the concepts of revolution of Huntington, Davies, and Johnson. We have subtracted the adjectives, if you will, that deal with system-wide changes, the "social" part of Skocpol's definition. We now have what for Skocpol and Moore would be *political* revolutions, e.g., the American Revolution. Here again we see an adjective appearing.

If we continue to remove dimensions, those dealing with (1) minor political structural change and (2) change of governing body, we arrive at the concept of Gurr. Taking the lead from the title of his book we might call them "rebellions," since they do not necessarily involve social or political change.

Because the attributes used to define revolution can vary so widely, one needs adjectives to fix the meaning of the concept for the author. Skocpol had to affix "social" or some other term to revolution because she had to distinguish her dependent variable from other common uses of the term revolution. So whether it is concepts plus or minus adjectives depends on what is taken as the basic-level concept. From Skocpol's perspective "political revolution" subtracts the system-wide and societal dimensions from the social revolution concept. From the other side, "social revolution" works classically by adding new attributes to the view of revolution as working only on government structures.

[6]In fact, however, in some cases it is not so clear that the author really thinks they are necessary: recall that within Sartori's framework the necessary condition structure is a given.

TABLE 3.2

Concepts with Adjectives: Unstable Basic-Level Concept of "Revolution"

Scholar	Violence	Popular Involvement	Change in Governing Body	Minor Political Structural Change	Major Political Structural Change	Stratification Changes
Social Revolution						
Skocpol	Y	Y	Y	Y	Y	Y
Moore	Y	Y	Y	Y	Y	Y
Political Revolution						
Huntington	Y	Y	Y	Y	N	N
Johnson	Y	Y	Y	Y	N	N
Davies	Y	Y	Y	Y	N	N
Rebellion						
Gurr	Y	Y	N	N	N	N

Source: Adapted from Kotowski (1984, 422)

Concepts/−adjectives

Collier and Levitsky specifically deal with what happens when you subtract an attribute from a concept, i.e., concepts/−adjectives, as well as adding one. It is not so much the logic of their analysis but how they visualize it which does not fit within the conceptual framework laid out in this volume. Of particular importance is their concept of a "diminished subtype" which is what one gets by subtracting a secondary-level dimension. It is worth citing them at length:

> An alternative strategy of conceptual innovation, that of creating "diminished" subtypes, can contribute both to achieving differentiation and to avoiding conceptual stretching. It is a strategy widely used in the literature on recent democratization. Two points are crucial for understanding diminished subtypes. First, in contrast to the classical subtypes discussed above, diminished subtypes are not full instances of the root [basic level] definition of "democracy" employed by the author who presents the subtype. For example, "limited-suffrage democracy" and "tutelary democracy" are understood as less than complete instances of democracy because they lack one or more of its defining attributes. Consequently, in using these subtypes the analyst makes a more modest claim about the extent of democratization and is therefore less vulnerable to conceptual stretching.
>
> The second point concerns differentiation. Because diminished subtypes represent an incomplete form of democracy, they might be seen as having fewer defining attributes, with the consequence that they would be higher on the ladder of generality and would therefore provide less, rather than more, differentiation. However, the distinctive feature of diminished subtypes is that they generally identify specific attributes of democracy that are missing, thereby establishing the diminished character of the subtype, at the same time that they identify other attributes of democracy that are present. Because they specify missing attributes, they also increase differentiation, and the diminished subtype in fact refers to a different set of cases than does the root definition of democracy. (Collier and Levitsky 1997, 437–38)

The figure that they use to represent the diminished subtype (reproduced as figure 3.1) and its relationship to the basic-level concept ("root" concept in Collier and Levitsky's terminology) misses some important distinctions. In particular, they portray the diminished

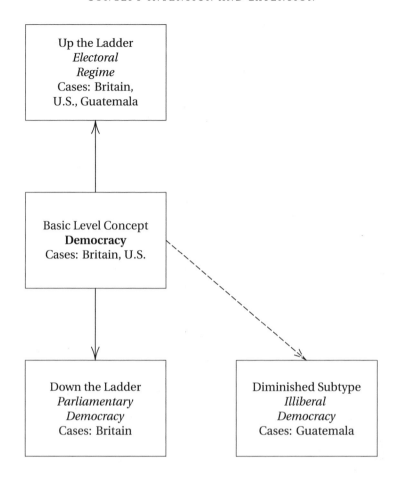

FIGURE 3.1
Diminished subtypes and the ladder of generality. *Source*: Collier and
Levitsky 1997, figure 2.

subtype at the level below the root-level democracy concept whereas
in reality one has moved *up* the ladder of generality. Thus in figure 3.1 the diminished subtype "illiberal democracy" appears at the
same level as "parliamentary democracy." Parliamentary democracy
is a classic concept+/adjective. So in visual terms these seem to be at
the same level even though in one case (illiberal democracy) we have
removed an attribute and in the other (parliamentary democracy) we
have added one.

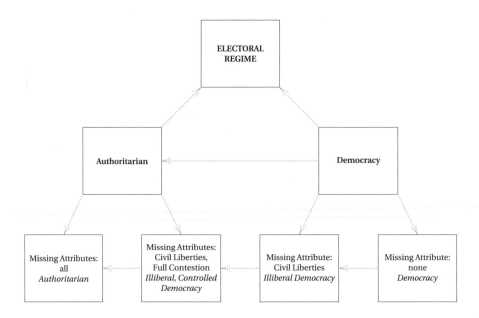

FIGURE 3.2

Concepts+/−adjectives and the authoritarianism-democracy continuum. *Note*: The arrows in this figure are used in the sense of Collier and Levitsky.

Collier and Levitsky are working very much in the context of Sartori's ladder of generality, so as one removes characteristics one moves up. In figure 3.1 the level up from democracy is the more general "electoral regime." Democracy is one type of electoral regime. So while Guatemala is not a democracy in the full sense, it does fall under the higher-level electoral regime concept.

This is a situation where I think they have become prisoners of the the ladder metaphor (Lakoff and Johnson 1980). If you are thinking in terms of ladders all you can do is go up or down. As I stressed in the previous chapter one must conceptualize not only the positive concept, e.g., democracy, but also its negative pole, e.g., authoritarianism. In short, my metaphorical universe also runs from left to right, from negative to positive pole, while Sartori's runs up and down the ladder.

Within my framework, then, to remove a dimension is to move left along the authoritarianism-democracy continuum. Figure 3.2 represents how things look from the perspective of a three-level concept framework (omitting the indicator/data level). As we remove attributes—create diminished subtypes—we have regimes that are less and less democratic. Movement is horizontal from democracy to authoritarianism. The difference between Collier and Levitsky and myself is that I stress lateral movement while they portray up-and-down changes.

Collier and his colleagues have made a major contribution to clearing up significant confusions on this key point of concept-building. They have made it clear that when one sees a concept with adjective in the literature one cannot assume the classical subsetting operation whereby the adjective adds a new dimension to the concept. Often the scholar is focusing on a configuration of the concept *without* some core attribute. The suggestions made in this section constitute some friendly amendments to Collier's argument. The main differences arise because I have attacked the problem within my three-level model of concepts instead of the ladder of generality.

IDEAL TYPES: ZERO EXTENSION

One concept-building strategy known to most social scientists uses the "ideal type" construction. This chapter focuses on concepts and their extensions; an ideal type usually has the empty set as its extension. It is an *ideal* type because it never or rarely can be found in practice. In practice, the principle meaning of ideal type is that the concept has zero extension.

The ideal type concept traces its historical origins back to Max Weber (1949). Burger describes Weber's view: "Ideal types are statements of general form asserting the existence of certain constellations of elements which are empirically only approximated by the instances of the class of phenomena to which each type refers" (Burger 1987, 133–34). There has developed a small literature devoted to Weber and his methodology including the ideal type. Unfortunately, these analyses and debates about Weber are conducted in a very abstract and philosophical way (e.g., Heckman 1983). There is very little in the way of guidelines that permit one to evaluate what a good (or bad) ideal type looks like, and hence very little guidance on how to construct an ideal type concept.[7]

More useful than the controversial subject of what Weber said about ideal types is what sociologists and political scientists have done when

---

[7] It is striking to notice how often ideal types are used and the almost complete absence of any discussion of them in methodology texts.

they have created ideal types. So my analysis may not capture what Weber thought, but I do hope to be faithful to common practice when scholars make and use ideal types.

An ideal type in my framework would mean those cases that score 1 (i.e., the maximum) on all the secondary-level dimensions. In many ways I think this is the best way to think about ideal types. Inherent in the notion of an ideal type is that it lies at the extreme, usually positive, pole of the continuum. There can be nothing, conceptually at least, which is more ideal. It is useful to think of ideal types in geometric terms. The ideal type (like the ideal point in spatial utility models) is the point where all dimensions are at the maximum. One can contrast, that is, measure the distance between, any given empirical object and that ideal point (Gärdenfors 2000).

What seems to typify ideal types in practice is that while they do not necessarily differ from ordinary concepts on intension they do differ from them on extension. Typically, when a scholar proposes an ideal type, she is thinking that the extension of the ideal type is likely to be zero or very small: "I shall take it that a distinguishing characteristic of ideal type concepts is that they have no instances" (Papineau 1976, 137). The ideal generally is one that cannot be attained in practice. George W. Bush may aspire to being a man without sin, but he is unlikely to achieve his ideals. This certainly lies behind Weber's use of the term. Ideal types were useful as a means—really a standard—for thinking about a less-than-ideal reality.

An important part of concept design is whether one can find actual cases with the maximum or minimum values on the scale of the basic-level concept. The advice to the concept-builder is to think seriously about this issue. One might want to stretch out the scale so that there are very few (if any) cases at either extreme. The underlying idea is that if there are large clumps of cases at either extreme then in reality the end points are not the ideal types and one could go further in either direction. For example, in chapter 5 we shall see concepts of dyadic democracy that generate large spikes at the maximum value on the democracy-authoritarianism scale.

I would like to consider an example of ideal type concepts that I think brings out many of the important questions that need to be answered in making an ideal type concept. Robert Dahl's concept of democracy and polyarchy serves as one very good example, an ideal type in action which clearly uses a necessary and sufficient condition structure.

Robert Dahl's conceptualization of democracy is perhaps one of the most famous ideal types in the literature.[8] Dahl has developed the same basic view of democracy over forty years (1955, 1971, 1989, 1998). He is interesting because he clearly distinguishes between the ideal type "democracy," which no country has every achieved, and "polyarchy," the term he prefers for those states that are closest to the democracy ideal. Dahl is quite unusual in separating so clearly the ideal type from the lower levels; most scholars prefer to keep the same word for the ideal type and those phenomena that get close. He quite clearly expresses his views on democracy in terms of ideal types:

> In this book I should like to reserve the term "democracy" for a political system one of the characteristics of which is the quality of being completely or almost completely responsive to all its citizens. Whether such a system actually exists, has existed, or can exist need not concern us for the moment. Surely one can conceive a hypothetical system of this kind; such a conception has served as an ideal, or part of an ideal, for many people. As a hypothetical system, one end of a scale, or a limiting state of affairs, it can (like a perfect vacuum) serve as the basis for estimating the degree to which various systems appropriate this theoretical limit. (1971, 2)

Here we see most of the typical features of an ideal type. The extension of the concept may well be zero or near zero. The usefulness of the ideal type is as a standard against which one can compare existing objects.

It is worth noting that Dahl views democracy in a three-level fashion typical of complex concepts (1971).[9]

I.   Formulate preferences

    A. Freedom to form and join organizations

    B. Freedom of expression

    C. Right to vote

    D. Right of political leaders to compete for support

    E. Alternative sources of information

---

[8] Max Weber's ideal type analysis of bureaucracy is another very famous example.
[9] See Dahl (1989, 222) for a different three-level model of democracy.

II.   Signify preferences

    A. Freedom to form and join organizations

    B. Freedom of expression

    C. Right to vote

    D. Eligibility for public office

    E. Right of political leaders to compete for support

    F. Alternative sources of information

    G. Free and fair elections

III.   Have preferences weighted equally in conduct of government

    A. Freedom to form and join organizations

    B. Freedom of expression

    C. Right to vote

    D. Eligibility for public office

    E. Right of political leaders to compete for support

    F. Alternative sources of information

    G. Free and fair elections

    H. Institutions for making government policies depend on votes and other expressions of preference

One way to build into the concept that its extension is likely to be zero is to use the necessary and sufficient condition structure for the concept. Dahl quite clearly uses AND at both levels of his concept of democracy. Everything at all levels is connected via AND. This makes it very difficult to find any real world phenomenon that satisfies such exigent conditions. To make things even more difficult Dahl says that the above structure is necessary but *not* sufficient: "These, [secondary-level dimensions] appear to me to be three necessary conditions for a democracy, though they are probably not sufficient" (Dahl 1971, 2).[10]

In short, democracy remains a pretty unattainable ideal: "polyarchy is one of the most extraordinary of all human artifacts. Yet it unquestionably falls well short of achieving the democratic process" (Dahl 1989, 223). Polyarchy describes well those states that have made significant progress. "Democracy" is an ideal we should strive for but which we are unlikely to ever achieve.

It is not hard to find others with a similar take on ideal types. For example, in the context of concepts of political parties:

> It is important to note that the models of political parties that we describe below are ideal types, in the strictest Weberian sense of that term. As such, they are heuristically useful insofar as they give easily understandable labels that will help the reader more easily comprehend otherwise complex, multidimensional concepts. Moreover, they facilitate analysis insofar as they serve as baselines for comparisons involving real-world cases, or as extreme endpoints of evolutionary processes that might never be fully attained. As with all ideal types, however, one should not expect that real-world political parties fully conform to all of the criteria that define each party model; similarly, some parties may include elements of more than one ideal type. Perhaps most importantly, individual parties may evolve over time, such that they may have most closely approximated one party type in an earlier period, but shift in the direction of a different type later on. (Gunther and Diamond 2003, 172)

Given the framework for concept construction of the previous chapter, thinking in terms of ideal types provides no additional benefits. From chapter 2 we have guidelines for thinking clearly about the positive and negative poles of the basic level. Similarly, the positive and negative poles almost by definition provide a standard of comparison. In reality, when most scholars use the term "ideal type" all they really mean is that the extension is zero at the pole. Whether or not the extension is large or small near these poles is an empirical puzzle

---

[10] Schmitter and Karl adopt the Dahl list of prerequisites and add two more necessary conditions: "Popularly elected officials must be able to exercise their constitutional powers without being subjected to overriding (albeit informal) opposition from unelected officials [e.g., army].... The polity must be self-governing; it must be able to act independently of constraints imposed by some other overarching political system" (1991, 81).

that calls for a causal explanation. For example, there are good casual reasons why it is hard to achieve absolute zero temperature. The existence of few or zero cases *anywhere* along the continuum from the negative pole to the positive—for example, in the gray zone between democracy and authoritarianism—generally poses questions worth examination.

THEORETICAL IMPLICATIONS OF CONCEPTS+/−ADJECTIVES: GENDER AND THE WELFARE STATE

Much of my analysis of concepts+/−adjectives has been devoted to clarifying issues of concept structure and its relationship to empirical extension. It could appear that the mundane maneuver of adding or subtracting adjectives has little in the way of up- or downstream ramifications on theory. In this concluding section I would like to illustrate that the addition of a dimension can have widespread and very important implications for theory and how we view the phenomenon described by the concept.

The concept of the welfare state has been and will continue to be a core example in this volume. A major new development in the literature on the welfare state over the last decade has involved the analysis of the gender bias both in the welfare state itself and in the scholarly literature on it which has reproduced that bias.

In these few pages I cannot even begin to cover all the ramifications of the gender critique of the welfare state literature (for reviews see Orloff 1996 and Pierson 2000). Of direct concern to me is how gender issues modify our concept of the welfare state and the implications for both theory and methodology, in terms of both the concept itself and its links to theories about the welfare state.

The classic idea of a welfare state at its core involves the provision of goods and services to some large part of the population. One can reasonably ask (independent of gender really): (1) Who are the main target populations? (2) What kinds of goods and services get delivered? Virtually all social welfare programs targeted male workers in nonagricultural occupations, typically an industrial employee. Implicit in welfare state policies was a typical recipient who was male, married, and head of a household with children. Clearly, the wife/mother provided (unpaid of course) child care, health care, and often services to aged parents in addition to basic household duties.

If you examine the list of services typically included in the operationalization of the welfare state and which reflect quite faithfully the
concept, almost all deal with problems of the working man. What
happens if there is an accident on the job? What happens when he is
unemployed? What happens when he gets old? Using the example of
Hicks discussed above (p. 75), you can see that his four dimensions of
the welfare state deal with these kinds of services. The goods and services for the household/family are thus funneled through the principal
(male) wage earner.

One can then ask what kinds of goods and services would be appropriate for a female head of household to keep her alive and well.
In addition to worker compensation, she would need maternity leave.
To maintain her income (i.e., remain employed) she would need child
care. She would need a pension plan tied not just to the income of her
spouse (not just survivor benefits). Thus to really take into account the
concerns of women in the population, particularly as (single) heads of
households, we need to reconceptualize the welfare state.

Orloff (1993) provides a very nice example of what this means. She
takes Esping-Andersen's (1990) very influential view of the welfare
state and asks what would have to be "added" to incorporate the concerns of women. She starts with the three secondary-level dimensions
of the welfare state according to Esping-Andersen. The first dimension involves the extent to which the welfare state provides services in
contrast to the use of some market mechanism:

> A fundamental dimension that varies across welfare states concerns the
> "range, or domain, of human needs that are satisfied by social policy"
> instead of by the market (Esping-Andersen and Korpi 1987, 41), that is,
> "how state activities are interlocked with the market's and the family's
> role in social provision" (Esping-Andersen 1990, 21).... Thus, there will
> be class-influenced debates over the content of social policy and over the
> relative roles of markets and policies in determining welfare outcomes.
> (Orloff 1993, 310)

The second dimension for Esping-Andersen deals with "stratification," or how welfare states get involved with redistribution of income
and problems of income inequality:

> A second dimension of policy regimes is stratification.... power resources
> analysts [e.g., Esping-Andersen] argue that systems of social provision
> have stratifying effects: some policies may promote equality, cross-class

solidarity, or minimize economic differences, while others may promote social dualism or maintain or strengthen class, status, or occupational differentiation. (Orloff 1993, 311)

This is the question about who benefits from the policies of the welfare state. Do these policies reinforce or mitigate inequalities generated by the market or other mechanisms?

Finally, the third dimension deals with the extent to which the welfare state creates "citizenship rights" and results in the "decommodification" of goods and services. The first dimension already talked about the state versus the market in terms of the delivery of services. The third dimension reinforces this by saying that some goods are decommodified because of welfare state policies:

> The third dimension of the welfare state concerns the character of social rights of citizenship. Some benefits are *universal*, that is, they are available to all citizens of a certain age or condition (e.g., sickness, unemployment, parenthood); some benefits depend on *labor market participation and financial contributions*; and some benefits are *income-tested*, that is they are available only to those with incomes assets below a certain level.... Esping-Andersen argued that the extent to which the rights embodied in social programs promote or circumscribe decommodification of labor is a critical dimension that varies across welfare states. (Orloff 1993, 311)

Orloff argues that to take into account gender one must *add* two dimensions to the Esping-Andersen concept of the welfare state. The first dimension requires that in addition to maintaining the basic wage of (male) workers, the strength of a welfare state should depend on the degree to which it supports paid labor by women:

> Thus, the decommodification dimension must be supplemented with a *new* analytic dimension that taps into the extent to which states promote or discourage women's paid employment—the right to be commodified. I call this fourth dimension of welfare-state regimes *access to paid work*.... Thus, I contend that the extent to which the state ensures access to paid work for different groups and the mechanisms that guarantee jobs (e.g., reliance on private employment, creation of tax incentives, legal regulation of private employment, or public jobs programs) are dimensions of all policy regimes. (Orloff 1993, 318)

The second new gender dimension argues that in addition to including the degree to which state policies encourage paid work for women one needs to extend the range of concern from individual men or women to the household and family. Most dramatically, the group of people most excluded from the traditional model was single-mother families. In the traditional system, all monies and services to the family, wife/mother, and children, were funneled through the working father. One thus needs to think about what services would be appropriate to keep a *household* going that might be headed by a single woman:

> If decommodification is important because it frees wage earners from the compulsion of participating in the market, a parallel dimension is needed to indicate the ability of those who do most of the domestic and caring work—almost all women—to form and maintain autonomous households, that is, to survive and support their children without having to marry to gain access to breadwinners' income. (Orloff 1993, 319)

If we conceive of the welfare state along these new lines then there are important downstream implications for measures of the welfare state, as traditionally defined. Most quantitative studies of the welfare state use spending data [usually from the International Labor Organization (ILO)] for programs typically part of the male welfare state.[11] ILO spending data (International Labor Organization 1949–) do cover "family allowances" and hence in part include programs that form part of Orloff's two additional dimensions. But Orloff argues that we also need to include all spending categories for programs that support (1) paid women's work and (2) women's capacity to maintain an autonomous household.

Beyond this, a gendered analysis of the welfare state suggests a more radical reconceptualizations of the welfare state along with common quantitative measures. With rare exceptions all post–World War II analyses of the welfare state use spending data.[12] However, the

[11]Welfare spending is defined by the ILO as government spending related to schemes, transfers, or services that (1) grant curative or preventive medical care, maintain income in case of involuntary diminution of earning, or grant supplementary income to persons with family responsibilities, (2) are legislatively sanctioned, and (3) are administered publicly or quasipublicly.

[12]I have had frequent recourse to the welfare state concept as a family resemblance one. In terms of substitutability, money is perhaps the ultimate substitutable factor.

gender analysis of the welfare state often focuses quite explicitly on *rights.* For example, O'Connor, Orloff, and Shaver (1999) in their analysis of Australia, Canada, the United States, and the United Kingdom include abortion rights as a central dimension of comparison. Rights to divorce, contraception, and abortion are absolutely fundamental to women's welfare. In addition to the spending dimensions of the welfare state, one could well add to the welfare state concept a series of rights as new secondary-level dimensions.

I have argued throughout this volume that how we conceptualize a phenomenon has deep and intimate links with basic-level causal theories. One of the important, if not the most important, signs of this in welfare state literature is how gendered analyses have moved the welfare state variable from the dependent variable side of the equation to the independent variable side. Before the nonsilent revolution in the literature of the 1990s, the welfare state often appeared as the dependent variable: one explained the causes of its origin or expansion. In contrast, much of the gender literature looks at the impact (or not) of the welfare state on women's quality of life. A core question is the influence of the welfare state, not its causes. Not surprisingly, this is one area where rights play a key role. For women, it is not just spending but control over their bodies that determines many aspects of their well-being (back to Nussbaum again). We add new secondary-level dimensions to the concept of the welfare state because we now know that they have important causal powers in the lives of women (and of course men). We add these new dimensions to the concept because we cannot understand how the welfare state works for 50 percent of the population without them.

A gender analysis of the welfare state illustrates what I mean by an ontological, realist, and structural analysis of concepts. It is not really about definitions as much as about analyzing how welfare policies work. You cannot make gender analysis go away by saying "This is what I mean by the welfare state" (the Red Queen strategy). The concept of the welfare state matters because it is embedded in important theories about the welfare state and its impact on individuals. It is not surprising that when the welfare state was viewed through the male model one of the key independent variables was labor union strength.

Because of its fungibility, lack of spending on one or more dimensions of the welfare state can be completely compensated for by spending on others. One might think of the United States with its high spending for the aged compared with little spending for the nonaged poor.

Because we see the dependent variable now in a new light we can then look to new kinds of independent variables. Because we have a new perspective on the welfare state we can ask causal questions about its impact on women's lives (e.g., Skocpol 1992). Going back to my chemical metaphor, finding out about the nuclear structure of copper means we understand better the properties of copper. Now that we understand better the gendered character of the welfare state we can better understand its policies, their causes and effects.

Conclusion

The act of adding or subtracting secondary-level dimensions—concepts+/−adjectives—has tremendous repercussions on the theory and methodology of concepts. The issues surrounding conceptual stretching are really about how empirical extension varies depending on changes in the concept structure (intension). The most striking distinguishing characteristic of an ideal type concept involves a claim about its empirical extension. As Collier and his colleagues have noted, to use adjectives does not always mean adding a secondary-level dimension but sometimes subtracting one.

To analyze effectively all of these kinds of questions requires a clear notion of concept structure. Once we have the three-level framework in hand and once we are clear about the character of the necessary and sufficient condition and family resemblance structures, we can begin to gain a clear understanding of the relationship between intension and extension. For example, the well-known claim that extension is inversely related to intension holds in general only for necessary and sufficient condition concepts. For family resemblance concepts the relationship can go in the other direction.

Much remains to be done on the concepts+/−adjectives front. It is not at all clear that concepts+/−adjectives always work as I have described them here. A big class of examples is gendered concepts. If we were to follow the standard (necessary and sufficient condition) procedure "women's (social) movement" is a subset of the class of all social movements. It is not clear that many working in the area would agree with this (e.g., Mazur and Stetson 2003). If the literature on cognitive psychology is any guide, the use of necessary and sufficient conditions is rare in natural social settings. There are good reasons why philosophers and social scientists continue to use the necessary and sufficient condition concept, but it might well be the case that when one uses concepts+/−adjectives the end result is something quite different from what one would predict using the procedures discussed in this chapter.

The gendered welfare state literature illustrates that adding secondary-level characteristics can generate whole new research agendas. By including dimensions of special relevance to women and by putting the welfare state on the independent variable side of the equation, we gain dramatic new insights into the workings and nature of public policy in developed countries. By including these dimensions on the dependent variable side, we begin to think differently about the role of groups like labor unions in the creation of the welfare state. Here again we see the core and intimate relationship between causal theories and concepts. To include a new dimension in a concept is to see a new cause or a new effect.

Increasing Concept-Measure Consistency

Almost all metaphysicians prior to Locke, as well as many
since his time, have a made great mystery of Essential
Predication, and of predicates which were said to be of the
essence of the subject. The essence of a thing, they said, was
that without which the thing could neither be, nor be
conceived to be.
J. S. Mill

In sum, measurement is valid when the scores [numeric
values] derived from a given indicator, can meaningfully be
interpreted in terms of the systematized concept that the
indicator seeks to operationalize.
Robert Adcock and David Collier

T HE LAST TWO CHAPTERS focused on basic issues all concept-builders
should consider when designing or analyzing a concept. If you will,
the last two chapters laid out a basic theoretical framework for designing concepts. One might well pose the practical and pragmatic
question about the implications of all these theoretical considerations
for the construction of numeric measures. When designing numeric
measures one needs to be concerned about how faithful the measure
is to its theory (i.e., concept). The degree of faithfulness is what I call
"concept-measure consistency." This is the degree to which the numeric measure reflects well the basic structure of the concept. While
there are a variety of aspects to this consistency, I will focus on the
degree to which the structure of the measure matches well the structure of the concept. Structure, as I outlined it in chapter 2, is basically
defined in terms of the levels of the concept and how indicators or
secondary-level dimensions are "aggregated"—to use the appropriate
word in the context of measure construction—to produce the next
higher level. Adcock and Collier ask important questions of the relationship between concepts and measures: "Does a given measure
adequately capture the full content of the systematized concept? This

'adequacy of content' is assessed through two further questions. First, are key elements [indicators in my terminology] omitted from the indicator [measure or dimension in my terminology]? Second, are inappropriate elements included in the indicator?" (2001, 538). In this chapter I add a question to their list: "Is the structure of the 'systematized concept' consistent with that of the numeric measure?"

The idea of concept-measure consistency is very similar to the relationship between theory and testing. If the theory predicts a U-shaped relationship between dependent and independent variables then a statistical test that is linear in form will not be appropriate. The statistical test must allow for the possibility of a U-shaped form in order to test the theory. The same is true of concepts and numeric measures: if the measure has a different structure from the concept then it is a measure of a different concept. Throughout this chapter I shall use the term "measure" to refer to numeric measures while I continue to use "concept" to refer to the theory of the phenomenon.

In this chapter I focus on the concepts and measures of democracy, in particular the widely used polity measure of democracy (Gurr 1974; Gurr, Jaggers, and Moore 1990; Jaggers and Gurr 1995). More generally, the concepts and measures of democracy provide a natural—and important—case for examining the issues of concept-measure consistency. There is both an extensive literature on the concept of democracy and a wide variety of numeric measures.

We shall see that when a measure has multiple indicators these are combined most often via *addition* or *averaging*. In contrast, concepts almost always use the structure of necessary and sufficient conditions. The fundamental methodological question of this chapter then is the implication—methodological, statistical, and empirical—of this kind of inconsistency between the concept and its numeric measure.

Table 4.1 describes the polity measure of democracy. There are five indicators in the measure (indicated by roman numerals) each of which can receive a value (in the "JG Weight" column), where positive ones indicate democracy and negative ones represent autocracy. The final measure of democracy used in most international relations work is the sum of the values of the score on the five elements for a country.[1] Here we see a standard way to construct numeric measures: add

---

[1] In the original version Jaggers and Gurr have separate indicators for democracy and autocracy. In terms of table 4.1 all the positive values go into the democracy scale and all the negative ones go into the autocracy scale. The final measure proposed is "democracy minus autocracy" (in the original the autocracy values are positive, but they become negative in the subtraction procedure) which is exactly what I have done in table 4.1.

TABLE 4.1

The Polity Numeric Measure of Democracy

Authority Coding	JG Weight	∆JG Weight
I. Competitiveness of Political Participation		
(a) competitive	3	5
(b) transitional	2	4
(c) factional	1	3
(d) restricted	−1	1
(e) suppressed	−2	0
II. Regulation of political participation		
(a) factional/restricted	−1	1
(b) restricted	−2	0
III. Competitiveness of executive recruitment		
(a) election	2	5
(b) transitional	1	3
(d) selection	−2	0
IV. Openness of executive recruitment		
(a) election	1	5
(b) dual: hereditary/election	1	3
(c) dual: hereditary/designation	−1	0
(d) closed	−1	0
V. Constraints on chief executive		
(a) executive parity or subordination	4	5
(b) intermediate category 1	3	4.5
(c) substantial limitations	2	4
(d) intermediate category 2	1	3
(e) slight to moderate	−1	2
(f) intermediate category 3	−2	1
(g) unlimited power of executive	−3	0

Source: Jaggers and Gurr (1995, 472), with modifications

∆JG—The polity concept and measure reformulated; see below figure 4.1 and following discussion

(or average) the values of the various indicators. For another example, Bollen (1980) suggests that a simple and quite valid measure of democracy can be formed by averaging three indicators of democracy.

However, if one examines the polity *concept* of democracy it involves the necessary and sufficient condition structure:

At its theoretical core, we argue that there are three essential interdependent elements of democracy as it is conceived of in Western liberal

1. pref

philosophy. The first is the presence of institutions and procedures through which citizens can express effective preferences about alternative political policies and leaders. This is accomplished through the establishment of regular and meaningful elections.... a second component of Western-conceived democracy is the existence of institutionalized constraints on the exercise of executive power.... The third dimension ... is the guarantee of civil liberties to all citizens in their daily lives and their acts of political participation. (Jaggers and Gurr 1995, 471; this repeats almost verbatim Gurr et al. 1990, 83).

2. limit

3. civ. lib

Hence we have the most common form of concept-measure inconsistency: a necessary and sufficient condition concept with an additive (or averaging) measure.

This chapter shows that in general most *concepts* of democracy use the necessary and sufficient condition theoretical structure, while most *measures* use the family resemblance strategy, which as we have seen is typified by addition or the logical OR. Thus in terms of concept-measure consistency they do poorly.

On the face of it, the essentialist and family resemblance structures are quite different and much debate has focused on the differences (e.g., Lakoff 1987; Collier and Levitsky 1997). What is less well known are the empirical and statistical differences between the two. I show that the mathematical properties of these two structures differ in important and coherent ways. I first demonstrate this with independent, random data on each dimension to highlight the structural differences. Then using the polity data I compare the polity measure of democracy which falls into the family resemblance category with a modified (by me) polity measure that incorporates the essentialist concept structure. In contrast with the literature on measures of democracy (see Inkeles 1991 and Munck and Verkuilen 2002 for surveys of the most prominent efforts), I find significant differences between the two measures using *exactly the same data.* In addition, the patterns with real-world data match closely the basic structural analysis done with computer-generated random data.[2]

THE STRUCTURE OF CONCEPTS OF DEMOCRACY

If one examines the most prominent scholars on the concept—not numeric measures—of democracy one finds that the necessary and

[2] Gurr (1972) in the original article on the polity concept in fact talks about democracy in terms of family resemblance more often than in necessary condition terms.

sufficient condition structure is very often used to define and conceptualize democracy. The only other common option is to list the dimensions of democracy (e.g., Karl 1990). The list approach is a structureless one. We have an undertheorized concept in the sense that the theory is insufficient to provide any guidance in measure construction. In this case the reader has basically three options: (1) take the list as is in its undertheorized form, (2) assume the standard necessary and sufficient condition structure, or (3) infer the concept structure from the measure structure.[3] Here are some concepts of democracy by prominent scholars; they—and all others I have seen—fall into the list or the necessary and sufficient condition category.

> In sum, I have defined political democracy to be the extent to which the political power of the elite is minimized and that of the nonelite is maximized. Political rights and political liberties are two major dimensions of the concept and these encompass most of the traits usually attributed to democratic system. (Bollen 1991, 8; he divides Dahl's eight necessary dimensions among the political rights and political liberties dimensions)

> Procedural minimum definition: (1) full suffrage, (2) full contestation, and (3) civil liberties. (Collier and Levitsky 1997, figure 3)

> I should like to reserve the term "democracy" for a political system one of the characteristics of which is the quality of being completely or almost completely responsive to all its citizens ... to be responsive ... all full citizens must have unimpaired opportunities: (1) to formulate their

---

[3]I suspect that this kind of confusion between necessary and sufficient conditions and simple lists is not uncommon. For example, Bendor, Moe, and Schott find the same conceptual confusion in the classic article by Cohen, March, and Olsen on the garbage can model of organizational choice. This illustrates as well how a list approach to concepts can be interpreted in necessary condition terms:

> What, then, are organized anarchies [garbage cans]? Cohen, March, and Olsen (1972) define them "organizations characterized by problematic preferences, unclear technology, and fluid participation." But this definition, though widely cited, suffers from serious ambiguities that subsequent work has done little to clarify.
> The first problem arises from the 1972 article's ambiguous statements about whether organized anarchies must have all three properties or just some of them. Much of the discussion suggests that each property is necessary [see, for example, the preceding quote, where the three properties are linked by "and"]. Yet, in the conclusion, organized anarchies are described as situations that depart from classical decision models "in *some or all* of three important ways: preferences are problematic, technology is unclear *or* participation is fluid" (p. 16, emphasis added); that is, each property suffices to identify an organized anarchy. (Bendor, Moe, and Shotts 2001, 173, the authors then go on to discuss the implications of this confusion for the garbage can research agenda.)

preferences, (2) to signify their preferences . . . by individual and collective action, (3) to have their preferences weighed equally in the conduct of government. . . . These, then, appear to me to be three necessary conditions for a democracy, though they are probably not sufficient. . . . Some requirements for a democracy among a large number of people: (1) Freedom to form and join organizations, (2) freedom of expression, (3) right to vote, (4) eligibility for public office, (5) right of political leaders to compete for suppose, . . . (6) alternative sources of information, (7) free and fair elections, (8) institutions for making government depend on votes. . . . Upon closer examination, however, it appears that the eight guarantees might be fruitfully interpreted as constituting two somewhat different theoretical dimensions of democratization. [He then discusses the dimensions of (1) public contestation and (2) right to participate in elections and office.] (Dahl 1971, 2–7)

A government is democratic if it exists in a society where the following conditions prevail:
1. a single party is chosen by popular election to run the governing apparatus;
2. such elections are held within periodic intervals, the duration of which cannot be altered by the party in power acting alone;
3. all adults who are permanent residents of the society . . . are eligible to vote in each election;
4. each voter may cast one and only one vote in each election;
5. any party receiving the support of a majority of those voting is entitled to take over the powers of government until the next election;
6. the losing parties in an election never try by force or any illegal means to prevent the winning party from taking office;
7. the party in power never attempts to restrict the political activities of any citizens or other parties as long as they make no attempt to overthrow the government by force;
8. there are two or more parties competing for control of the governing apparatus in every election. (Downs 1957, 23–24)

Democracy in a complex society may be defined as a political system which supplies regular constitutional opportunities for changing the governing officials, and a social mechanism which permits the largest possible part of the population to influence major decisions by choosing among contenders for political office. This definition . . . implies a number of specific conditions: (1) a "political formula" or body of beliefs specifying which institutions—political parties, a free press, and so forth—are legitimate. . . .(2) one set of political leaders in office; and (3) one or more sets of recognized leaders attempting to gain office. (Lipset 1960, 27; he goes on to imply that these are necessary)

Thus "democracy" for us, is a regime in which those who government are selected through some contested elections. This definition has two parts: "government" and "contestation.". . . What is essential in order to consider a regime as democratic is that two kinds of offices be filled, directly or indirectly, by elections: the chief executive office and the seats in the effective legislative body. . . . Contestation occurs when there exists an opposition that has a some chance of winning office as a consequence of elections. (Przeworski et al. 2000, 16–17)

I use "democracy" to refer to a political system in which ideologically and socially different groups are legally entitled to compete for political power, and in which institutional power-holders are elected by the people and are responsible to the people. We should apply the same criteria for democracy to all countries because it is reasonable to assume that human nature basically is similar everywhere. (Vanhanen 2000, 252)

One can see the necessary condition requirement in many of these descriptions. The sufficient condition part of the structure is almost always absent. In this case, one must infer the joint sufficiency part of the theoretical construction. Jaggers and Gurr say there are three essential requirements that must be satisfied for a country to fall under the democracy concept; they do not explicitly say that these three are sufficient. Dahl along with Collier and Levitsky (1997) seem explicitly or implicitly, respectively, to reject the sufficiency part. However, a concept structure without sufficiency is incomplete. This has downstream consequences for the construction of numeric measures: to code a country as a democracy requires a sufficiency criterion; hence sufficient conditions must be given. The essential elements alone do not suffice to make a final *positive* classification choice. To code a country as a democracy is to have some sufficiency criterion.

The key point in terms of concept-measure consistency is that one must be clear about the theoretical structure of the concept. This is all the more important because the theoretical structure rarely receives formal or mathematical representation. Jaggers and Gurr once again illustrate that the theoretical structure of the concept often slides into measure construction. The discussion of the concept of democracy quoted above (p. 97) appears in a section entitled "Operationalizing Democracy." In a similar vein, with Vanhanen when you get to indicator construction you find that each dimension of the concept is necessary ["Because I see both dimensions of democratization as necessary for democracy, I have weighted them equally in my Index of Democratization" (2000, 255–56)]. This same phenomenon occurs with Hadenius's (1992) concept and measure of democracy. Nothing in the conceptual discussion leads to a necessary condition view, but once one gets to index construction then necessary condition arguments appear.

One reason why the issue of concept-measure consistency does not exist in the methodological (or applied) literature is because the two are rarely seen as distinct entities. In practice, the concept, its dimensions and structure merge with those of the numeric measure, thus producing concept-measure inconsistency. Implicitly it is assumed that there is some sort of coherence between the two, but as we shall see, there can be a great deal of theoretical slippage with the end result being that the measure is in fact quite loosely connected to the concept.

Since this chapter focuses in particular on the polity measure of democracy the view of Gurr, Jaggers, and Moore is particularly relevant. While some, like Bollen, do not think of democracy in terms of essential dimensions, most prominent thinkers (e.g., Dahl, Downs, Gurr, Lipset, Przeworski) have used the necessary and sufficient condition concept structure, though in some cases this must be teased out of the text since it is not directly stated (e.g., Lipset). The necessary and sufficient condition idea is the structural glue that most thinkers use to put the various secondary-level dimensions together to build a concept of democracy. This is not surprising given the hegemonic status of the essentialist structure in defining concepts.

As we have seen, the other common approach to concept structure uses the family resemblance framework. The basic idea of family resemblance incorporates two basic principles. The first is that one has to have a minimum number of characteristics to become a member of the family. The second is that there need be no common feature shared by all members of the family. These two characteristics describe very well the polity *numeric measure* of democracy. None of the five indicators is necessary: all that matters is that a country has a high enough sum of indicators to pass the democracy threshold.

We can work our way backward from the numeric measure to concept structure. Given a particular measure structure, like the polity one, we can ask what is the corresponding concept structure. If the indicator is built with an OR or a "+" then implicitly we have a family resemblance concept structure.

Basically then the following broad generalization holds:

If the concept uses the necessary and sufficient condition structure then it is very likely that there will be concept-measure inconsistency.

Why? Because all the common, default means of building measures—addition, averaging, latent variables—are not faithful to the necessary and sufficient condition concept. One can certainly find exceptions, e.g., Mainwaring, Brinks, and Pérez-Liñán (2001), Munck and Verkuilen (2003), and Bowman, Lehoucq, and Mahoney (2005). This is because these authors are very conscious that they have a necessary and sufficient condition concept and hence choose appropriate measures.

INCREASING CONCEPT-MEASURE CONSISTENCY: REFORMULATING THE POLITY CONCEPT AND MEASURE OF DEMOCRACY

Since I am particularly interested in the polity concept and measure, how they score on concept-measure consistency merits an extended discussion. As with most of the democracy concepts and their corresponding measures, the polity concept of democracy is an essentialist one (see above, p. 97) while the measure belongs to the family resemblance group. The overall scale—democracy minus autocracy—is the *sum* of the scores of the five elements. The measure structure is a series of "+"s, while the conceptual theoretical structure is a series of ANDs. These are two radically different theoretical structures. This means that the concept-measure consistency of their enterprise is low.

Jaggers and Gurr are quite explicit in rejecting the necessary condition view democracy, for their measure at least: "[T]he Polity databases are constructed on the premise that there is no "necessary condition" for characterizing a political system as democratic or autocratic; rather each dimension [indicator] can be measured independently. In fact, many historical and some contemporary polities have mixed authority patterns" (1995, 472).

103

This quotation expresses two important confusions. Jaggers and Gurr imply that a necessary condition conceptualization of democracy is inconsistent with indicators being measured "independently." It is not clear what this can possibly mean. As they well know, the various dimensions are in fact highly correlated. This does not mean that they cannot be independently *measured*.

The second confusion is that the existence of mixed regimes contradicts the necessary condition view of democracy. What underlies this claim is an unrecognized—but very common—view that necessary condition variables are dichotomous. If the secondary-level dimensions are measured dichotomously then a necessary condition theoretical structure will only generate zeros and ones as a basic-level democracy score for a political entity.

In terms of numeric measure construction, the necessary condition requirement can be seen as an issue of weighting dimensions. A necessary dimension is more heavily weighted than nonnecessary dimensions. An additive, family resemblance measure can have de facto necessary dimensions if a dimension's sufficiency weight is high enough. For example, take a three-dimensional concept with a family resemblance structure and secondary-level weights of 5, 3, and 2. If the rule is that a sum of 6 or more is required to be in the family then dimension 1 is necessary because 2+3 does not get over the bar.

It is important to recall that the weights of each indicator in table 4.1 are arbitrary. Nowhere do Jaggers and Gurr describe how they arrived at them, or what the rationale for them is. In practice, they have arranged the weights so that de facto each dimension is in fact necessary for a state to be a "coherent" democracy. A coherent democracy is defined as a score of seven or more on the sum of the indicators. For example, the maximum possible on the indicator of "constraints on the executive" is four; while the maximum total on the indicator of "political competition and recruitment" is six. In short, it is impossible to be scored as a coherent democracy without at least a modest score on each indicator.

The polity measure implicitly considers one dimension to be more important than the other. The political competition and recruitment dimension has a maximum possible score of six, while the constraints on the executive has a maximum of four. This suggests that the political competition dimension is 50 percent more important than the constraints on the executive. I think that most people would agree with the general direction of this weighting since the idea of open, competitive elections and access to office is more central to the concept of a democracy than executive constraints.

In summary, the polity measure scores low on concept-measure consistency (along with many other concepts and measures of democracy) because the structure of their concept of democracy differs dramatically from the structure of their measure of democracy. What is necessary in the concept, expressed by a series of ANDs, becomes nonnecessary in the measure, and becomes a series of "+"s.

To increase the concept-measure consistency we need to rethink both the concept and its corresponding measure. The first order of business is then to take the polity democracy concept and measure and develop an explicit three-level concept keeping in mind the indicators that we have available for the numeric measure.

Jaggers and Gurr do not attempt to measure the secondary-level dimension of civil liberties: "However, given the paucity of the current, let alone historical, data on civil liberties, we have not attempted to single out, and then quantify, this dimension of democracy" (p. 471). They defend this with a collinearity argument: "While serious violations of human rights may occur despite the effective functioning of these [democratic] institutional structures ... we contend that when political participation is fully open and competitive, executive recruitment is elective, and the constraints on the chief executive are substantial, the correlation between democratic institutions and practices will be relatively high" (p. 471).[4]

That leaves us with the two essential dimensions of "political competition and recruitment" and "constraints on executive power." The political competition and recruitment dimension seems in fact to consist of two subdimensions. One is a "system whereby citizens are expressing preferences about alternative policies and leaders" (1995, 471), which is accomplished through "regular and meaningful competition among individuals and groups" (1995, 471). Conversely, having several candidate choices and no right to vote is not democratic either (e.g., the U.S. South for most of U.S. history or Great Britain pre-1832). In short, people must have two freedoms: (1) to vote and (2) to run for office. Indicators I and II refer to the basic freedom to vote while indicators III and IV refer to who is eligible to be a candidate for office.

---

[4]Vanhanen (2000) makes the same argument.

Hence there seem to be two key subdimensions in the competition and recruitment dimension. The fact that I have referred to this as the "competition and recruitment" dimension already indicates that there is no easy one-word label. One subdimension is the ability of individuals to express policy and leadership preferences. The second is how open the recruitment process is, which can have a major impact of the choice electors have. Basically, the "competition" factor corresponds to indicators I and II, while the "recruitment" factor fits with indicators III and IV. Munck and Verkuilen (2002, 14) make this same basic critique: they see that there are two general elements, (1) competitive elections and (2) offices filled by elections. Hence I think it makes sense to promote them into full-fledged secondary-level dimensions.

Of course, by dividing the competition and recruitment dimension into two new dimensions we have not solved the problem. In fact, we have added an issue to the agenda: what is the theoretical relationship between these two new dimensions?

When both dimensions score high or low the answer is easy; the crux of the issue is how does one think, theoretically, about situations where one is high and the other is low. I think all would agree that being able to vote but having the choice of candidates very restricted and controlled is not a democracy at all. Communist elections with 100% participation rates but with candidates preselected by the party are meaningless. In short, such mixed cases should score very low, i.e., the necessary and sufficient condition structure.

We have then a conceptual structure as illustrated in figure 4.1. The concept of democracy now has four secondary-level dimensions. Following the literature on democracy, the new concept of democracy uses the necessary and sufficient condition structure to aggregate from the secondary level to the basic level.

Models of Individual Secondary-Level Dimensions: Sufficiency and Substitutability

Since the polity measure just sums across all indicators, the multilevel structure of the democracy concept does not appear at all in the measure. Here we see another aspect of concept-measure consistency: if the concept has three levels then one should take that into account when constructing the measure. If all we had was the measure construction description—sum of five indicators—then it would be reasonable to infer that the polity concept of democracy has just two levels: the five indicators and the basic-level concept of democracy.

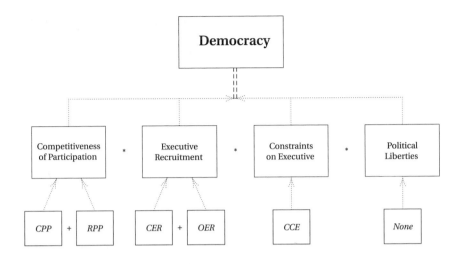

CPP – Competitiveness of political participation

RPP – Regulation of political participation

CER – Competitiveness of executive recruitment

OER – Openness of executive recruitment

CCE – Constraints on chief executive

None – No indicator available

FIGURE 4.1
A modified polity concept and measure of democracy

This is in fact another test of concept-measure consistency: given the indicator structure can one correctly infer the concept structure?

However, if we take the multilevel structure of the concept seriously then a new problem arises. For example, the competitiveness of participation secondary-level dimension has two indicators, (1) competitiveness of political participation and (2) regulation of political participation. How do we combine the indicators to arrive at a score for the secondary-level dimension?

There are various possible solutions. Much of the answer depends on developing the concept side of things. As given, Jaggers and Gurr provide no guidance on this question (again because it does not matter in the final measure). One obvious, pretty atheoretical, approach would be just to add the two indicators together as Jaggers and Gurr do in general.

I think a common and often reasonable response is to consider these indicators as substitutable. In other words, as long as we have a high score on one of the indicators then the secondary-level dimension receives a high score. Mathematically, this means taking the maximum of the indicators as the dimension score. Figure 4.1 shows this by placing an OR between the indicators of a dimension. A high score on either indicator suffices to give the dimension a high score. Hence the relationship between the indicator level and the secondary level is one of substitutability.

One can see this by asking about substitutability in the substantive context of democracy. For example, take the indicators of the executive recruitment dimension; if we know that there is an election on the competitiveness indicator, does it really "add" anything to have a value of one on the openness indicator? In some ways it might be worse to add: does "dual: hereditary election" plus "transitional" really equal a competitive election? This is exactly the point that Munck and Verkuilen make in their critique of the polity measure:

> On the other hand, attributes at the same level of abstraction should tap into mutually exclusive aspects of the attribute at the immediately superior level of abstraction. Otherwise the analysis falls prey to the distinct logical problem of redundancy. . . . The problem of redundancy is evident in two indices. Polity IV falls prey to this problem because it identifies a pair of attributes (competitiveness and regulation of participation) that grasp only one aspect of democracy, the extent to which elections are competitive, and another pair of attributes (competitiveness and openness of executive recruitment) that also pertain to a single issue, whether offices are filled by means of elections or some other procedure. (2002, 13–14)

Munck and Verkuilen are absolutely correct in pointing out this serious problem of redundancy. However, their principle that attributes at the same level of analysis should be mutually exclusive is not necessarily correct. If the final measure is constructed via addition then they are on target, but if there exists a clear principle of substitutability then it is actually *desirable* to have redundancy. In summary, the redundancy issue is key, but cannot be resolved independent of the specifics of the structure of the measure at both the secondary and indicator levels.

I think substitutability and sufficiency form the dominant theoretical structures when thinking about how indicators combine to determine the scores of secondary-level dimensions. In the context of the polity measure, this becomes the maximum of the scores of the indicators. Unlike on the secondary level, where it is completely inappropriate to a necessary condition theoretical structure, addition is also a plausible mechanism for combining indicators (as we have seen for the welfare state). Here much more will depend on the specific theory of the concept. The key point is that one must use knowledge of what democracy is and how it works to make a decision.

Some Details of the Modified Polity Measure

This section briefly discusses a number of practical decisions that have to be made in order to produce a numeric measure of the concept outlined in figure 4.1. As such this section can be skipped by those not interested in the details of how my modified polity measure is constructed. Nothing in the rest of the chapter depends on a knowledge of this material.

To get to actual numeric values involves revisiting the polity scaling scheme in the context of the modified concept structure. Since each dimension has a different maximum this means that there are different scales, which translates into different weights in the additive indicator construction scheme. Munck and Verkuilen (2003) stress the same point: "there remains yet one more weighting scheme implicit in the Polity IV indices—apparently not recognized by Marshall et al.—due to the different scales used to measure each attribute [see my table 4.1]. As a result, executive constraint is implicitly assigned a larger weight in the aggregate scores, which makes Gleditsch and Ward's (1997, 378–79) finding that this attribute, more than anything else, drives aggregate scores less surprising and noteworthy." Given their premise that the overall democracy score will be the sum of the individual elements, the issue of scaling is not so important. However, if we have three necessary dimensions then the comparability of the scales becomes critical.

We generally want the domain of the scales to be the same for all essential dimensions. Otherwise, when we combine them we get "scale effects." For example, Bollen (1980, 1990) automatically rescales various indicators into a common scale, be it 0–10, 0–100, or statistical standardization.

This becomes more important when we use the minimum as the means of combining secondary-level dimensions. If the maximum on one dimension is five, while it is only two on another, then the overall score cannot be greater than two. Given the polity scale we have the following maxima for the three dimensions (assuming the maximum option for aggregating indicators to dimensions):

Competitiveness of participation—maximum three
Executive recruitment—maximum two
Constraints on executive—maximum four

Adding these up, one gets the polity maximum democracy score of 10. However, for the modified measure the highest possible score is four. In short, the polity scales need to be changed.

Table 4.1 (column ΔJG) gives my revised scales. In order to give each secondary-level dimension the same weight I have made five the maximum. This, somewhat ironically, makes a move back to the original Gurr scales of polity I (Gurr 1974) which had a number of 1–5 scales. But I have not done so for the various indicators of the dimensions. The rescalings of the indicators are as follows:

1. Competitiveness of political participation: add two to all (a)–(g).
2. Regulation of political participation: add two to all.
3. Competitiveness of executive recruitment: 2, 1, –1 become 5, 3, 0.
4. Openness of executive recruitment: I have considered that "hereditary/election" is significantly less open than "election." This in fact goes back to the original polity I coding (Gurr 1974).
5. Constraints on chief executive: here there are four categories with three intermediate values. I coded the main categories 5, 4, 2, 0 and the intermediate ones in the middle.

The modified polity measure thus ranges from zero to five. It can thus be compared to the original measure which goes from –10 to 10. While the choice of five is arbitrary, at least the scales are coherent, which fixes the problem noted by Munck and Verkuilen.

THREE-LEVEL CONCEPTS AND MEASURES OF DEMOCRACY

Now that I have reformulated the polity concept and measure so that concept-measure consistency is high, it worth exploring the degree of concept-measure consistency for other concepts/measures of democracy. Concept-measure consistency means that the theoretical and mathematical structure of the measure corresponds to that of the concept. If the correspondence is weak then concept-measure consistency is low. The particular—but common—theoretical structure that I focused on in the previous section was one of multiple necessary conditions that are jointly sufficient. The concept-measure consistency question then becomes: does the measure and its theoretical structure—at both the indicator/data and secondary levels—match that of the concept?

Munck and Verkuilen published a survey (2002) of the literature entitled "Conceptualizing and Measuring Democracy." Their analysis confirms in many key ways the arguments I am making here. Table 4.2 basically reproduces, with some light editing, their summary table. First of all, they break down the indicators that they discuss into two parts that correspond to my secondary-level dimensions and indicators (in the original they use "attributes" for my dimensions and "components of attributes" for my indicators). Hence, my three-level framework fits easily with their analysis.

Most important for this section is that they describe the structural rules that each indicator applies to aggregate indicators and dimensions. Hence we can see to what degree, at least in the measures that they survey (which is not a complete list since they only looked at measures associated with major data-collection efforts), necessary condition or family resemblance logics are used to construct them.

One can see that addition among dimensions is quite common with Bollen, Freedom House, Hadenius, and Jaggers and Gurr using this measure structure (see also Jackman 1973), with Arat partially using it. Hence, addition is the dominant structure for secondary-level dimensions.

While addition is the most common aggregation rule in table 4.2 multiplication is also often used. How does multiplication fit in terms of concept-measure consistency? With the proper scale—usually the [0,1] interval—multiplication is one possible way to implement the necessary condition conceptual structure. It is, however, not the most obvious choice, which is the minimum. For most people the minimum makes more sense because necessary conditions are often thought of in terms of the "weakest link" (see the next chapter for much more on this). Conceptually this means that a country is as democratic as its weakest dimension. The usual verbal expression of the necessary condition structure is "Dimension 1 AND dimension 2 AND dimension 3 are necessary for nation A to be a democracy." The canonical translation of AND into mathematical terms is the minimum operator.

TABLE 4.2
Existing Quantitative Measures of Democracy: An Overview

Creator of Index	Dimension	Indicator	Measure Structure
Alvarez et al.	Contestation	Multiple parties	Multiplicative at all levels
		Executive turnover	
	Offices	Election executive	
		Election legislature	
Arat	Participation	Executive selection	Mostly additive at dimension level,
		Legislative selection	Additive at dimension level
		Legislative effectiveness	
		Competitiveness of nominations	
	Competitiveness	Party legitimacy	
		Party competition	
	Coerciveness		
Bollen	Political liberties	Press freedom	Additive at dimension level,
		Freedom of group opposition	Factor analysis at indicator level
		Government sanctions	
	Popular sovereignty	Fairness of elections	
		Executive selection	
		Legislative selection	

Coppedge & Reinicke	Contestation	Free and fair elections Freedom of organization Freedom of expression Pluralism in media	Guttman scale
Freedom House	Political rights Civil rights	9 indicators 13 indicators	Additive at all levels
Gasiorowski	Competitiveness Inclusiveness Civil/political liberties		None
Hadenius	Elections Political freedoms	Suffrage Elected offices Meaningful elections Freedom of organization Freedom of expression Freedom from coercion	Additive at dimension level, Additive/multiplicative at indicator level
Jaggers and Gurr	See table 4.1		Additive
Vanhanen	Competition Participation	Election results Voters/total population	Multiplicative

Source: Munck and Verkuilen (2002). I have changed the terminology to match mine along with some light editing.

With multiplication as the AND function (all components scaled in the [0,1] interval) one gets scores equal to or lower than the minimum. Almost always the overall democracy level will be significantly lower than the minimum. So, for example, if the scores on the two dimensions are .70 and .50 the overall democracy score is .35, significantly less than the minimum of .50.

In addition, there are substitutability effects with multiplication. In general higher values on one dimension can compensate for lower values on other dimensions (see Goertz 2003, chapter 10 for a discussion of this point). It is in fact substitutability effects that lead Vanhanen to add a third criterion in order to make a dichotomous coding of democracy. He explicitly used multiplication because each dimension of his indicator is necessary: "The second combination [first combination is addition, second is multiplication] is based on the assumption that both dimensions are necessary for democracy and that a high level of competition cannot compensate the lack of participation, or vice versa" (Vanhanen 2000, 256). But when faced with coding countries dichotomously as democracy or not he uses the minimum of three criteria:

> The selected threshold values [for democracy] of Competition (30 percent) and Participation (10 percent) are arbitrary, but I believe that they are suitable approximations for distinguishing more or less autocratic systems from political systems that have crossed the minimum threshold of democracy. Because both dimensions of democracy are assumed to be equally important, a country must cross both threshold values if it is to be classified as a democracy. It is not enough to define a threshold value of democracy solely for the ID [Index of Democracy]. In the case of the ID, I have used 5.0 index points as the minimum threshold of democracy, which is clearly higher than the ID value 3.0 produced by the minimum threshold values of Competition and Participation. Countries that have reached all three minimum threshold values (30 percent for Competition, 10 percent for Participation, and 5.0 index points for the ID) can be regarded as democracies. It should emphasized, however, that it is also possible to define threshold values differently, by raising or lowering them. (Vanhanen 2000, 257)

Notice that dichotomous democracy is *not* based on the overall democracy measure (i.e., ID) but uses the minimum of the two components Competition and Participation along with the overall ID indicator. This need for a convoluted procedure (which obviously has double counting since the two components appear in the overall ID) is because multiplication is used in the construction of ID and has substitutability effects.

In short, clearly addition is not appropriate for a necessary condition concept. The best choice is the minimum (e.g., Bowman et al. 2003), but multiplication is a possible alternative to the minimum (e.g., Munck and Verkuilen 2003). I use the minimum for this chapter because it is the most obvious choice for a necessary and sufficient condition concept and since the main point is to illustrate the contrast with family resemblance concepts. An important item on the agenda for future work is which among the acceptable necessary and sufficient condition possibilities is the best, but that is beyond the scope of this chapter.

A second issue raised here is that one often uses the maximum or addition to construct secondary-level dimensions from their indicators. Table 4.2 sheds some interesting light on current practice in this regard. The basic three-level structure that I suggest makes most sense is one that uses the minimum for the dimensions and either the maximum or addition for the indicators. *None* of measures presented in table 4.2 gets close to this structure. Alvarez et al. use multiplication at the dimension level as I suggest is appropriate, but they also apply multiplication at the indicator level which makes less sense.

Munck and Verkuilen's survey of democracy measures brings out very clearly the three-level structure of almost all democracy concepts and measures. In all almost all cases one must think about the structural glue used to make dimensions out of indicators and the structural cement used with dimensions to construct the basic-level democracy concept.

COMPARING ESSENTIALIST AND FAMILY RESEMBLANCE MEASURES OF DEMOCRACY

The next obvious agenda item is the more concrete effects of the differences in measure construction. To what extent does the original polity measure, from now on the JG measure, differ from the one with

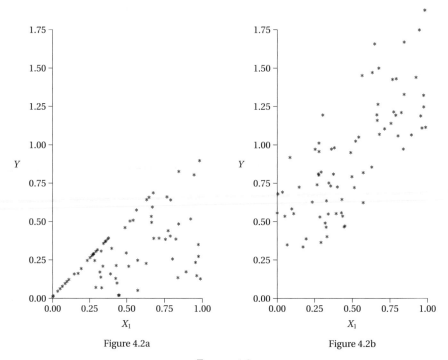

Figure 4.2a   Figure 4.2b

FIGURE 4.2
Minimum versus additive structures, two dimensions

greater concept-measure validity one outlined above, henceforth the
ΔJG measure?

The most important structural difference between the JG and ΔJG
concepts lies in the contrast between the five additive indicators in
the JG measure and the three essential dimensions of ΔJG. Obviously
$\min(E_1, E_2, E_3)$ is not the same as $\text{sum}(E_1, E_2, E_3)$. Beyond their not-
sameness it is useful to examine some concrete aspects of the move
from sum to minimum.

The differences are best seen by simplifying the situation to two
or three dimensions and taking random observations over the same
domain [0,1]. The collinearity and particularities of the actual data
can obscure key structural differences so it is best to use independent,
uniform, random variables.

Figures 4.2a and 4.2b illustrate that the differences between the
essentialist and family resemblance structures are not trivial. I have
graphed this in two dimensions instead of three. Since both the

minimum and sum are symmetric the basic points I want to make come through in two-dimensional plots. The X-value is the value of X_1 variables while the Y-value is either the sum or the minimum of X_1 and X_2.

First, note that the variance of Y in the additive procedure is significantly larger than in the minimum case (0.087 versus 0.048). Not only that, the variance in the additive case is constant while in the minimum case it increases with X.

Also, the more essential dimensions one adds the bigger the difference in variance becomes. This is because necessary conditions put ceilings on the outcome variable (see Ragin 2000 or Goertz 2003 for analyses of this ceiling effect). Intuitively this makes sense since the addition of a necessary condition can only *reduce* the overall score. The contrast can be seen in figures 4.3a and 4.3b which replicate figures 4.2a and 4.2b but with three dimensions instead of two. Now the variances are 0.032 for the essentialist indicator and 0.24 for the additive one. As we move from two to three essential dimensions the ratio of the variances increases from 1.8 to 7.5.

In addition to decreasing the variance, the minimum operator generates heteroscedastic data. Clearly, the minimum in figures 4.2a and 4.3a shows heteroscedasticity. In contrast, the scatter plots for the sum have constant variance. Necessary conditions produce heteroscedasticity, and some, e.g., Tsebelis (1999), have used that as evidence for necessary condition theories. If one regresses X_1 on the various Y's in figures 4.2 and 4.3 the standard White (1980) test for heteroscedasticity is significant in both two and three dimensions for the minimum and not significant for the sum.[5]

Not only is the range of variation diminished by the minimum operation but it is limited to the region below the $X = Y$, $45°$ angle line. Again, this follows directly from the logic of the minimum operator. In contrast, the sum can range over virtually the whole domain.

In summary, the sum is a "looser" view of democracy, or in other words, the necessary and sufficient condition structure generates more autocracy categorizations. If we split the Y values in figures 4.2 and 4.3 into three categories corresponding to the final level of

---

[5]The statistics are as follows:

  Sum, two dimensions: d.f., 2; χ^2 value, 0.29; Prob> χ^2, 0.86.
  Minimum, two dimensions: d.f., 2; χ^2 value, 21.86; Prob> χ^2, 0.00.
  Sum, three dimensions: d.f., 2; χ^2 value, 4.05; Prob> χ^2, 0.13.
  Minimum, two dimensions: d.f., 2; χ^2 value, 19.45; Prob> χ^2, 0.00.

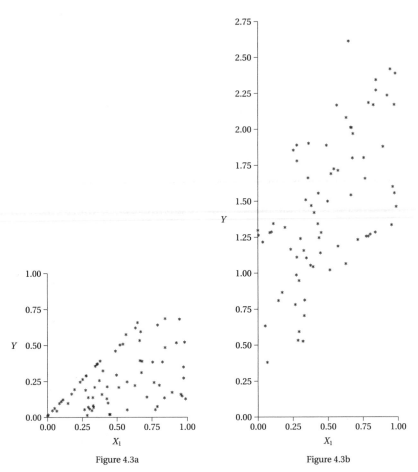

Figure 4.3a

Figure 4.3b

FIGURE 4.3
Minimum versus additive structures, three dimensions

democracy[6] (see table 4.3) we find that the minimum produces many more autocracy ratings than does the sum. For two dimensions the sum produces 25 percent autocracies versus 61 percent for the necessary condition structure; with three dimensions this difference increases to 13 percent against 71 percent. Hence with essential

[6] I have divided the range into three equal categories (note that the range stays constant for the minimum (i.e., [0,1]) but increases by one for each element of the sum). Since the values of the basic indicators are uniform random variables, the starting line is basically an equal distribution of cases between autocracy, gray, and democracy.

TABLE 4.3
Stricter (Minimum) and More Liberal (Sum) Conceptual Structures

	Minimum		Sum	
Category	N	Percent	N	Percent
Two Dimensions				
Nondemocracy	46	0.61	19	0.25
Gray zone	20	0.27	37	0.49
Democracy	9	0.12	19	0.25
Three Dimensions				
Nondemocracy	55	0.73	10	0.13
Gray zone	16	0.21	54	0.72
Democracy	4	0.05	11	0.15

dimensions the necessary condition procedure produces five and half times more autocracies than does the family resemblance approach.

Gray Cases

In terms of both concepts and measures a decisive issue revolves around the gray zone cases. Unlike Przeworski et al. (2000), who code democracy/autocracy only—and unrealistically—as dichotomous, the polity approach clearly understands the need to allow for intermediate degrees of democracy.

One issue of importance to international relations as well as comparative politics is the status of transitional regimes. As countries move from authoritarian to democratic they often pass through intermediate stages (this does not seem to be the case in reverse). This is particularly important in foreign affairs where often the King or Kaiser retained substantial control after losing much of domestic policy-making to the parliament.

The decline in the number of democracies as the number of dimensions increases is quite precipitous for the minimum. The addition of new essential dimensions just augments the ceiling effect of the minimum operator. Figure 4.2a shows a large number of values near the $X = Y$ line. This is the ceiling effect graphically at work. Most of these cases had high (i.e., $> .5$) values on X_2 (recall that only X_1 is given in the figures), but the minimum forces the overall value down to the $X = Y$ line. Adding another dimension (figure 4.3a) pushes the values down even further; now we have a significant number of points below the $X = Y$ diagonal. The additional essential dimension thus is pushing democracy values into the gray zone and gray zone cases into the autocracy category. With the minimum operator there is nowhere to go but down, so adding more dimensions just keeps pushing the overall value further and further down. In table 4.3 we find that as one moves from two to three dimensions the percentage in *both* the democracy and gray categories declines, to the benefit of the autocracy category.

The sum works quite differently. Here as we add new categories the gray zone increases significantly at the expense of *both* the democracy and autocracy categories. Table 4.3 shows this pattern quite clearly. The pattern arises because of the Central Limit Theorem. If one adds random variables (i.e., *i.i.d.* random variables with finite variance) then the sum becomes more and more like the normal distribution. Flipping a coin is the dichotomous version of what I have done here. The number of heads with a reasonable number of flips begins to look like the Gaussian bell curve. In short, the sum will tend to force countries into the gray zone, as illustrated in table 4.3. Unlike the minimum, which drives states out of the democracy category, the sum will continue to keep roughly equal numbers in both the democracy and autocracy slots.

Summary

The point of this section is not that one conceptual structure is better but rather that they are quite different. As the literature on democracy abundantly shows, there are widely varying views on the basic concept of democracy. For example, some early measures of democracy (notably Cutright 1963) included stability factors. This practice was criticized by many (e.g., Jackman 1973; Bollen 1991) and seems to have been abandoned as not a valid part of the democracy concept. As I have briefly outlined above, essentialist conceptualizations of democracy dominate the literature, but certainly family resemblance ones can be defended.

Different concept structures have quite different empirical properties. When thinking about the concept one must keep an eye out for the statistical and mathematical characteristics that will emerge in the quantitative measure. The gray cases are fundamental to thinking about the concept of democracy. In terms of measure construction the minimum produces fewer and fewer gray cases while the sum produces more and more. These analyses also clearly show that the essentialist approach to democracy is much stricter. It produces significantly fewer democracies than does the sum. This is more and more the situation as one adds dimensions to the concept. These factors are important design considerations when building concepts and measures.

The goal of this section is point out some of the practical consequences of different theoretical choices. The following differences between the necessary and sufficient condition, and family resemblance approaches are significant:

1. The variance of the sum is significantly larger than the variance of the minimum.

2. The more essential dimensions the larger the difference in variance between the two becomes.

3. The sum has a constant variance while the minimum is heteroscedastic, with the variance increasing with X.

4. The minimum produces relatively more cases with autocracy scores than does the sum.

5. The sum produces more gray zone cases than does the minimum.

6. Increasing the number of dimensions increases the percentage of gray zone cases for the sum and the percentage of autocracy cases for the minimum.

7. The minimum is a stricter standard for democracy than the sum.

An Empirical Comparison of the JG and ∆JG Measures

If scholars vary widely in their views on the concept, measures, and indicators of democracy, they all say with one voice that quantitative measures used on real-world data produce highly correlated results. Without exception (that I am aware of) all studies agree on this point.

We have seen above that the mathematics of the necessary and sufficient condition and family resemblance models produce very different results when dimensions are independent of each other (and when using uniformly distributed data). Hence low concept-measure consistency *can* have a dramatic impact. In this section I examine the extent of that impact in one case, democracy. More specifically, I use the standard polity measure which falls under the family resemblance school of measure construction and contrast it with $\triangle$JG which I have built using the necessary and sufficient condition approach. It should be kept in mind that I am using exactly the same data for both measures.

The key question in this section is the extent to which the structural differences demonstrated above with independent and uniform random data appear in real-world data. Almost all the differences documented above related in one fashion or another to the ceiling effect of the minimum. One ceiling effect shows itself in decreased variances. As we saw above, the addition of dimensions increases the variance of the sum indicator and decreases the variance of the minimum one. Comparing the JG and the $\triangle$JG measures (using the Polity IV data, version 2000) on this characteristic, we find that there is in fact little difference between the variances, 50 for the JG and 58 for the $\triangle$JG (converting the 0–5 $\triangle$JG scale to the –10 to 10 scale of JG). So in fact the tendency is opposite to the one generated by independent, uniform variables.

In real-world data collinearity can mitigate and hide structural effects. When data are highly correlated, as is the case with democracy indicators, and when they are quite bimodal at the extremes, as is the JG measure, we can see the variance increase. Collinearity acts to concentrate values at either end of the spectrum. This of course then means that the variance should increase.

Another way the ceiling effect can be seen is in reduced means. I find that the JG indicator has a mean of −1.7 while the $\triangle$JG has a mean of −3.8 (staying with the −10 to 10 scale of the JG measure). Here we see one concrete manifestation of how the minimum operator drives down the values in general.

The difference in means shows a general tendency for the $\triangle$JG values to be lower than the JG ones. Above we also saw that the minimum operator really concentrated values in the lowest category with three dimensions. It is not easy to directly compare the JG and with $\triangle$JG indicators, but if we consider zero on $\triangle$JG to be a "coherent" autocracy,

TABLE 4.4
ΔJG Cross JG

ΔJG	JG							
	0	1	2	3	4	5	*Total*	%
0	2828	2891	1073	298	0	0	7090	51
	40	41	15	4	0	0	Row%	
1	0	524	278	347	2	0	1151	8
	0	46	24	30	0	0	Row%	
2	0	0	904	499	47	0	1450	11
	0	0	62	34	3	0	Row%	
3	0	0	15	364	522	262	1163	8
	0	0	1	31	45	23	Row%	
4	0	0	0	33	189	535	757	6
	0	0	0	4	25	71	Row%	
5	0	0	0	2	127	2049	2178	16
	0	0	0	0	6	94	Row%	
Total	2828	3415	2270	1543	887	2846	13789	100
%	21	25	17	11	6	21	100	

which matches pretty well the official polity definition of an autocracy as −7 to −10 then we find that for JG that there are 33 percent coherent autocracies versus 51 percent for ΔJG. Correspondingly at the top, the JG codes 23 percent of the observations as coherent democracies versus 16 percent for ΔJG.

The ceiling effect of the essentialist measure structure comes out quite clearly in table 4.4. (Here I convert the −10 to 10 scale of JG to the 0–5 scale of the ΔJG.) If the two measures produce identical results then all observations will lie on the diagonal. The table, however, reveals a distinct asymmetry; there are very few values below the diagonal (177 out of 13,789) while there are many above it. At almost every level the JG indicator codes states significantly higher than ΔJG. In almost all relevant rows (except row 3) at least 50 percent of the time the JG indicator is higher than the ΔJG and is almost never less.

We have seen with *independent* dimensions that the two structures produce quite contrasting patterns, but with highly correlated data

TABLE 4.5
Correlations of Essential Dimensions

	CP	ER	CE
CP	1.00	0.33	0.69
ER	0.33	1.00	0.39
CE	0.69	0.39	1.00

CP—Competitiveness of participation

ER—Executive recruitment

CE—Constraints on executive

differences can be attenuated. This makes sense intuitively since a high score on one dimension implies a high score on the others. Hence the ceiling effect of the minimum operator is reduced. Table 4.5 shows that in fact the correlations between the secondary-level dimensions of the ΔJG measure are not as large as one might expect. Two of the correlations are less than .40 and the third is a moderate .69. These modest correlations mean that the minimum operator can have some bite because high values on one dimension do not automatically mean high values on other dimensions. That we have three dimensions instead of two increases the impact of the essentialist structure.

The literature on democracy measures stresses how highly correlated they are. Here we can see that part of what might be going on is an aggregation effect. If we look at the secondary level, we see that the correlations between the essential elements of democracy are not as high as one would expect given the reputation of collinearity among measures of democracy.

The standard claim that various measures produce very correlated results in general masks a key issue. We have seen above that the situations where a country scores high on one dimension but low on another are crucial. We expect that, no matter what the concept or measure construction technique, if a state scores high or low on all dimensions, the various measures will agree (see the next chapter for more on this point). The key question is: what happens in the gray zone?

Since democracy data are such that there are relatively few cases in the gray zone (no matter how that zone is defined) overall correlations between measures are relatively meaningless. They will be driven by the overwhelming number of cases that agree on the high and low ends. This is all the more crucial since many key questions in comparative politics and international relations revolve around transitions to and from democracy. For example, Mansfield and Snyder (1995) have argued that transitional democracies are more war- and conflict-prone. If the measure of democracy is to be used for analyses that focus particularly on the Third World, then a much more relevant comparison between measures must focus on the gray zone cases.

Table 4.4 permits one take on this question. We can trichotomize into autocracy, gray zone, and democracy for both the JG and ΔJG measures. We can then ask to what extent they disagree on putting cases in or out of the gray category. Discordance occurs when one measure puts an observation into the gray category while the other does not. Given the ceiling effect, clearly the biggest category of discordance lies between the ΔJG measure classifying an observation as autocracy and the JG putting that same observation in the gray zone: this happened for 4,262 observations. Next most common is JG coding a case as a democracy while the ΔJG puts it into the gray category (797 times). Finally, on rare occasions ΔJG categorizes a state as a democracy while JG would put it into the gray zone, which happened 129 times. Overall, a striking 38 percent of the total number of observations (13,789) were discordant. Given the importance in many theoretical settings of transitional democracies these differences assume great relevance.

As I noted in the beginning of the section, most scholars have found high correlations between democracy measures, implying in effect that it does not matter what one uses in practice. This is true of JG and ΔJG: they are correlated at .93! Looking at table 4.4 from this angle the high correlation is not so surprising; most values lie on or near the diagonal. Nevertheless, we have seen that a high correlation can mask clear and significant differences that exist between the family resemblance and essentialist measure structures. These differences are neither random nor due to measurement error. They are systematic and coherent in character. The ceiling effect of the necessary condition structure has multiple ramifications, in terms of reduced means, reduced variances, systemically lower values, and extensive disagreement on categorization.

125

It must be emphasized that neither measure is necessarily better per se. They operationalize different—and defensible—concept structures. In terms of concept-measure consistency, the ∆JG concept and measure are clearly better since they correspond to the essentialist view of democracy held by most scholars.

Conclusion

This chapter has explored the idea of concept-measure consistency. This kind of consistency—in contrast with reliability and external validity—focuses on the relationship between concept and measure. I have examined one facet of concept-measure consistency, the extent to which the mathematical structure of the measure reflects the theoretical structure of the concept. When this correspondence is low then concept-measure consistency is low.

Traditionally and in standard usage concepts are defined in terms of necessary and sufficient conditions, what I have referred to as an essentialist perspective on concepts. As the various quotes on p. 99 above show, this conceptual strategy has dominated thinking about democracy.

While the necessary and sufficient condition perspective has dominated the concept side of things an implicit family resemblance strategy has guided most quantitative measure construction. On the measure side by far the most common practice has been to sum up (or average) the score of various indicators. The combination of an essentialist concept and a family resemblance measure results in low concept-measure consistency.

The conventional wisdom is that all the various measures of democracy produce very similar results, i.e., they are highly correlated. My analysis confirms and challenges this traditional wisdom. The family resemblance (JG) and essentialist (∆JG) measures were highly correlated (.93). However, a series of empirical analyses showed that they were quite different from each other. The high correlation masks a series of major differences.

Most of the differences can be traced back to what Ragin (2000) calls the ceiling effect of necessary conditions. This effect reduces average values as well as the variance, along with producing heteroscedasticity. With rare exceptions the JG measure had values equal to or greater than those generated by ∆JG. This had some dramatic effects; if one trichotomizes into autocracy, gray zone, and democracy then the two approaches disagree on the classification of an observation 38 percent of the time. This has major implications for much comparative politics and international relations work dealing with democratic transitions.

The point of this chapter is not that the necessary and sufficient condition view of concepts is better or worse than the family resemblance one. The key fact, in many respects quite obvious, is that they are different, and different in some very important and systematic ways.

Substitutability, Aggregation, and Weakest-Link

Measures

WITH WILLIAM F. DIXON

Tthis chapter addresses a very common problem (and common solution) that appears constantly in the literature on international conflict: how to form a dyadic-level concept from individual-level attributes. If we consider conflict to be between dyads (by far the most common research design over the last twenty years) and if we have attributes of each member of the dyad, say, level of democracy, how do we form the concept of "dyadic democracy"?

Substantively the problem of dyadic concepts in the literature on international conflict seems far removed from the concepts of corporatism, welfare state, and others that I have discussed as my principal examples. However, formally and substantively we have the same basic problem of moving between levels that occurs at the heart of the three-level approach to concepts. We need to think about how to "aggregate" individuals into a dyad just as we need to structure secondary-level dimensions to form a basic-level concept. We shall see that the three-level approach gives us ways to think about this common problem in the conflict literature. One sign of the power of the three-level framework is its ability to provide leverage and guidance in situations which on the face of it have little in common.

In this chapter we focus on two particular variables that are at the core of arguments about the "liberal peace," democracy and international trade. For example, how should we characterize the level of democracy of a dyad comprised of an authoritarian dictatorship and a competitive parliamentary government? Similarly, how should we think about the level of trade interdependence of a dyad when state A relies heavily on trade with state B, but very little of B's commerce is conducted with A?

With answers to these questions not at all obvious, the international relations research community has formed a relatively strong consensus around what is known as the "weakest-link" approach to dyadic measure construction.[1] Initially proposed as a solution to the question of dyadic democracy in studies of the democratic peace (Dixon 1993, 1994), the weakest-link logic is easily illustrated. If we begin with the theoretical assumption that *both* members of a dyad must possess sufficiently democratic norms, institutions, or incentive structures to achieve a genuine "democratic peace," then we can infer that the norms or institutions of the *less* democratic state are primarily responsible for the peacefulness of dyadic relations and thus serve as a simple but sound measure of *dyadic* democracy. The metaphor of links in a chain is quite apt, since a dyad is conceived to be only as democratic as its less democratic member no matter how much more democratic the other state. This same logic has been extended to the measurement of trade interdependence at the dyadic level by Oneal and Russett (1997, 1999) and numerous others (e.g., Cornwell and Colaresi 2002; Gleditsch 2002; Jungblutt and Stoll 2002; Lai and Reiter 2000; Mousseau 2000).[2]

This chapter illustrates in one concrete setting the claim that concepts involve important causal arguments. The use of the weakest link arises from theoretical arguments about how democracies in conflict interact with each other. The necessary and sufficient condition structure is used for dyadic democracy because scholars have found these substantive propositions convincing. However, as a theoretical and causal proposition this way of constructing dyadic-level concepts is open to challenge. The literature on trade and conflict provides a case where the weakest-link approach has been contested (Barbieri 2002). Of course, Barbieri chooses a different measure of dyadic trade because she has a different theory about how trade influences war. Thus the weakest-link approach to dyadic concepts hinges on a falsifiable

---

[1]Weakest-link measures of dyadic democracy have been used in research on international collaboration (Mousseau 1997), trade agreements (Mansfield and Pevehouse 2000), trade grievances (Sherman 2001), dispute settlements (Dixon 1994), and rivalry termination (Cornwell and Colesari 2002), as well as in studies of the liberal peace (Oneal and Russett 1997, 1999; Russett and Oneal 2001). Weakest-link measures of trade interdependence are not quite so ubiquitous and, as we will discuss, somewhat more controversial.

[2]The weakest-link approach is also commonly applied to dyadic measurement of economic development (e.g., Mansfield and Pevehouse 2000; Mousseau 2000; Sherman 2001).

empirical claim, though to our knowledge it has never been treated as a testable hypothesis. Indeed, the weakest-link logic has long been regarded as generally accepted background knowledge exempt from critical scrutiny.[3]

One can contrast the family resemblance with the necessary and sufficient condition concept structures, with one as the positive pole and the other as the negative pole of a concept structure continuum. I have frequently contrasted the AND of the necessary and sufficient condition structure with the OR of family resemblance concepts. At the same time one needs to theorize the continuum lying between the two poles. It is substitutability that forms the underlying continuum between AND and OR. In short, OR allows for maximum substitutability while AND permits no substitutability.

Once we understand that the weakest-link democracy concept can be formulated by measures with differing degrees of substitutability then we have the tools to conduct an empirical test of the theory embedded in the concept. We do so by assessing the performance of alternative dyadic measures in capturing the assumed causal relations, a standard approach that Adcock and Collier (2001) refer to as "nomological" validation.[4] We will assume the truth of the hypothesis that dyadic democracy reduces the likelihood of conflict in order to assess which concept and measure best capture that relationship.

In summary, the three-level approach provides a framework for dealing theoretically and methodologically with a very common problem in the conflict literature, that of dyadic concepts. Many have felt that the weakest-link measure is plausible, but have had no conceptual framework within which to place it. As we shall see in the next section, many conflict variables must deal with the problem of aggregating from the individual to the dyadic level.

---

[3]For example, Dixon (1993, 52) states "the weakest link principle implies that . . . [conflict] management is most directly fostered or impeded by the norms of the less democratic party to the dispute." Similarly, Maoz and Russett contend that "The anarchic nature of international politics implies that a clash between democratic and nondemocratic norms is dominated by the latter rather than the former" (1993, 625). Neither study actually tests this weakest-link logic.

[4]Others (e.g., Carmines and Zeller 1979) use the term "construct" validation.

Dyadic Concepts and the Analysis
of International Conflict

The reason that the three-level framework applies to dyadic concepts is because one frequently faces the same structural problem. In the context of dyadic studies of international conflict it is more natural to talk about "individual-level" variables, e.g., the democracy level of each country, rather than secondary-level dimensions. Likewise, it proves more natural to speak of the aggregation of two individuals into a dyad rather than the basic level. The disadvantage of the aggregation language is that it hides the fact that we are dealing with a concept—e.g., dyadic democracy—that is not necessarily an "aggregation" in a theoretical sense of its parts. While we will use the term aggregation one should constantly keep in mind that the theory used to justify a particular kind of basic-level concept may differ from that used to identify the component, secondary-level, parts.

To understand the problem of dyadic concepts it is useful to survey the independent variables commonly used in quantitative conflict studies. We have surveyed the major journals that regularly publish this work (i.e., *Journal of Conflict Resolution, Journal of Peace Research, International Interactions, American Journal of Political Science,* and *International Studies Quarterly*) for the years 1990–2002 looking at those studies that were large-N quantitative and that had war, militarized dispute, or crisis as their dependent variables. While there is quite a variety of variables that are specific to one or a few studies, there is a set of variables that can be called the usual suspects, a line-up of which can be found in table 5.1. The Russett and Oneal analysis that we replicate below—that is, tables 5.4 and 5.6—uses most of the variables that appear in table 5.1. The goal here is not an exhaustive survey of dyadic variables, but rather an overall view of the extent and characteristics of the dyadic concept problem.

The dyadic concepts listed in table 5.1 can be broken into two categories based on the relationship between the individual-level indicators. The first category consists of what we call "relational" dyadic concepts. The dyadic concept is inherently a *relation* between the two countries. "Alliance" provides a prototypical example: by definition an alliance is a relationship *between* two or more countries. In contrast, "aggregation" concepts are ones where the individual parts can stand alone. The level of development or democracy is an attribute of each

TABLE 5.1

Dyadic Concepts and the Study of International Conflict

Dyadic Concept	Sample Citation	Structural Relationship	Dominant Structure
Democracy	Dixon (1993)	Aggregation	Weakest link
Trade	Barbieri (2002)	Aggregation	Weakest link
Major/minor power	Mousseau (2000)	Aggregation	None
Level of development	Hegre (2000)	Aggregation	Weakest link
Militarization	Goertz and Diehl (1986)	Aggregation	None
Arms race	Sample (2002)	Aggregation	None
Alliance	Gibler and Vasquez (1998)	Relational	n.a.
Contiguity	Bremer (1992)	Relational	n.a.
Power	Organski and Kugler (1980)	Relational	n.a.
IGO	Oneal and Russett (1999)	Relational	n.a.
Issue, territory	Senese and Vasquez (2003)	Relational	n.a.

n.a.—not applicable

Trade—level of trade dependence

Level of development—e.g., GNP/capita

Militarization—military spending as a percentage of national resources

Contiguity—geographical contiguity

Power—military capabilities, potential or actual

IGO—memberships in intergovernmental organizations

Territory—conflict is over territory

nation separately; to get a dyadic concept we must aggregate these individual values.

Table 5.1 suggests that about half of the time the researcher faces the problem of forming a dyadic concept. The last column of the table gives the dominant—if any—approach to the dyadic measure. In some cases, like democracy, the weakest-link measure clearly has been adopted by almost all. For other variables, such as major power status,[5] there is no clear pattern.

If we examine patterns over time, the weakest link comes out the clear winner. While early work on the democratic peace did not use this approach, since it was proposed by Dixon in 1993 it has reigned pretty much uncontested. As we shall see below, Barbieri has seriously challenged the hegemonic status of the weakest-link approach for the trade, economic dependency, variable. However, a clear majority of people who include this variable in their analyses apply the weakest-link procedure. The influence of the weakest link also extends to variables such as level of development (e.g., gross national product (GNP) per capita) where it is commonly used. As such the weakest-link procedure has almost achieved conventional wisdom status. But it is often useful to challenge the conventional wisdom. The contrast between the family resemblance and necessary and sufficient condition concepts with the underlying substitutability continuum provides us with the methodological tools for this task.

In the larger context this survey shows how common the problem of concept structure is. It also illustrates how this problem has not been directly addressed by methodologists. With the methodological and conceptual tools developed in the previous chapters we can address the logic and methods used to construct dyadic concepts. All conflict scholars know that using the weakest link means using the minimum to construct the measure, but this exists as an isolated fact. This chapter provides a systematic theoretical and methodological framework for making informed choices about dyadic concept construction.

---

[5]This variable is whether there is one or more major powers in the dyad. The weakest link is the rule that this dichotomous variable is coded one, weakest link, if both states are major powers. The maximum is used when the variable is coded "at least one major power."

SUBSTITUTABILITY AND MEASURE CONSTRUCTION

As chapter 2 discussed in detail, one can think of the family resemblance and necessary and sufficient condition concept structures as sitting on the two ends of the substitutability continuum. The weakest-link metaphor implies using the minimum, which is exactly what the fuzzy logic of the necessary and sufficient condition structure suggests. To illustrate, suppose we have an indicator of democracy ranging from 1 (lowest) to 10 (highest) and a pair of states rated [10,1] constituting a dyad of interest. Because the weakest-link approach takes the minimum of these two values, the dyadic level democracy score is 1. We see that individual democracy scores are assumed to be nonsubstitutable. The use of a continuous democracy measure demonstrates another important point as well—that no matter how high the rating of the more democratic state, it cannot compensate for the other's lack of democracy when characterizing the dyad as a whole. Weakest-link measures thus necessarily entail assumptions of strict nonsubstitutability. In this case such assumptions are justified by our theoretical understanding of democracy as representing norms or institutions of democratic governance that serve to constrain aggressive or belligerent behavior. In our [10,1] example with only one democratically constrained state, we would expect the dyad to exhibit little in the way of democratic constraint. The weakest-link approach thus derives its credibility from its underlying theoretical context, not from the simplicity of its combinatorial scheme.

The strict nonsubstitutability of democratic constraints is now a common working assumption among democratic peace researchers due to the widespread use of weakest-link measures. But this is certainly not the only plausible assumption one could adopt. For example, we could postulate partial substitutability in the sense that one state's highly democratic norms or institutions actually entail some limited constraining effect on other states irrespective of their form of governance. We know that people behave differently in different social contexts: why might this not also be true of state behavior in a dyadic setting? It is at least imaginable that states unburdened by their own democratic constraints nevertheless choose to moderate their behavior when dealing with highly constrained democracies. Just this sort of partial substitutability is found in the most familiar and intuitive of all combinatorial algorithms—the arithmetic mean. Returning to our example [10,1] dyad, the arithmetic mean of 5.5 would imply that the higher democracy score of 10 can now partially compensate for the lower score of 1, but only by one-half.

It is also possible to conceive of fully substitutable characteristics, though dyadic democracy is probably not the best example with which to develop this idea. Instead, let us consider the problem of characterizing formal alliance ties for a dyad where both states happen to be parties to two different alliances, one obligating them to mutual defense and the other, an entente, requiring only consultation in the event of attack. Should one alliance take precedence over the other, or should dyadic alliance ties be portrayed as some combination of the two? Small and Singer (1969, 263), the original compilers of the Correlates of War (COW) alliance data, "begin with the assumption that—in terms of the obligations undertaken—a defense pact imposes greater commitments than a neutrality or non-aggression pact, and that each of these imposes greater commitments than an entente."[6] Following Small and Singer, we characterize our example dyad as being bound by the mutual defense pact rather than the lesser obligation of the entente. By doing so, however, we also assume full substitutability in the sense that the greater obligation of stronger alliances completely offsets the lesser commitments of weaker alliances. Here we see scholars following implicitly the family resemblance approach when thinking about multiple alliance commitments. The use of the maximum signals that one has complete substitutability between the alliance commitments of two states.[7]

The case of dyadic alliance ties is illuminating because it demonstrates the broad applicability of our notion of substitutability. It also shows that the maximum, like the minimum, can also serve as a legitimate aggregating device. The idea of full substitutability can be conveyed metaphorically by designating the maximum as a "best-shot" approach to aggregate measurement. Just as the theoretical notion of democratic constraint is best depicted by the weakest-link *minimum* level of democracy, the best-shot *maximum* degree of obligation provides the best representation of how two states are legally bound to

---

[6]Gibler (1999) follows this rule in his update of the COW alliance data.

[7]Other examples of the use of the maximum and hence complete substitutability are by Fortna (2004), who codes multiple peacekeeping missions as the value of the strongest one, and Pevehouse (2002), who codes an international organization variable based on the most democratic of the organizations a state belongs to.

TABLE 5.2
The Substitutability Continuum: Its Metaphors and Representations

| *← Substitutability Continuum →* | | |
Necessary and Sufficient Condition	*Average*	*Family Resemblance*
Minimum	Mean	Maximum
Weakest link	Correlation	Best shot
Noncompensatory	Partial compensation	Compensatory
$t = -\infty$	$t = 1$	$t = \infty$

t is the substitutability parameter in the generalized mean, equation (5.1)

one another by a formal alliance. Moreover, issues of substitutability are also relevant to other types of aggregate units, not just dyads. Consider, for example, how to assess the nuclear deterrent capability of an alliance. Here again a best-shot approach would seem to be most appropriate since it treats the deterrent capability of an alliance as equivalent to that of its most powerful member under the assumption that nuclear forces are fully compensatory among allies.[8]

Here we have an important set of translation equivalences. Depending on various traditions, scholars have used different terms or metaphors to tap into the two canonical concept structures of necessary and sufficient condition or family resemblance. Table 5.2 shows how these all refer in their different ways to the substitutability continuum and points in between.

There are, of course, infinitely many algorithms delineating degrees of substitutability in addition to the minimum, mean, and maximum. We can make this combinatorial complexity substantially more manageable by employing the generalized mean to establish discrete markers along this continuum of substitutability. The generalized mean of the positive real numbers $a_1, \ldots, a_n$ is defined by equation (5.1):

$$m(t) = \left(\frac{1}{N} \sum_{i=1}^{N} a_i^t \right)^{1/t} . \tag{5.1}$$

[8]For more on weakest-link and best-shot approaches in the context of collective defense by alliances, see Conybeare, Murdoch, and Sandler (1994).

Note that when the exponent $t = 1$ this expression conveniently yields the arithmetic mean. Moreover, as t approaches ∞, $m(t)$ approaches the maximum of a_i and as t approaches $-\infty$, $m(t)$ approaches the minimum, thus defining the endpoints of the continuum (as illustrated in table 5.2). Additional discriminating markers can be added to this basic structure as needed. For example, the geometric mean used by Lemke and Reed (2001) to measure dyadic democracy serves well as a marker of quite modest substitutability situated between the partial substitutability of the arithmetic mean and the strict nonsubstitutability of the minimum value. The geometric mean also fits nicely within this general framework since $t = 0$ is the geometric mean.[9] Although never used in the literature to our knowledge, the quadratic mean, equivalent to $t = 2$, might serve as a similar marker at the opposite end of the substitutability continuum since it is always larger than or equal to the arithmetic mean. We can illustrate these inequalities more formally; for any pair of real numbers $[a, b]$, the inequality in equation (5.2) necessarily follows, with equality if and only if $a = b$:

$$\min(a, b) \leq (a * b)^{1/2} \leq \frac{a + b}{2} \leq \left(\frac{(a^2 + b^2)}{2} \right)^{1/2} \leq \max(a, b). \quad (5.2)$$

For the values $[10,1]$ used earlier in our dyadic democracy example, these quantities are $1 < 3.2 < 5.5 < 7.1 < 10$, respectively.

Although substitutability is a property of considerable theoretical interest, in practice its significance depends on the degree of heterogeneity among constituent units. Obviously all combinatorial algorithms yield exactly the same result under conditions of perfect homogeneity [e.g., $a = b$ in equation (5.2)]. Even under conditions of near homogeneity the measurement procedure may be of little consequence since aggregate measures are apt to be highly correlated. But as the homogeneity of individual units decreases, the choice of aggregation strategy is increasingly likely to have significant empirical implications. We believe this to be the case for measurement of dyadic democracy since there are quite a few states that are completely democratic, just as there are many states that are fully autocratic.

Viewing aggregate measures in terms of substitutability also helps to dispel a common criticism of weakest-link measures. It is sometimes said that the weakest-link approach is flawed because by setting the dyadic score equal to that of only one state it fails to use all of the

---

[9]This is because as t approaches 0 the limit of $m(t)$ is the geometric mean.

information available in the dyad. This criticism is mistaken for two reasons. First, the minimum is a mathematical function that by definition uses information from all observations in a set to return a single value.[10] The fact that the minimum returns a value equal to one of the observations does not imply that information from only that particular observation was used in generating the result. Second, and more importantly, the weakest-link logic is based on a theoretical claim about the nonsubstitutability of democratic constraints on state behavior. If this logic is correct then the minimum is indeed an appropriate measure of dyadic democracy. If this conceptual model is mistaken and democratic constraints are compensable to some degree, then we should abandon the weakest-link approach. But the issue at stake has to do with measurement validity and substitutability, not the amount of information contained in the measure.

ASSESSING NOMOLOGICAL VALIDITY

Nomological validity concerns the extent to which a particular measure of interest conforms to theoretically derived expectations. Adcock and Collier (2001, 541) "propose an acronym that vividly captures the underlying idea: AHEM validation; that is, 'Assume the Hypothesis, Evaluate the Measure.'" Usual practice, of course, is just the reverse: assume the measure to be valid and use it to evaluate the hypothesis. Assuming the hypothesis means accepting the veracity of the expected causal relationship and treating it as part of our accumulated background knowledge not to be criticized or questioned.[11] But do propositions of the liberal peace warrant such treatment?

Although there remain a few exceptions (e.g., Gowa 1993; Henderson 2002), most scholars now accept at least some variant of the democratic peace proposition. To do otherwise flies in the face of a remarkably consistent accumulation of empirical evidence acquired from assorted research designs, data sets, analysis procedures, and

---

[10]The minimum function is formally defined for any two real numbers $[a, b]$ as $\min(a, b) = (1/2)(a + b - (a^2 + b^2)^{1/2})$. See Wolfram Research's mathematical functions, http://functions.wolfram.com/01.34.02.0001.01.

[11]This element of nomological validation sometimes generates skepticism; see Adcock and Collier (2001) for a discussion of the relevant issues.

operational definitions of both democracy and conflict.[12] Indeed, if any area of international relations is suited to nomological validation by having well-established theoretical expectations and corroborating evidence, it is surely the democratic peace.[13] The same cannot be said of the hypothesized pacifying effects of trade interdependence. Although this proposition has also received sustained attention from researchers using alternative designs, procedures, and indicators, the findings have been decidedly more mixed.[14] At issue is whether or not the unsettled status of the trade interdependence hypothesis undermines our validation effort. We think not for two reasons.

One rests on the general principle that there is no recognized epistemological rationale for privileging causal hypotheses over measurement hypotheses. Both begin as conjectures, both must be conceptually coherent, and in the end both must meet certain empirical standards for acceptance. But, again as a matter of principle, both cannot be evaluated simultaneously; one must always be assumed while the other is tested. Moreover, as Adcock and Collier rightly point out, "To take a causal hypothesis as given for the sake of measurement validation is not to say that the hypothesis is set in stone" (2001, 543). It can always be revisited later, suggesting the possibility of a kind of iterative process of alternating improvements in measurement and hypothesis testing.

The second reason is tied more specifically to our present application. We are not asking whether a particular measure of trade interdependence is judged nomologically valid by confirming an assumed

[12]The literature is immense so only a flavor of its variety can be given here. The most prominent current stream of research is that of Russett and Oneal (2001) and its predecessors (e.g., Maoz and Russett 1993; Oneal and Russett 1997, 1999). Many others have also contributed key findings and propositions using different definitions of both conflict (Rummel 1985; Hewitt and Wilkenfeld 1996; Rousseau et al. 1996; Dixon 1998) and democracy (Chan 1984; Lemke and Reed 1996; Dixon 1998; Rioux 1998; Elkins 2000) as well as different estimation procedures (Beck, Katz, and Tucker 1998; Oneal and Russett 1999; Reed 2000). Nor is all the evidence from large-scale statistical studies, as the superb qualitative studies by Doyle (1986), Ray (1993), and Weart (2001) demonstrate.

[13]Although much of this corroborating evidence is based on weakest-link measures of democracy, a substantial portion is not (e.g., Maoz and Russett 1993; Hewitt and Wilkenfeld 1996; Oneal et al. 1996; Oneal and Russett 1999; Lemke and Reed 1996, 2000).

[14]Whereas a majority of studies reviewed by McMillan (1997, 52) "support the liberal hypothesis that interdependence reduces conflict, many also pose important questions and qualifications." It is perhaps telling that two recent books on the matter reach precisely opposite conclusions (Barbieri 2002; Russett and Oneal 2001).

causal hypothesis. Instead, we are evaluating alternative measures of a single concept to ascertain which best exposes a presumed relationship. In this case the trade interdependence hypothesis serves only "as a point of reference for comparing the performance of . . . indicators and thereby gaining evidence relevant to choosing between them." (Adcock and Collier 2001, 543). The case is bolstered even further by the fact that we are working with a particular design and data set in which the interdependence hypothesis has been repeatedly confirmed.[15] In sum, the tentativeness of the interdependence hypothesis is not in and of itself sufficient to undermine our analysis.

EVALUATING WEAK-LINK MEASURES

Our plan is to replicate Russett and Oneal's (2001, 316) logistic regression analysis on the probability of militarized interstate disputes and to compare the performance of the original weakest-link measures to three alternative aggregate measures reflecting different degrees of substitutability. In addition to the weakest-link minimum measure, our analyses encompass the limited substitutability entailed by the geometric and arithmetic means as well as the full substitutability implied by the maximum.[16] If the weakest-link hypothesis is correct we should observe two empirical outcomes. First, the minimum measures of dyadic democracy and trade interdependence should outperform all others by carrying the strongest impact on the probability of disputes. Second, we should observe a discernible pattern of decreasing performance across measures as substitutability increases. Thus the marginal substitutability entailed by the geometric mean should generate the second-best estimate, followed by the arithmetic mean and maximum measures, respectively.

Note that in order to focus on dyadic level aggregation procedures it is necessary to accept as given the constituent state-level indicators of democracy and trade dependence used by Russett and Oneal (2001). Even so, our use of these particular indicators should not imply our unconditional endorsement of the validity of either. While the polity democracy scale has demonstrated its utility in recent years, especially for studies over long time spans, it is not without certain shortcomings

---

[15]The data set has evolved over time partly as a result of different methods of handling missing data (Oneal and Russett 1999; Gleditsch 2002).

[16]We include the latter measure to provide a point of maximal contrast; we do not regard full substitutability as a theoretically defensible hypothesis in the present context.

as the previous chapter showed in detail.[17] Trade dependence data are subject to a whole different set of problems since researchers routinely rely on official statistics initially collected and reported for a variety of purposes by bureaucracies of varying competence, then compiled together and transformed by often unreliable exchange rate figures (Barbieri and Schneider 1999; Gleditsch 2002). Our aim is not to gloss over such problems but rather to temporarily suspend scrutiny of them to make manageable our central task of assessing the weakest-link approach to dyadic measure construction.

Dyadic Democracy

To reiterate the logic, students of the liberal peace argue that procedures, norms, and institutions of democratic governance serve to constrain aggressive or belligerent foreign behavior. This suggests that for any pair of states, particular attention should be paid to the *less* constrained actor. Indeed, Russett and Oneal hypothesize "that the likelihood of conflict depends primarily on how strong the constraints are on the less constrained state in each pair. In effect, that state is the weak link in the chain of peaceful dyadic relations" (2001, 99). But is it in fact a weak link? We intend to find out by examining the performance of a weakest-link measure against others that admit of at least some degree of substitutability.

The measures are constructed in the usual fashion by first assigning each state a democracy score based on the familiar Jaggers and Gurr (1995) 21-point scale. For present purposes we assume this state-level indicator to be a valid reflection of democracy and thus outside the purview of our validity assessment. Next we adjust the scale to range from 1 to 21 to avoid taking the square root of a negative number when calculating the geometric mean. We then create the four contending dyadic-level measures from pairs of these adjusted scores by taking the minimum, the geometric mean, the arithmetic mean, and the maximum. Observations are dyad-years from 1886 to 1992, yielding nearly 40,000 cases. We begin by examining some descriptive properties of these alternative measures in table 5.3.

The top panel of table 5.3 presents correlations among the four dyadic democracy measures. Note that the minimum measure is most strongly related to the geometric mean, followed by the arithmetic

---

[17]We use the polity measure, not ΔJG, in order to make our results comparable with the liberal peace literature, which almost without exception uses the polity measure.

TABLE 5.3

Measures of Dyadic Democracy: Correlations and Descriptive Statistics

	Minimum Democracy	Geometric Mean	Arithmetic Mean	Maximum Democracy
Geometric Mean	.96			
Arithmetic Mean	.85	.86		
Maximum Democracy	.47	.69	.96	
Mean	7.7	10.2	11.7	15.7
Standard deviation	6.6	6.1	5.8	6.8

Observations are 39,996 dyad-years from Russett and Oneal (2001)

mean and the maximum, with correlations of .96, .85, and .47, respectively. This pattern of correlations makes sense when each measure is placed along the substitutability continuum. We would expect that those measures that lie closer to each other on this continuum should be more highly correlated than those that lie far apart, and that is exactly what we see. The means at the bottom of the table reveal a similar pattern. If we think of democracy as a proxy for the degree of constraint in a dyad, then it comes as no surprise that on average the most constraint is registered with the minimum measure. Once we assume that higher democracy scores can partially compensate for lower scores, as is the case with the geometric and arithmetic means, the average level of constraint begins to decline. And, of course, the highest average scores are produced by the maximum.

Although the means in table 5.3 increase as a function of substitutability, there is no similar pattern in the standard deviations. A different view of the distributional properties of these measures is seen in the histograms in figure 5.1. Note that the minimum democracy measure manifests a distinct clustering of dyad-years toward the lower end of the scale, a pattern consistent with its low average value. The maximum measure produces an even more striking spike at the maximum democracy value. Once again we observe the geometric and arithmetic means arrayed in between these two extremes.

The first column of table 5.4 reproduces the Russett and Oneal (2001, 339) estimation while the remaining columns replicate their results

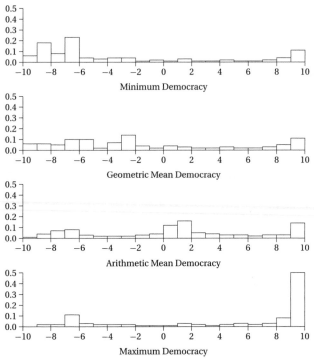

FIGURE 5.1

Measures of dyadic democracy: Frequency distributions

with the three alternative dyadic democracy measures.[18] As noted earlier, our test of the weakest-link substitutability logic rests on two critical observations: (1) the relative performance of the minimum democracy measure and (2) the pattern of estimates across all four measures. Of course raw logit coefficients are not necessarily indicative of substantive effects even when estimated on identical scales. We expose these effects in two ways at the bottom of table 5.4, first as a percentage change in odds and then as the change in predicted probabilities while holding all other variables at their mean values. For each case we examine effects of both absolute changes in democracy and relative changes based on the standard deviation of each measure.

The upper row of the percentage change panel shows how the odds of a dispute drop with a one-unit increase in dyadic democracy while

[18]We follow Russett and Oneal (2001) in using a general estimating equation framework with a binomial distribution, a logit link function, and AR1 error.

the lower row takes account of distributional differences by reporting the change in odds associated with an increase of one standard deviation. In both cases the largest impacts occur when dyadic democracy is measured by the weakest-link procedure. Furthermore, the magnitudes of effects in both cases correspond exactly to the pattern we would expect based on the weakest-link reasoning with the largest values observed for the minimum measure followed by those resulting from the geometric mean, the arithmetic mean, and the maximum, respectively. The pattern is repeated again in the lower row of the probability panel which lists changes in the likelihood of a dispute associated with change from one standard deviation below to one standard deviation above the mean democracy scores. Despite the high collinearity evident from table 5.3, a standard nonnested significance test encompassing both measures clearly favors the minimum ($z = 3.2$) over the geometric mean ($z = 1.8$).

Adding further to the weight of evidence is the fact that the error surrounding the logit estimates increases along with the substitutability implied by the measures. The ratio of the minimum democracy estimate to its standard error (-6.4) easily exceeds the ratios of the geometric mean (-5.3), the arithmetic mean (-3.9), and the maximum (-0.4), a pattern necessarily mirrored in the Wald χ^2 values. Overall, then, these results tend to support what would be expected of the weakest-link logic on both criteria. In the first place, the minimum measure does outperform all others in revealing the assumed causal relationship between democracy and militarized conflict. And secondly, the overall pattern of results is consistent with our conception of substitutability, with the performance of measures inversely related to their degree of substitutability.

The results from this first systematic empirical test of the weakest-link hypothesis will be welcome news to researchers who routinely employ the minimum as a measure of dyadic democracy. Evidence from table 5.4 strongly supports the weakest-link proposition. The weakest-link logic asserts that democratic constraints are strictly nonsubstitutable and this is exactly what our analysis has confirmed, at least in the theoretical context of the liberal peace. In practical terms this means that for any pair of states it is the less democratic one that establishes the norms and procedures governing the interactions between them. If the pair is democratic then democratic norms prevail, but if one or both is not democratic then realist power politics govern their interactions.

145

TABLE 5.4
Logistic Regression of Dispute Occurrence Using Alternative Measures of Dyadic Democracy

Variable	Minimum Democracy	Geometric Mean	Arithmetic Mean	Maximum Democracy
Democracy	-.0608	-.0529	-.0413	-.0045
	(.0094)	(.0099)	(.0099)	(.0106)
Allies	-.5392	-.5938	-.6120	-.5474
	(.1589)	(.1382)	(.1646)	(.1756)
Power Ratio	-.3182	-.3231	-.3270	-.3414
	(.0432)	(.0438)	(.0444)	(.0470)
Trade Dependence (lower)	-.5292	-.5775	-.6538	-.9084
	(.1341)	(.1382)	(.1464)	(.1870)
International Organizations	-.0135	-.0130	-.0131	-.0150
	(.0043)	(.0042)	(.0042)	(.0043)
Noncontiguity	-.9892	-.9880	-.9924	-1.033
	(.1675)	(.1690)	(.1721)	(.1823)

Log Distance	−.3762	−.3710	−.3699	−.3757
	(.0647)	(.0651)	(.0657)	(.0657)
Only Minor Powers	−.6472	−.6740	−.6680	−.5818
	(.1781)	(.1811)	(.1855)	(.1977)
Constant	.5406	.6037	.5895	.3880
	(.5353)	(.5409)	(.5475)	(.5553)
Wald χ^2	228.1	211.4	195.0	177.3
Percentage change in odds of a dispute with a change in democracy of				
1 unit	−5.9	−5.1	−4.0	−0.5
1 standard deviation	−33.3	−27.6	−21.2	−3.0
Change in probability of a dispute with a change in democracy from				
25th to 75th percentile	−.016	−.017	−.011	−.001
−1 s.d. to +1 s.d.	−.024	−.020	−.015	−.002

Observations are 39,988 dyad-years from Russett and Oneal (2001); standard errors in parentheses

Trade Interdependence

Although the weakest-link approach has been extended to measurement of dyadic trade dependence by Oneal and Russett (1997, 1999), the research community has not yet formed a consensus on this procedure. The logic of their approach once again rests on the idea of constraints, albeit with a somewhat different reasoning than in the case of the dyadic democracy concept. They begin with an indicator of dependence consisting of one country's total bilateral trade with another divided by its gross domestic product in order to control for the size of the economy. They then argue that for any pair of countries it is the more dependent one that is apt to be more constrained in its behavior to the other. Here constraints arise from self-interest in protecting a valuable trading relationship rather than from democratic norms or institutions. To construct a dyadic-level measure they once again rely on the weakest-link principle to model the constraints on the more dependent trading partner.

A weakest-link measure is appropriate for Oneal and Russett because the logic of their argument appears to preclude even marginal substitutability. They assume, first, that bilateral interactions are largely a function of constraints, and, second, that the modest behavioral constraints associated with low levels of trade dependence are completely independent of one's dyadic partner no matter how extreme the dependence. Put differently, one actor's high degree of dependence can in no way compensate for its dyadic partner's relative lack of dependence. But is this necessarily the case?

Barbieri (2002) assumes just the opposite when she proposes that the more constrained state in an asymmetrical relationship may well strive even harder to avoid or resolve potential conflicts. For Barbieri, it matters how much more dependent the more dependent state is. This is because a substantially more dependent state will perceive its own disadvantage in dealing with its less dependent dyadic partner and will thus moderate its behavior in order to protect its valuable trade relationship. This clearly implies some degree of substitutability since the high constraints of one actor in effect compensate for the other's lack of constraints. Whether or not the constraints derived from trade dependence are substitutable in this way is an empirical question that deserves systematic investigation.

Our inquiry into the measurement validity of trade dependence follows the same strategy used to investigate dyadic democracy. We again

TABLE 5.5

Measures of Trade Interdependence: Correlations and Descriptive Statistics

	Minimum Dependence	Geometric Mean	Arithmetic Mean	Maximum Dependence
Geometric Mean	.89			
Arithmetic Mean	.54	.80		
Maximum Dependence	.42	.72	.99	
Mean	.23	.54	1.22	2.21
Standard Deviation	.72	1.26	2.42	4.50

Observations are 39,996 dyad-years from Russett and Oneal (2001)

replicate Russett and Oneal's (2001) logistic regression estimation, this time comparing the performance of alternative dyadic measures of trade dependence.[19] If the weakest-link logic is appropriate, as Russett and Oneal contend, then the minimum measure of trade interdependence should outperform all others and the estimates should decline in magnitude as substitutability increases. On the other hand, if more dependent states do moderate their behavior in line with Barbieri's conjecture, then we would expect the strongest performance from the geometric or arithmetic mean since these measures are able to accommodate some degree of substitutability.[20]

Table 5.5 reports means, standard deviations, and correlations for trade interdependence.[21] The interrelationships among the measures correspond remarkably well to the pattern observed for democracy in table 5.4. Here again the minimum is most strongly correlated with the geometric mean, followed by the arithmetic mean and then the maximum. It is also apparent that the means of the measures reproduce the lowest to highest pattern extending from the minimum

[19] Also as before we presume the state-level indicator to be valid in order to focus our assessment on the validity of the weakest-link procedure.

[20] We should acknowledge that Barbieri (1996, 2002) would interpret the geometric mean as a measure of salience rather than interdependence.

[21] Raw trade dependence ratios from Russett and Oneal (2001) were multiplied by 100 prior to constructing the dyadic-level measures.

149

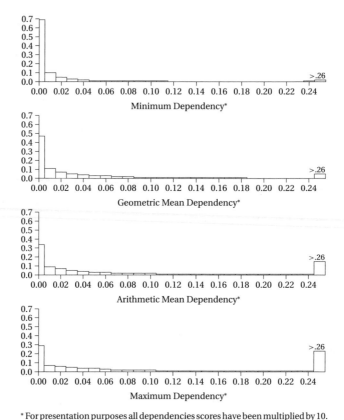

* For presentation purposes all dependencies scores have been multiplied by 10.

FIGURE 5.2

Measures of trade interdependence: Frequency distributions

to the geometric and arithmetic means and finally to the maximum. In fact, the only entries in table 5.5 that betray a substantially different pattern from table 5.4 are the standard deviations. The reason for this becomes evident in figure 5.2.

The histograms in figure 5.2 reveal the very highly skewed distributions of the trade interdependence measures. Although there are some similarities to the democracy distributions shown in figure 5.1, there are also striking differences. While the values of all four measures are heavily concentrated in the region near zero, this concentration is much more pronounced for the minimum than for the other measures. In addition, the maximum has a much longer tail than any of the others. Given these characteristics it is not surprising that we found a systematic pattern in the standard deviations.

Table 5.6 presents the same logistic regression analyses as before except that now we substitute dyadic measures of trade dependence, allowing for increasing levels of substitutability. Consider first the percentage change in odds resulting from changes in trade interdependence. The weakest-link measure once again reveals the strongest substantive effects from both an absolute change of one unit and a relative change of one standard deviation, though in the case of the latter the minimum (-32.2) just barely outperforms the geometric mean (-31.9). Interestingly, it is the geometric mean that surpasses all other measures when it comes to changes in predicted probabilities. Here we examine an absolute change in dyadic trade dependence from zero to five percent and a relative change from zero to one standard deviation above each measure's mean.[22] The geometric mean is also the best fitting measure with an estimate at 4.2 times the size of its standard error, followed by the minimum (4.0), the arithmetic mean (2.9), and the maximum (2.4).[23]

The analysis in this section has attempted to adjudicate between conflicting arguments regarding the substitutability of trade dependence measures. If the tenor of bilateral relations is primarily determined by the less dependent—and, hence, less constrained—state and the more dependent state plays no compensatory role at all, then a weakest-link measure of interdependence should be most effective. But if a more dependent actor recognizes its position and take pains to moderate its behavior so as not to provoke a less dependent partner, then an appropriate measure must accommodate some substitutability. The evidence adduced here, while by no means definitive, has highlighted the efficacy of the geometric mean, thus suggesting at least some measure of substitutability.

Notice that we have recast the debate between Russett and Oneal, and Barbieri in terms of substitutability. Their views of how trade dependence influences military conflict have implications in terms of substitutability that we have used to evaluate the merits of their respective arguments. The examination of democracy and trade links to

[22]We use zero percent as a baseline for both change calculations to maintain a positive level of dependence. Five percent is an arbitrarily chosen high level of dependence that falls below the maximum but above the ninetieth percentile for all but the maximum measure. The relative efficacy of the geometric mean at the bottom of table 5.6 is unaffected by this choice.

[23]Both the standard nonnested F test and the Davidson and MacKinnon (1981) J test proved indeterminate in distinguishing between the minimum and geometric mean measures of trade interdependence.

TABLE 5.6

Logistic Regression of Dispute Occurrence Using Alternative Measures of Trade Interdependence

Variable	Minimum Dependence	Geometric Mean	Arithmetic Mean	Maximum Dependence
Trade interdependence	-.5292	-.3062	-.0942	-.0416
	(.1341)	(.0737)	(.0330)	(.0174)
Minimum Democracy	-.0608	-.0598	-.0661	-.0680
	(.0094)	(.0094)	(.0094)	(.0094)
Allies	-.5392	-.5938	-.6120	-.5474
	(.1589)	(.1597)	(.1595)	(.1593)
Power Ratio	-.3182	-.2966	-.2693	-.2669
	(.0432)	(.0419)	(.04185)	(.0419)
International Organizations	-.0135	-.0129	-.0131	-.0133
	(.0043)	(.0043)	(.0041)	(.0041)
Noncontiguity	-.9892	-1.028	-.9687	-.9504
	(.1675)	(.1679)	(.1728)	(.1738)

Log Distance	-.3762	-.3853	-.3549	-.3470
	(.0647)	(.0657)	(.0660)	(.0660)
Only Minor Powers	-.6472	-.6958	-.5940	-.5673
	(.1781)	(.1800)	(.1793)	(.1179)
Constant	.5406	.5116	.3125	.2725
	(.5353)	(.5365)	(.5842)	(.5500)
Wald χ^2	228.1	230.1	215.8	213.9
Percentage change in odds of a dispute with a change in trade interdependence of				
1 unit	-41.7	-26.4	-9.0	-4.1
1 standard deviation	-31.8	-31.9	-20.4	-17.1
Change in probability of a dispute with a change in trade interdependence from				
25th to 75th percentile	-.002	-.005	-.004	-.003
0 s.d. to +1 s.d.	-.006	-.015	-.010	-.008

Observations are 39,988 dyad-years from Russett and Oneal (2001); standard errors in parentheses conflict shows how important the theoretical arguments are in creating concepts and their corresponding measures. In both cases, most of the measures did show a significant relationship with dispute initiation. We suspect that in many situations this will be the case. So scholars will almost inevitably be confronted with choosing among various (dyadic) measures, most of which will produce significant results. At the same time our analyses show that the strength of these positive results can vary significantly across measures; hence an attitude that "they are all about the same" is not confirmed at all.

CONCLUSION

The family resemblance and necessary and sufficient condition concept structures lie at opposite poles of the concept structure continuum. This continuum consists of the degree of substitutability between secondary-level factors. Beyond the specific analyses in this chapter, we provide a general procedure for thinking about and testing hypotheses embedded in concepts. By choosing measures of differing degrees of substitutability we can build and evaluate different concept theories. When Dixon first introduced the weakest-link idea into the democratic peace literature, he saw the tie between the theoretical argument about democracy and a quantitative measure. In this chapter we have put that insight into a larger framework.

One should not come away from this chapter with the view that the weakest-link democracy measure is always the appropriate one. It all depends on the the theory and the empirical phenomenon under examination. If one is looking at democracy and the outcome of disputes and wars, then perhaps the maximum might be more appropriate (Goertz, Jones, and Diehl 2005), since there is evidence that democracies are more likely to win wars (e.g., Reiter and Stam 1998). If one of the parties to the dispute/war is a democracy then we might expect the outcome to be a victory rather than the very common (65–70 percent) stalemate.

Both the last chapter on democracy and this one on dyadic concepts have shown that a concern for the theory embodied in concepts has important downstream consequences for quantitative measure construction. This volume has stressed throughout the theoretical nature of concept building. The choice of the mean, geometric mean, or maximum in conflict studies reflects theories about the mechanisms that generate or hinder the occurrence of militarized disputes.

The analyses of this chapter also foreshadow the discussion of two-level theories in chapter 9. The theories examined in this chapter have two levels. The secondary-level consists of the hypotheses embedded in dyadic concepts. The basic level is the statistical model with other independent variables. Chapter 9 examines in much greater detail and with many examples the issues surrounding such theories. While this chapter uses statistical techniques, the final chapter tests two-level theories using fuzzy set methods.

This chapter has also illustrated how the theories embodied in concepts cannot be divorced from basic-level theories. The AHEM principle of Adcock and Collier proposes that for the purposes of evaluating concepts and measures we suspend analysis of the causal relations at the basic level. Our evaluation of the various concepts of dyadic democracy and trade interdependence hinges critically on assumptions about the causal relationships at the basic level. If joint democracy does not hinder the outbreak of militarized disputes then our analysis of the validity of the concepts has little value. However, if we choose inappropriate concepts and measures (e.g., the maximum) we might find no relationship at all between democracy and conflict.

PART TWO

CONCEPTS AND CASE SELECTION

*

Concepts and Selecting (on) the Dependent Variable

WITH J. JOSEPH HEWITT

CONCEPTS PLAY TWO IMPORTANT ROLES in the research enterprise, as constituent parts of theoretical propositions and as means to select cases for empirical analysis. This chapter and the next two deal with some important aspects of the relationship between concepts and case selection. These issues constantly face qualitative researchers because they usually have to construct their populations themselves. The same problems are less pressing for the large-N quantitative literature because most scholars rely on preconstituted populations and their corresponding concepts. However, all large-N data sets provoke discussion on key conceptual points when they first appear on the scene. The next generation of researchers takes these data sets as given and is often unaware of the conceptual debates that surround their birth. Hence it is useful to examine two very widely used preconstituted data sets and their connection with concept structures. In this chapter we examine the well-known International Crisis Behavior (ICB) data set (Brecher and Wilkenfeld 2000), while in chapter 7 we take a look at the widely used Correlates of War data set on militarized disputes. In between, I focus on the most severe problem facing qualitative researchers, the selection of negative, control cases.

We can think of concepts playing a role in case selection because different concepts can be used to select different kinds of cases. Figure 6.1 illustrates this with a Venn diagram. The set of positive ("+" in the figure) cases is usually constituted by the phenomenon that the researcher seeks to explain (e.g., cases of revolution or crisis). This set of positive cases intersects with a set of negative cases (indicated by "−" in the figure). The negative (or control) cases are used to test the theory in question. The third big group is the set of "irrelevant" cases (symbolized by "0" in the figure). These are the many other potential cases that lack the outcome of interest, but which are seen as not useful for testing the theory in question.

Scope conditions

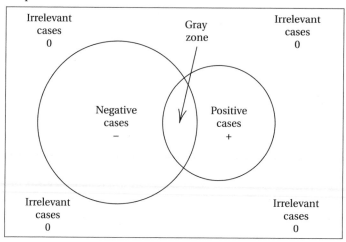

FIGURE 6.1
Case selection: Positive, negative, and irrelevant cases

This chapter examines one crucial boundary decision: how to separate the positive from the negative cases. In figure 6.1, the intersection of the positive and negative sets is nonempty. This nonempty space is the gray zone. In this chapter we focus on the concept of "crisis," which is a positive concept. The negative concept is frequently not very well defined; it is not clear at all what the set of "noncrises" consists of. Depending on how we structure and define the concept of crisis we can expand or shrink the set of positive cases; this means that depending on how we think about crisis the cases in the gray zone can be placed either in the set of noncrises or in the set of crises.

We shall focus in this chapter on the canonical strategy that defines concepts in terms of necessary and sufficient conditions. The International Crisis Behavior Project developed the concept of an international crisis (see the next section) using this default strategy. For any state under consideration as a potential crisis actor, the absence of any of the components of the concept removes the state from the population of cases. By requiring additional necessary conditions, concepts become increasingly restrictive in terms of the cases that qualify for selection into an analysis. In this way, one can conceive of concept-building strategies in terms of the intension-extension relationship. As chapter 3 discussed in detail, with necessary and sufficient condition concepts the size of the noncrisis set will shrink or enlarge as we add or subtract dimensions to or from the concept of crisis. Decreasing intension allows more cases into the positive population—i.e., increasing extension. Below, we illustrate how changes in the intension of the ICB crisis concept lead to important consequences for case selection which, in turn, have ramifications for causal inferences about crisis behavior.

Concept construction issues are absolutely crucial because the concept structure used interacts in various, usually hidden, ways with theories and hypotheses that researchers want to test. In this way we point out a type of selection bias that stems from the manner in which we define our concepts. Given that there are various ways to construct a concept, and hence to select a population, different concept structures can then bias the results because they choose different populations for analysis. In terms of chapter 3, variation in the intension of a concept produces changes in extension. The extension of the concept in the terms of this chapter is the population of cases selected for analysis. Hence, the intension-extension relationship has implications for selection bias.

For the phenomenon of international crisis, we suggest that among the more important causal inferences affected by the intension-extension connection to selection rules is that between power and crisis behavior. Due to the logic of deterrence, differences in power between disputants, which affect their resolve in pursuing their demands in crisis bargaining, play an important role in determining whether a particular contest between states will be selected into the pool of international crises (Morrow 1989; Fearon 2002). Since changes to intension involve selection effects, we expect the relationship between power and crisis behavior to be particularly affected by changes to the crisis concept.

Selection effects have received much attention lately (e.g., Reed 2000, 2002; Signorino 1998; Smith 1998). Perhaps the most well-known selection effect is due to selection on the dependent variable. Typically, this appears as a problem in qualitative studies when researchers choose cases based on the value (usually positive) of the dependent variable. More generally, selection bias occurs when the dependent variable is correlated with the selection rules used to choose cases. King, Keohane, and Verba (1994) discuss a form of selection bias that occurs when cases are selected such that the full range of variation in a particular dependent variable is truncated. In such cases, the

161

selection rule can potentially correlate with dependent variables of interest. When the selection rule implied by a concept intension correlates with the dependent variable of interest, research that tests the relation between that dependent variable and explanatory variables will be affected. Specifically, King, Keohane, and Verba write, "if the explanatory variables do not take into account the selection rule, *any selection rule correlated with the dependent variable attenuates estimates of causal effects on average*" (1994, 130, emphasis in original).[1] Since choices about concept intension amount to implicit decisions about case selection, it follows that construction of concepts can generate selection bias.

To illustrate how this works in practice, we focus on the concept of international crisis developed by the International Crisis Behavior (ICB) Project (Brecher, Wilkenfeld, and Moser 1988; Wilkenfeld, Brecher, and Moser 1988; Brecher and Wilkenfeld 1989; Brecher 1993; Brecher and Wilkenfeld 2000). It is a good illustrative example for two reasons. First, the concept of a crisis is defined using the standard necessary and sufficient condition strategy. As we know from chapter 3, extension decreases with increasing intension for necessary and sufficient condition concepts. We can thus add or subtract secondary-level dimensions to or from the crisis concept and explore the downstream effects. We shall see that there is a clear correlation between intension of a crisis and common ICB dependent variables. In addition, we shall illustrate that crisis intension influences causal inference in a typical multivariate statistical analysis. In short, the intension-extension relationship has important influences on selection bias and causal inference.

Crisis Concept Structures

The ICB concept of international crisis applies the classic necessary and sufficient condition concept structure:

> [A crisis is] a situation with three necessary and sufficient conditions deriving from a change in a state's external or internal environment. All three are perceptions held by the highest level decision-makers of the

[1] We shall see below, e.g., table 6.4, that in multivariate analyses causal effects can be attenuated or accentuated when selection rules are correlated with the dependent variable.

actor concerned: (1) *a threat to basic values*, along with (2) the awareness of *finite time for response* to the external value threat, and (3) a *high probability of involvement in military hostilities*. (Brecher, Wilkenfeld, and Moser 1988, 3)

The three conditions are the secondary-level dimensions of the concept. They are applied to each participant in the interstate confrontation to identify which states are crisis actors. That each of these three factors is necessary and together they are jointly sufficient forms the first key structural principle. The second key structural principle specifies that an international crisis is said to exist whenever at least one state satisfies the three crisis conditions. Notice that the concept of international crisis is composed of two different levels of analysis. On one level, the actor level, we have the set of participants. The other level, the crisis level, refers to the aggregated group of crisis actors, and is characterized, at least in part, by features of crisis interactions between the actors.[2] This issue should already be quite familiar since the previous chapter dealt with the creation of dyadic concepts in the context of the liberal peace (e.g., dyadic democracy and interdependence).

Due to the manner in which the ICB Project conceptualizes crises, it is possible for a state to satisfy each of the three crisis conditions while its main adversary does not. Hewitt and Wilkenfeld term these crises "one-sided crises" and explain that they

emerge from the coding process when no evidence can be found indicating that one of the parties to the crisis experienced all three conditions necessary for inclusion as a crisis actor. Thus, while a nation-state may trigger a crisis for another state by some action (e.g., Germany in the Remilitarization of the Rhine or Syria in the Syrian Mobilization Crisis), it may not be included as a crisis actor if the conditions for inclusion are not satisfied. (Hewitt and Wilkenfeld 1999, 310)

Earlier, we suggested that concept-building strategies could be conceived of in terms of the intension-extension relationship and how that influences the extent to which differing numbers of cases enter into the population. It would be possible to increase the ICB intension of crisis by adding an additional necessary condition for international

[2]To be clear, the empirical analyses we present below will be carried out at the crisis level of analysis.

crisis. Specifically, if the structural principle were to require that an international crisis exists only when at least two adversarial states satisfy the three crisis conditions, all one-sided crises would be removed from the population. That is, this change in intension would imply a change in the selection rule for identifying crises. This modification to the concept structure would truncate the variation in the degree of hostility in the set of crises; low levels of hostility in one-sided crises would be removed from the population, and hence extension would be reduced.

A contrasting approach to concept construction can be seen in the concept of the militarized interstate dispute widely used and incorporated in the militarized dispute data set (Gochman and Maoz 1984). Here is the definition of a militarized dispute according to Jones, Bremer, and Singer: "The term 'militarized interstate dispute' refers to united historical cases in which the threat, display or use of military force short of war by one member state is explicitly directed towards the government, official representatives, official forces, property, or territory of another state (Jones, Bremer, and Singer 1996, 168)."

The main dimension of the dispute concept is whether a state threatens or uses force short of war. The structural principle for constructing militarized disputes from this single dimension is different from crises. Any potential militarized dispute is investigated by looking at all the participants. If any of the participants has a level of hostility above the threshold of a "serious threat to use military force" then that state *and the target* of the threat or use of force joins the population of dispute actors. The threat or use of force is *not* a necessary condition for dispute involvement for a particular state. A target in a dispute can become an actor in a militarized dispute even when it does not reciprocate threats or uses of force. To be clear, a threat, display, or use of force is a sufficient condition for a militarized dispute to exist, but an actor is not required to commit such an action to be an actor in a militarized dispute. The structural principle used is the maximum level of hostility exhibited by any of the participants. Once one participant surpasses the threat threshold, any target state of such an action is included as a dispute actor even if it does not meet the threshold itself. The concept of a militarized dispute is thus an excellent example of the family resemblance use of the maximum for dyadic (or multilateral) concepts.

Thus the concept of a militarized dispute has greater extension than the concept of a crisis for two reasons. To be a crisis actor means satisfying three necessary conditions that are jointly sufficient, while to be a militarized dispute actor does not require military action at all. As long as another militarized dispute actor has satisfied the one sufficient condition by acting with a level of hostility above a certain threshold, targets of that action are included regardless of their actions. The second difference concerns criteria about when a dispute or crisis occurs. The militarized dispute procedure looks at the the one dimension of level of hostility; if the maximum of all the actors is above the threshold then a dispute has occurred. In contrast, a crisis uses the three conditions that are necessary and jointly sufficient. These strategies clearly indicate which conceptual families these two concepts belong to: crisis belongs to the necessary and sufficient condition group, while dispute belongs to the family resemblance category. I have stressed throughout this volume that one has various alternatives in building concepts; here we can see how the ICB group has taken one route, while the COW group the other.

DEPENDENT VARIABLES AND SELECTION EFFECTS

As discussed above, a change in the concept structure of crisis that adds a requirement that crises must comprise at least two states satisfying the three crisis conditions would amount to making the original ICB concept have reduced empirical extension. All one-sided crises, confrontations characterized by less reciprocated hostility, would be removed from the population. Here then is an excellent illustration of the argument we advance about how concept structure relates to selection bias. A change in concept structure (excluding one-sided crises) implies a change in the selection rule that correlates with a feature of crises—extent of reciprocated hostility. We argue below that the extent of reciprocated hostility is, in turn, quite likely to be correlated with dependent variables often studied in the crisis literature. In analyses that focus on these dependent variables, the potential for selection effects is, therefore, appreciably high.

To demonstrate the centrality of this issue, we choose as our dependent variables those that have been most commonly used in crisis research. We will focus on overall crisis violence, the primary crisis management technique, and gravity of threats. At least one of these variables has been the focus in studies of crises and the democratic peace (Rousseau et al. 1996), international rivalries (Colaresi

165

and Thompson 2002), presidential decision-making (Wang 1996), ethnic conflict (Carment and James 1995), the political economy of the use of force (DeRouen 1995), and the diversionary use of force (Gelpi 1997). Let us now elaborate on the theoretical reasoning underlying the expectation that the intension of the crisis concept is correlated with these dependent variables.

We expect the likelihood of crisis violence to be significantly lower in one-sided crises than in two-sided crises. Similarly, we expect that the central manner in which crisis adversaries handle the crisis—the primary crisis management technique—will less likely be violent in one-sided crises. Typically, one-sided crises occur when a state engages in a foreign policy action that triggers a crisis for a target state, but when the reaction of the target state does not trigger a crisis for the initiator. In such cases, the target's reaction is not sufficiently provocative or challenging to cause leaders in the initiating state to perceive a heightened probability of military hostilities or any of the other crisis conditions. Although the initiator's action has caused the target to believe that the probability of future hostilities has increased, the initiator perceives the situation differently, especially in light of a less provocative response from the target. It follows that, in these conflict settings, the likelihood of violent escalation is expected to be lower than in settings with greater reciprocated hostility. Lower levels of reciprocated hostility in one-sided crises contribute to a lower likelihood of overall crisis violence and especially to a reduced likelihood that violence would be utilized as the primary crisis management technique by the adversaries.

We also expect one-sided crises to feature lower-level threats than in two-sided crises. One of the conditions for crisis is that leaders must perceive a threat to national values. When the target state responds to the actions of the initiating state and that response does not elicit all of the necessary perceptions to qualify the state for crisis involvement, then it is reasonable to assume that the level of threat made by the target against the initiator, if any, is generally low.

In sum, we expect one-sided crises to be less likely to feature military hostilities (overall and as part of the primary crisis management technique) and high-level threats. If this expectation is supported, we will have prima facie evidence that a particular secondary-level dimension of the concept, i.e., selection rule for identifying crises, is correlated with common dependent variables. Let us now test this expectation, beginning with a brief description of our underlying data.

Our approach for identifying one-sided crises is slightly different from Hewitt and Wilkenfeld's (1999) original approach, so a brief comment is warranted about how we proceed. To identify a one-sided crisis for this research, we examine the members of the two opposing coalitions in each crisis and define a one-sided crisis as any crisis where one of the crisis coalitions is composed entirely of noncrisis actors. We identify all active participants in each coalition by utilizing data from the dyadic-level ICB data collection (Hewitt 2003). That project involved a complete examination of the historical background for each crisis to identify pairs of states involving at least one crisis actor and any actor that perceives that the other has directed a threatening or hostile action against it. In this way, our use of the dyadic-level data to identify one-sided crises represents a slight improvement over Hewitt and Wilkenfeld's (1999) original approach because it is based on a more thorough inventory of the actors involved in each case.

From the original ICB data collection of 434 cases, we eliminate a total of 91 cases. First, we eliminate 15 crises for which it was not possible to identify opposing crisis coalitions.[3] From the remaining 419 crises, we eliminate 76 intrawar crises (crises initiated in the midst of an ongoing war). The final data set contains information about 343 international crises that occurred during the 1918–2001 period. Within this sample of cases, 116 (34 percent) of the crises are one-sided crises and 227 (66 percent) are two-sided crises.

To assess whether one-sided crises have a lesser propensity toward military hostilities than two-sided crises, we examine the bivariate relationship between crisis type (one sided or two sided) and each of the three variables discussed above (overall violence, violence in crisis management technique, gravity of threat).

Tables 6.1 through 6.3 present 2×2 contingency tables depicting the association between the concept that determines the population, that is, whether a crisis was one sided or not, and three different common dependent variables found in the crisis literature. Table 6.1 presents the relationship between crisis type and overall crisis violence. The variable indicates whether there were military hostilities (minor clashes, major clashes, or war) in the crisis regardless of whether that use of force was coded by ICB as the primary crisis management technique. For two-sided crises, 74 percent of the cases

---

[3] Many of these crises involve nonstate actors as a primary crisis adversary (e.g. Russian Civil War I or Spanish Civil War I).

TABLE 6.1
Overall Crisis Violence

Crisis Type	No Violence	Violence	Totals
Two-sided	58	169	227
	26%	74%	100%
One-sided	50	66	116
	43%	57%	100%
Total	108	225	343
	31%	69%	100%

$\chi^2 = 10.96, p = .001,$ 1 d.f.

TABLE 6.2
Crisis Type and Primary Crisis Management Technique

Crisis Type	No Violence	Violence	Totals
Two-sided	88	139	227
	39%	61%	100%
One-sided	79	37	116
	68%	32%	100%
Total	167	176	343
	49%	51%	100%

$\chi^2 = 26.45, p = .001,$ 1 d.f.

featured military hostilities. In one-sided crises, the percentage of cases involving violence was 57 percent. The difference is statistically significant ($\chi^2 = 10.96, p = .001$).

Table 6.2 presents the relationship between crisis type and whether the primary crisis management technique involved the use of military force. In two-sided crises, the primary crisis management technique

TABLE 6.3
Crisis Type and Level of Threat

Crisis Type	No Violence	Violence	Totals
Two-sided	63	164	227
	28%	72%	100%
One-sided	54	62	116
	47%	53%	100%
Total	117	226	343
	34%	66%	100%

$\chi^2 = 12.07, p = .001$, 1 d.f.

involved the use of force in 61 percent of the cases. In comparison, one-sided crises were about half as likely to involve the use of force as the crisis management technique. The primary crisis management technique involved the use of force in only 32 percent of the one-sided crises ($\chi^2 = 26.45, p < .001$).

Finally, table 6.3 presents the association between crisis type and the level of threat in crises. Using the ICB variable GRAVTY, we code high-level threats as any threats to influence in the international system, threats to territory, threats of grave damage, or threats to existence. Political or economic threats are coded as low-level threats. We hypothesize that one-sided crises will be less likely to involve high-level threats. Looking at the table, it can be seen that one-sided crises exhibit high-level threats 53 percent of the time while two-sided crises involve high-level threats 72 percent of the time. The difference, 19 percent, is highly significant ($\chi^2 = 12.07, p = .001$).

Tables 6.1 through 6.3 clearly show that variation in intension of the crisis concept—and, hence, attributes of the selection rule for identifying the population for analysis—has a strong correlation with common crisis dependent variables. In all three cases there is a strong relationship between the concept of crisis and the dependent variable. These bivariate analyses provide prima facie evidence for selection effects. The next obvious question is how these selection effects can affect causal inference in a typical multivariate analysis.

SELECTION EFFECTS AND CAUSAL INFERENCE

We now test a multivariate model that includes a number of factors that past research indicates are strong predictors of military violence in international crisis. By testing the multivariate model on different subsets of the crisis population, we intend to assess how concept structures and selection effects influence causal inference regarding the use of force in crises. The seven variables in the multivariate model are violence in crisis trigger, capability ratio of the opposing coalitions, gravity of threats, whether the crisis included rival dyads, major power involvement, the presence of democratic states in the opposing coalitions, and the number of crisis actors.[4]

Due to space considerations, we offer only a brief discussion about our expectations for the independent variables and their measurement. According to the logic of trigger-response transitions (Leng 1983; Wilkenfeld 1991), we hypothesize that violent crisis triggers will be followed by a higher overall likelihood of crisis escalation. High-level threats are expected to lead to a higher probability of crisis escalation. Wilkenfeld, Brecher, and Moser (1988, 80) found that such threats are associated with a significantly higher likelihood of escalation to full-scale war. Another relevant variable is the number of crisis actors. Based on findings reported by Brecher and James (1989), we expect that the probability of crisis escalation increases with increases in the number of crisis actors.

The theory of the democratic peace argues that democracy should inhibit the onset of international crisis, but past research has also reported that the presence of democracies also inhibits escalation once the crisis begins (Rousseau et al. 1996; Hewitt and Willkenfeld 1996). The democracy variable, DEM, is computed by averaging the polity scores for the states in each of the two opposing crisis coalitions (Jaggers and Gurr 1995). Then, following the logic discussed at length in the previous chapter, we use the weakest link as a measure of the extent to which democratic constraints operate on crisis escalation.

As we mentioned earlier, we expect the relationship between power and crisis escalation to be particularly susceptible to selection effects. Specifically, we expect large differences in power between adversaries to be especially important in reducing the likelihood of military force

[4]We use EUGene (version 3.03) to generate data for democracy and military capabilities (Bennett and Stam 2000).

in one-sided crises. Large differences in power explain why crisis actors in one-sided crises are apparently deterred from responding to the challenge issued by the initiator with an action that would trigger a crisis for that state.

One power factor is the relative military capabilities between the opposing crisis coalitions. Following the many reported findings that power imbalances reduce the likelihood of serious conflict (e.g., Bremer 1992; Kugler and Lemke 1996), we expect divergent capabilities to lower the likelihood of escalation. To measure the capabilities of the opposing crisis coalitions, we use the Correlates of War Project's National Material Capabilities data set to compute a capability index (CINC scores) for each state in the crisis (Bremer 1992). We then compute a coalition capability score by summing the actor scores in each coalition. The variable CAPRATIO is the logged ratio of the capabilities of the stronger coalition to the capabilities of the weaker coalition.

A second power variable is whether there is a major power involved as a crisis actor. We suggest that significantly more of the one-sided crises involve a major-minor power relationship. Given the deterrence effects of power asymmetry we suspect that a significantly greater proportion of asymmetric cases in the one-sided population will produce quite different statistical results than in a population of two-sided crises. Recent empirical findings demonstrate that dyads involving major powers are significantly more likely to experience both militarized disputes and international crises (Russett and Oneal 2001; Hewitt 2003). Further, Bremer (1992) reports that major power dyads are more likely to experience full-scale war.

While we expect variables associated with power to be more vulnerable to selection effects, there are other variables that we propose are more robust. In particular we suggest that the rivalry variable falls into the robust category. One aspect of militarized rivalries is that they generate much high and low level conflict. Hence, we expect to see less difference between the populations of one- and two-sided crises since rivalry will produce both. In summary, we think that the rivalry variable will prove less susceptible to selection effects in our multivariate analysis.

We define a rivalry as any pair of states who have experienced at least three crises over a period of fifteen years or more. Hewitt (2005) theorizes that the likelihood of observing long rivalry sequences containing many high-severity crises is low because the likelihood of finding highly resolved rival states with the fortitude to engage in frequent, repeated high-severity crises is itself very low. After accounting for many known predictors for crisis escalation in a multivariate model, Hewitt (2005) found strong support for this somewhat counterintuitive proposition.

We proceed by testing a logistic regression model that includes each of the explanatory variables described above. We would like to know if features of concept construction and intension interact in important ways with theories and hypotheses commonly investigated by researchers. For our analysis, the dependent variable is the use of force as the primary crisis management technique adopted by crisis adversaries (1 equals use of force; 0 equals no use of force). Specifically, the logistic regression model is expressed as

$$
\begin{aligned}
\text{CMT} \;=\; & \beta_0 + \beta_1 \text{TRIGGER} + \beta_2 \text{GRAVTY} + \beta_3 \text{MAJPOW} \\
& + \beta_4 \text{NUMACTRS} + \beta_5 \text{CAPRATIO} \\
& + \beta_6 \text{RIVALRY} + \beta_7 \text{DEM}.
\end{aligned}
\tag{6.1}
$$

As suggested above, the inclusion of one-sided crises in the overall population of crises represents a more permissive conceptualization of crisis than a concept-building strategy that restricts the population of crises to two-sided affairs. What are the consequences of intension-extension relationships on causal inference about factors related to the use of force in crisis? We expect our multivariate model for crisis escalation to perform differently depending on whether it is applied to all crises, only two-sided crises, or only one-sided crises.

Table 6.4 presents the results of each of the three logistic regression analyses. Column (a) reports the results for the model applied to all crises. Columns (b) and (c) give the results for two-sided and one-sided crises, respectively. As expected, causal inferences about the likelihood of crisis escalation diverge substantially depending on the extension of cases. In all, the estimates for three of the crisis escalation predictors appear to depend on the manner in which international crisis is conceptualized. These variables are capability ratio, major power involvement, and gravity of threats. Since we initially expected causal inference involving power to be especially sensitive to the selection rule, let us focus our discussion on the former two variables.

In the population of all crises, large differences in capabilities between crisis adversaries serve to inhibit the likelihood of escalation. From column (b) it can be seen, however, that this relationship appears to be entirely absent in the population of two-sided crises.

TABLE 6.4

Logistic Regression Models for Use of Force in Primary Crisis
Management Technique

| | (a) | (b) Two-Sided | (c) One-Sided |
	All Crises	Crises	Crises
Capability Ratio (CAPRATIO)	−0.22**	−0.14	−0.51**
	(0.09)	(0.10)	(0.19)
Major Power Involvement (MAJPOW)	0.69**	0.65*	0.76
	(0.29)	(0.36)	(0.56)
Rivalry (RIVALRY)	−1.25**	−1.15**	−1.77**
	(0.30)	(0.35)	(0.66)
Violent crisis trigger (TRIGGER)	2.01**	2.17**	1.78**
	(0.28)	(0.37)	(0.51)
Gravity of threats (GRAVTY)	0.77**	0.80*	0.47
	(0.28)	(0.37)	(0.48)
Number of Crisis Actors (NUMACTRS)	0.53**	0.31*	0.41*
	(0.14)	(0.18)	(0.25)
Democracy (DEM)	0.02	0.01	−0.01
	(0.03)	(0.03)	(0.07)
Constant	−1.68**	−1.19*	−1.34**
	(0.43)	(0.61)	(0.79)
−2 Log Likelihood	366.8	238.4	112.4
p of χ^2	<.001	<.001	<.001
N	338	222	116

$^*p < .05$; $^{**}p < .01$ (one-tailed tests)

On the other hand, looking at column (c), there is a strong inverse relationship between capability differences and the likelihood of escalation in one-sided crises. The finding supports the expectation we described earlier that power differences would be more influential at preventing escalation in one-sided crises.

In thinking about this relationship, we suspect that selection bias is at work involving the relationship between crisis escalation in one-sided crises and capability differences. From previous research, it is known that large power differences inhibit the likelihood of crisis onset (Hewitt 2003). Among those anomalous cases that do become crises despite large power differences between the adversaries, there is good reason to suspect that these would be one-sided crises. Sharp power imbalances between disputants increases the likelihood of the onset of a one-sided crisis (rather than a two-sided crisis) because weaker crisis actors typically lack the resolve to issue or carry out threats that would, in turn, trigger a crisis for the stronger state. Consistent with this reasoning, Hensel and Diehl (1994) find in a study of unreciprocated militarized disputes that targets are less likely to reciprocate a threat or use of force when they are substantially weaker than the dispute initiator. Once triggered, one-sided crises involving sizeable power imbalances are more likely to be settled without military hostilities because the weaker state makes the necessary concessions to avoid costly military exchanges that would likely end in defeat.

A similar logic appears to be at work in the major power variable. This is significant and positively related to crisis escalation for two-sided crises but not for one-sided crises. In two-sided crises, by the definition of crisis, both sides perceive important threats to national interests, while in one-sided crises we would expect major powers to rarely be involved as the sole crisis actor. Major powers, after all, are less likely to be deterred when challenged by another state and, therefore, would be more likely to respond with an action that would trigger a crisis for the initiator. Indeed, of the 116 one-sided crises, major powers are crisis actors in only 16 percent of them (compared to a 33 percent involvement rate in two-sided confrontations).

We suspect that when selection effects are important that it will often result in volatility of power variables. Because deterrence effects (either success or failure of deterrence) play such a powerful role in selection and because they are so closely related to power, we are not surprised that many of the key differences that appear in table 6.4 are related to power variables.

Some of the tested variables appear to be more robust in resisting selection effects. For example, consider the rivalry variable. In contrast to power variables the coefficients in both the one- and two-sided populations have the same sign and are both statistically significant. We see this as consistent with the hypothesis that rivalries produce fewer differences between populations because of their ability to produce high and low hostility crises. The estimated relationship between violent crisis management and two other variables, violence in the crisis trigger and the number of crisis actors, also proved to be consistently significant across different conceptualizations. Democracy, on the other hand, was not a significant inhibitor of crisis escalation in any of the models we tested.[5]

In sum, decreasing crisis intension produces an extension predisposed to admitting more crisis adversaries characterized by power imbalances. Within those particular crisis interactions, there is strong reason to expect the likelihood of crisis escalation to be low. In this way, the causal inference about the impact capability ratios on crisis escalation is conditioned by a particular attribute of the crisis concept—whether it is one-sided or two-sided. How we conceive of crisis has important downstream influences on causal inferences regarding key power politics factors.

CONCLUSION

The explicit choices researchers make about how to structure particular concepts are tantamount to decisions about which observations to select into an analysis. As such, particular concept structures carry the potential for selection biases.

We explored this phenomenon by looking at the ICB conceptualization of crisis. Modifications in the intension of this concept serve to shrink or enlarge the extension of crises selected for analysis. Changes in intension were correlated with standard dependent variables used in analyses of crisis behavior. We then explored how selection effects influence a multivariate analysis of crisis escalation by modifying the population of crisis. The results of that analysis demonstrated how selection effects can interact with hypotheses we aim to test and thus influence causal inference.[6]

[5] Since democratic peace theory is largely concerned with the onset of armed conflicts (as opposed to the escalation of crises), we do not interpret these results as contrary to the democratic peace hypothesis. Nonetheless, it is important to note that the findings reported here differ from those of Hewitt and Wilkenfeld (1995) who found that high levels of democracy in crisis significantly lowered the likelihood of escalation. The divergent findings could be due to several differences including the measurement of democracy, temporal domains, and model specification.

[6] Our results have important implications for the use of militarized disputes as well. If one considers that unreciprocated militarized disputes are the analogy to one-sided crises then it is sobering to note that nearly half of all militarized disputes are unreciprocated.

Unlike the usually uninterpretable ρ coefficient in Heckman selection models, we have seen that there is often a clear logic to the selection biases that reveals itself when we look at statistical analyses comparing different populations. Many have stressed how power and deterrence factors can produce selection effects. Our analyses have confirmed in a very clear fashion that these concerns are well founded. In contrast, there is almost no work on variables that should produce *no* selection effects. For example, we found that rivalry variables were much less susceptible to these kinds of problems. This chapter then confirms some well-founded hypotheses, but at the same time pushes the selection bias agenda forward.

In this chapter we have focused on the gray zone between the positive and negative concepts (see figure 6.1). As Sartori (1970) emphasized with his ladder of generality, there is a clear relationship between intension and extension for necessary and sufficient condition concepts. Scholars have the option of putting observations in the gray zone either into the positive or negative sets. As our analyses of international crises have illustrated, this can lead to significant selection effects. Often, decisions about gray zone cases are correlated with dependent variables, hence producing selection biases. These decisions then have downstream implications for causal inferences. The intension-extension relationship thus plays a large role in case selection and causal inference.

Negative Case Selection: The Possibility Principle

WITH JAMES MAHONEY

"I see nobody on the road," said Alice.
"I only wish I had such eyes," the King remarked,
in a fretful tone.
"To be able to see Nobody! And at that distance, too!"
Lewis Carroll

WHERE AND WHEN do "non–social revolutions" occur? Certainly the United States in 1900 qualifies, but Skocpol (1979) never considered this case in her famous study of social revolutions. Nor did she choose to analyze Canada in 1890, Australia in 1950, or most of the millions of non–social revolutions that have occurred in world history. Instead, she selected a sample of "negative cases"[1] that she regarded as relevant and appropriate for testing her theory of social revolution. In qualitative research, most analysts must—like Skocpol—select a set of negative cases to test their theories. However, the rules for choosing and justifying a set of cases defined by the occurrence of a nonevent are far from straightforward.

Intuitively, most qualitative analysts would claim that the United States in 1900 is not relevant or informative for testing theories of social revolution. Does this therefore mean that the case can be legitimately ignored when testing a theory of social revolution? Philosophers have puzzled over this question for half a century in the form

---

[1] One can think of "negative" cases as "control" cases. We prefer the term negative because the contrast group is constituted by the observations that are "positive" on the outcome variable. Here we assume that cases are coded dichotomously on the dependent variable, an assumption that we relax below. It bears emphasis, however, that case selection is largely a dichotomous affair in research: either an observation is included in the analysis or it is not.

of the "Raven Paradox" (Hempel 1945). The paradox begins with the hypothesis that "all ravens are black." The positive cases which clearly support the hypothesis are black things that are ravens and ravens that are black. The paradox arises from the logical fact that all nonblack, nonraven things also support the hypothesis. We intuitively feel that most—though probably not quite all—nonblack, nonraven things are not very useful in testing this hypothesis, just as the United States in 1900 is not an informative case for testing theories about the causes of social revolution. However, without any clear guidelines for differentiating relevant from irrelevant cases, it is hard to justify excluding these cases.

The previous chapter dealt with using concepts to select populations which are related to the dependent variable, and implications for the problem of selection bias. As is well known, selecting cases based on their value on the dependent variable can lead to the overrepresentation of positive cases in the sample, which can bias results in statistical analyses. This chapter and the next deal with the problem of determining the negative cases. The inclusion of irrelevant observations as negative ones does the opposite of selecting on the positive values of the dependent variable: one introduces too many negative cases into the population. In short, selecting on the dependent variable normally means too many positive cases, whereas including irrelevant observations means too many negative cases. Just as the solution for selecting on the dependent variable is to include more negative cases, so too the solution to the negative case problem is to exclude irrelevant cases.

As we saw in chapter 2, a key issue in building concepts is the negative pole. Frequently it is not clear what the negative concept is, e.g., nonwar, non–social revolution, etc. Yet it is exactly this set of cases that we need in order to test theories that focus on the positive pole of the dependent variable concept. In order to empirically examine theories of war and social revolution we need cases of nonwar and non–social revolution. So, while in terms of theoretical propositions, it is often not necessary to have a clear notion of what the negative pole consists of, for purposes of research design one must grapple with the problem and find a solution.

This chapter proposes a principle—the Possibility Principle— that provides explicit, rigorous, and theoretically informed guidelines for choosing a set of negative cases. The Possibility Principle holds that only cases where the outcome of interest is *possible* should be included in the set of negative cases; cases where the outcome is *impossible* should be relegated to the set of uninformative and hence irrelevant observations. We show that this principle can help scholars avoid errors and maximize leverage for making valid causal inferences. This principle applies to both strategies for defining the negative cases, defining the negative pole via "non" (e.g., non–social revolutions) or defining a complete population (e.g., politically relevant dyads; see the next chapter).

The Possibility Principle implicitly informs much experimental research. For example, when testing new varieties of crops, researchers do not usually put test plots in the desert. The use of these test plots would be a waste of resources, and their inclusion could grossly distort inferences about the efficacy of crop strands in settings where the outcomes of interest are possible. Or suppose scientists seek to test a drug to prevent breast cancer. Should they include men and children in the test population? Although men and children can develop breast cancer, it is quite rare. One might therefore argue that men and children are irrelevant when testing a drug to prevent breast cancer, given that the outcome of interest is such a low-probability event for them. The Possibility Principle states that the negative cases should be those where the outcome has a real possibility of occurring—not just those where the outcome has a nonzero probability.

We are particularly concerned with studies that seek to *test theory* about the causes of outcomes of exceptional interest such as revolution, war, genocide, welfare state development, and sustained economic growth. To explain these kinds of outcomes, nearly all research designs require the examination of negative cases. This is true both of research designs in large-N, quantitative work (see the next chapter) and of small-N research methods such as Mill's method of difference (Skocpol 1984), typological theory (George and Bennett 2005), Boolean algebra (Ragin 1987), and fuzzy-set analysis (Ragin 2000).[2]

The argument proceeds as follows. We first describe the case selection problems faced by qualitative and quantitative researchers, highlighting the challenge of distinguishing negative cases from irrelevant cases. We then introduce the Possibility Principle as a means of selecting negative cases. Subsequent sections consider how the

---

[2]Research designs focused on necessary causes are perhaps the only partial exception to this claim. As Dion (2003), Braumoeller and Goertz (2000), and Ragin (2000) have shown, one can test necessary cause hypotheses by selecting only cases with positive outcomes. However, Braumoeller and Goertz (2000) have argued that negative cases are required to test whether or not a necessary cause is trivial.

principle relates to theory formulation and the use of scope conditions. We end by considering the controversy surrounding Skocpol's selection of negative cases in *States and Social Revolution* (1979), showing how the application of the Possibility Principle generates new conclusions about this famous argument.

THE TOPOLOGY OF CASE SELECTION

A basic challenge involves drawing the boundaries between different kinds of cases. Most scholars have discussed this boundary challenge in terms of distinguishing positive and negative cases, as was discussed in the previous chapter. By contrast, we focus attention in this chapter and the next on the rarely discussed boundary issues involving negative and irrelevant cases. We suggest that these negative-irrelevant boundary issues must be resolved *before* scholars can implement procedures for choosing a representative sample of cases.

Negative-Irrelevant Boundary

The problem of negative case selection involves the difficulties of distinguishing nonpositive cases that should be included in the research design (i.e., negative cases) from nonpositive cases that should not (i.e., irrelevant cases). In figure 7.1, the zone of irrelevant cases next to the negative cases highlights the structure of this boundary problem. The question raised here is how should scholars draw the line between the negative and irrelevant cases?

To this point, methodologists have offered only very general answers. They do not explicitly declare certain nonpositive cases to be irrelevant, but rather advise that some nonpositive cases are more analytically useful than others. In particular, nonpositive cases that closely resemble positive cases, particularly on key hypothesized causal factors, are seen as highly useful. For example, in her discussion of the method of difference,[3] Skocpol suggests that negative cases

---

[3]Scholars have criticized Skocpol's characterization of Mill's method of difference as not consistent with what Mill himself was arguing (for example, Ragin 1987 believes Skocpol is actually characterizing Mill's indirect method of difference). Nevertheless, her codification of this approach has become the conventional understanding of the method of difference in the social sciences.

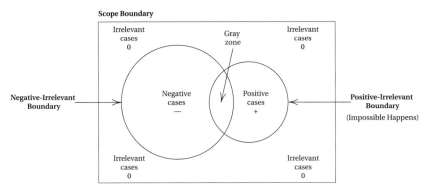

FIGURE 7.1
Case selection: Positive, negative, and irrelevant cases

should be "as similar as possible to the 'positive' cases in all respects except for their value on the dependent variable" (Skocpol 1984, 378). Przeworski and Tuene's "most similar system design," which examines positive and negative cases, is also grounded in the belief that cases "as similar as possible with respect to as many features as possible consti- tute the optimal samples for comparative inquiry" (1970, 32). Ragin frames the issue of negative case selection in similar terms: "Negative cases should resemble positive cases in as many ways as possible, es- pecially with respect to the commonalities exhibited by the positive cases" (2000, 60). Indeed, many scholars have sought to use time pe- riods within a given unit in order to maximize similarities between positive and negative cases (Haydu 1998).

These analysts encourage a focus on negative cases that resemble positive cases in part because this approach allows one to control for many background features and thereby facilitates causal inference. We consider this to be good advice for selecting a sample of negative cases in small-N research.[4] However, the advice still assumes that all negative cases are theoretically relevant or at least theoretically neu- tral, failing to note that serious problems may arise if certain negative cases are included in the analysis.

---

[4] Indeed, by virtue of focusing on negative cases that resemble positive cases on certain potential causal variables, the advice is consistent with the Rule of Inclusion that we develop below.

Positive-Irrelevant Boundary

It would seem unlikely that a boundary exists between positive observations and irrelevant ones. Indeed, according the Possibility Principle, irrelevant observations are those where the positive outcome is impossible. However, the impossible can happen if an observation is mistakenly put into the irrelevant category, but it in fact has a positive outcome. Thus, at the irrelevant-positive boundary we have a situation where the "impossible happens." The impossible is likely to happen in research designs where the analyst defines populations without consideration of their value on the dependent variable. This boundary decision will form a central part of the next chapter since it is likely to arise when the Possibility Principle is used to select the entire population, not just the negative cases. In contrast, it does not pose a problem for researchers who use all their positive cases and only apply the Possibility Principle to select the negative ones.

Scope Boundary

A well-known boundary involves the scope of a theory. In figure 7.1, this boundary is represented by the box itself; all observations within the box are assumed to meet the scope conditions of the theory. Typically, scope conditions define irrelevant cases as those where causal processes are not homogeneous. For example, Skocpol argues that the basic causal processes of social revolutions in states with colonial histories differ from those in noncolonial states, and her scope includes only the latter kind of cases. There might well be social revolutions outside this scope (i.e., in the area outside the box in figure 7.1), but these are irrelevant to testing her theory.

IRRELEVANT CASES: SELECTION BIAS VIA TOO MANY NEGATIVE CASES

A common reflex in statistical analysis is to consider all cases as relevant for testing theory. This reflex is grounded in the belief that excluding cases as irrelevant entails the loss of potentially helpful information. It finds philosophical support in the advice of Hempel (1945) who resolved the Raven Paradox by arguing that all things—i.e., nonblack, nonraven things—are relevant to confirming the propo-

TABLE 7.1
Democratic Peace and the Raven Paradox

	No Democracy	Democracy
War	36	0
No War	1045	169

Source: Russett (1995, 174)

sition that all ravens are black. Likewise, it is consistent with an "all-cases" design in qualitative analysis, which advises researchers to sample from the entire population when testing hypotheses about necessary or sufficient causation (Seawright 2002).

The inclusion of all cases will artificially inflate the number of observations that confirm a theory. In effect, this practice can make a false or weak theory appear much stronger than it really is. For example, consider the theory that most ravens are white. Although this theory will not be supported by black ravens, it will be confirmed by all nonraven, nonwhite things. Insofar as the number of confirming observations is orders of magnitude larger than the number of disconfirming observations, one could conclude that the theory is almost always supported by the data.[5]

We can see the Raven Paradox problem by looking at a simple 2×2 table, table 7.1, on the democratic peace. The democratic peace hypothesis is that all wars involve at least one nondemocracy, just as all ravens are black. We have a pretty good idea about the war cases, often used is the Correlates of War list, but what should count for the nonwar cases? Clearly no war between the United States and Great Britain counts as evidence for the democratic peace. It is not so clear that no war between Canada and Switzerland does.[6]

It is pretty clear that the no war–no democracy cell of table 7.1 can contain a very large number of observations—just as we can find

---

[5]Hempel (1965, 48) recognized this problem, and he suggested that some confirming observations may carry less weight than others when testing a theory (Earman 1992). This problem also motivated Popper (1968) to focus on disconfirming observations rather than confirming observations.

[6]The analyses of the weakest-link hypothesis in chapter 5 used politically relevant dyads; see the next chapter for more on this.

a large number of nonblack nonravens—depending on how we go about things. If statistical significance is what you are looking for then pumping more cases into this cell will eventually get you what you want.

This issue underlies a recent debate between Seawright and his critics (Seawright 2002; Clarke 2002; Braumoeller and Goertz 2002). Seawright suggests that all cases in an "appropriately defined universe" are relevant to testing a proposition about causal sufficiency, even negative cases that lack the hypothesized sufficient cause.[7] In context of the democratic peace, the hypothesis is that joint democracy (i.e., "Democracy" in table 7.1) is sufficient for "no war." He shows that the inclusion of all cases can substantially enhance statistical significance by increasing the number of confirming observations. By contrast, Clarke argues that including all cases will lead one to confirm a proposition through irrelevant observations, in much the same way that "most ravens are white" might be confirmed by observing yellow pencils and blue books. Braumoeller and Goertz's argument likewise suggests that, when testing a hypothesis about a sufficient cause, cases that lack both the cause and the outcome are irrelevant, since the hypothesis does not imply anything about the number or proportion of these cases that should be present.

For all of these reasons, the definition of the full population of relevant cases has large implications for theory testing and research findings. Yet, the literature on sampling techniques often makes it appear as if the definition of the population can be treated as unproblematic and given. Consider case-control sampling methods when studying rare events. Here the analyst strictly differentiates between positive and negative observations, and then selects all positive observations and a random sample of (perhaps matched) negative observations (King and Zeng 2001, 142; Goldstone et al. 2000). This approach simply assumes that the analyst has a good understanding of the full population of negative cases. In their discussion of militarized conflict among dyads of states, for instance, King and Zeng (2001, 144) assume that determining the fraction of positive cases is "straightforward" because "the denominator, the population of countries or dyads, is easy to count." By contrast, we think that determining the population

---

[7]The debate applies equally to necessary causes. We focus here on sufficient causes because of their close connection to theories that require negative cases.

size is quite problematic: it depends on how one defines a relevant dyad.[8]

Likewise, scholars who have sounded alarm bells about the dangers of selection bias assume that the scholar is working with a well-defined larger population of relevant cases. Yet, we believe that—unless the Possibility Principle is applied—the full population of cases may include many irrelevant observations. These irrelevant cases will often be systematically different from the relevant cases vis-à-vis their value on the independent variables. In addition, the inclusion of irrelevant cases will produce an explosive increase in the number of cases with zero values on the dependent variable, much as selecting on the dependent variable often leads to an overrepresentation of positive cases. Because samples selected from populations that include irrelevant cases have too many cases of zero on the dependent variable and frequently will be systematically different on many of the independent variables, one can say that failure to apply the Possibility Principle is a potential source of selection bias.[9]

The Possibility Principle

In this section, we more formally introduce and elaborate the Possibility Principle. Many qualitative and quantitative researchers already have implicitly applied the principle in making and justifying their case selection decisions, and thus we are in many ways only formalizing a widely held intuition. Nevertheless, we argue that greater explicitness and rigor in applying the principle can improve the quality of research and can help resolve debates about case selection in the social sciences.

---

[8]Note that any statistical calculations that involve $\Pr(Y=1)$ or $\Pr(Y=0)$, e.g., relative risk, will be significantly influenced by how the boundary between relevant and irrelevant observations is drawn.

[9]The consequences of selection bias for qualitative research are sharply debated. For different views, compare King, Keohane, and Verba (1994) and Geddes (2004) with Collier and Mahoney (1996); see also Brady and Collier (2004).

Basic Rules

The Possibility Principle of negative case selection has the basic form

Possibility Principle: Choose as negative cases those where the outcome of interest is possible.

Obviously, much depends on how we interpret the key concept of "possible," which is used to draw the boundary between the negative and irrelevant observations. We propose two rules for implementing this principle in qualitative analysis: a Rule of Inclusion and a Rule of Exclusion.

The *Rule of Inclusion* assumes that an outcome should be seen as possible if at least one independent variable of the theory under investigation predicts its occurrence. This is true even if other independent variables predict its absence. Thus, the basic rule is

Rule of Inclusion: Cases are relevant if their value on at least one independent variable is positively related to the outcome of interest.

We call this the Rule of Inclusion because it serves as a means of selecting observations into the population of relevant cases.

The Rule of Inclusion is applied in conjunction with the theory under investigation. In qualitative research, investigators usually develop parsimonious theories in which the number of independent variables is relatively limited. For example, five or fewer independent variables often constitute the core of the theory, whereas it is rare for more than seven or eight independent variables to be included. In this sense, in the context of qualitative research, a case with the presence of even one core independent variable that is hypothesized to be positively related to the outcome of interest should be considered within the domain of observations where the outcome is possible. In other kinds of research, theories may contain many more independent variables, and these variables may be seen as only weakly related to the outcome of interest. For these studies, the Rule of Inclusion can be adjusted such that the presence of more than one positively related independent variable is needed for a case to be included in the relevant category.

In contrast to the Rule of Inclusion, the *Rule of Exclusion* provides a means of declaring an observation to be irrelevant and thus excluding it from analysis. Under this rule, a case is considered irrelevant if it possesses a value on a variable that is known to make the outcome of interest impossible. For example, in her study of the causes of genocide, Harff (2003) discovers that almost all genocides (i.e., 36 out of 37) occur during or immediately after political upheavals. Accordingly, she excludes cases like France and Canada that lack political upheaval when testing her theory of genocide. These politically stable cases have such a low probability of experiencing genocide that their inclusion would distort inferences about other cases where the outcome of interest is possible.

The Rule of Exclusion depends on the analyst having good knowledge about one or more "eliminatory variables" that are important enough to remove a case from the domain of relevant observations all by themselves. These eliminatory variables may be necessary causes of the positive outcome of interest, or they may be sufficient causes of the negative outcome. It is not uncommon for multiple eliminatory variables to be present in a given case, and thus for the zero value on the dependent variable to be overdetermined. For example, one can come up with many reasons why social revolution in the United States in 1900 was theoretically impossible. Given that non–social revolution was overdetermined, it makes little sense to use the United States when testing theories of social revolution.

The Rule of Exclusion takes precedence over the Rule of Inclusion: eliminatory variables can lead an analyst to declare a case as irrelevant even if the case is considered relevant via the Rule of Inclusion. For example, one may have a theory of genocide that highlights ethnic divisions as a key independent variable. Under the inclusion rule, contemporary Canada could therefore be considered a relevant case. However, under Harff's (2003) exclusion criterion, Canada is irrelevant because its value on the political upheaval variable eliminates it from the analysis. In short, then, the Rule of Exclusion has the following basic form:

Rule of Exclusion: Cases are irrelevant if their value on any eliminatory independent variable predicts the nonoccurrence of the outcome of interest. This rule takes precedence over the Rule of Inclusion.

As we explore below, the Rule of Exclusion is closely related to the use of scope conditions in comparative research.

It is crucial to understand the differing roles of the Rules of Exclusion and Inclusion. The Rule of Exclusion *cannot* be used for core causal variables under test. For example, Harff cannot test the importance of political upheaval as a cause of genocide, since all her cases have that factor present (i.e., no variation on the independent variable). In the case of social revolutions, we cannot use the Rule of Exclusion with the state breakdown and peasant revolt variables because these are the central causal factors we want to examine. Hence, for these variables we must use the Rule of Inclusion. The Rule of Exclusion is almost always based on *existing empirical and theoretical knowledge*. Harff uses her knowledge that 36 of 37 cases of politicide/genocide occurred near political upheavals as her justification for applying the Rule of Exclusion. When testing varieties of corn, we apply existing knowledge about the importance of water to exclude testing in the desert. Hence:

Caveat: The Rule of Exclusion cannot be used with variables under test; the Rule of Inclusion must be used.[10]

Although the Possibility Principle is normally applied when a scholar seeks to test a finalized theory, testing theory and formulating theory are often quite interactive in qualitative research. As a result, analysts may choose to apply the principle at different points in the research process. Likewise, a community of scholars may use the Possibility Principle at different points in the research cycle. For example, an initial investigator may formulate and test a theory without exploring negative cases at all. A subsequent researcher may then test the theory using information from negative cases but without applying the Possibility Principle. A final researcher may then apply the Possibility Principle and test this theory by drawing on information from the full range of negative cases relevant to the theory. This practice of subsequent researchers testing theories formulated by an initial investigator with new cases is a central component of knowledge accumulation in comparative research (e.g., Mahoney and Rueschemeyer 2003). The Possibility Principle provides concrete rules to help structure the selection of negative cases in this kind of cumulative research.

[10]It is not uncommon in the quantitative conflict literature to include the variables used to define the population, e.g., contiguity or major power status, in the statistical analyses. This has significant implications for causal inference that are explored in detail in the next chapter.

Uses with Boolean Theories

To further investigate the Possibility Principle, it is helpful to consider some standard Boolean theories which are common in qualitative research. We define these as theories that use logical ANDs and/or ORs to specify hypotheses. For illustrative purposes, Skocpol's *States and Social Revolutions* is a helpful example. The theory is relatively straightforward: state breakdown and peasant revolt are individually necessary and jointly sufficient for social revolution (see chapter 9). Thus, Skocpol argues that

Social Revolution = state breakdown AND peasant revolt.

She claims that if state breakdown occurs at the same time as peasant revolt then social revolution will occur (given her scope conditions; see below).

Here we have a very simple Boolean theory that uses AND with two positively related causal variables. The Rule of Inclusion states that we should choose as negative cases those where either causal variable is present. Hence the set of negative cases consists of

Possible Social Revolution = state breakdown OR peasant revolt.

Notice that we have replaced the AND of the theory of the positive cases with an OR to capture the full relevant population. Here we see a key rule for linking Boolean theories with the Possibility Principle:

Change the AND in Boolean theories of the positive outcome to OR when selecting the population of relevant cases.

This procedure is a version of the Rule of Inclusion that we call the AND-to-OR replacement rule.

Ragin (1987, 2000) and others have pointed out that conjunctural causation is a common trait of theories in qualitative comparative analysis. Conjunction implies the use of AND to connect independent variables. Again, because AND makes reference to the positive outcome, a useful general rule when applying the Possibility Principle to conjunctural causation is to replace all ANDs in the theory with ORs. For example, a typical result from a preliminary Boolean analysis

189

might look like

$$Y = A * B + B * C + C * D. \tag{7.1}$$

This theory could then be tested using other techniques (e.g., process tracing) and perhaps examined in light of alternative cases.[11] At that point, one has enough information to apply the AND-to-OR replacement rule to arrive at

$$\text{Possible } Y = A \text{ OR } B \text{ OR } C \text{ OR } D. \tag{7.2}$$

In this example, the researcher should sample all cases where at least one of the independent variables is present. While the researcher might not be confident about which combinations are sufficient for the positive outcome (i.e., equation 7.1), knowledge about the basic causal factors is enough to select the negative cases.

Boolean results often include both the presence of some factors (indicated by capital letters) in conjunction with the absence of others (signaled by lower-case letters). The question then arises about how the *absence* of a certain variable should be used to select cases with the Possibility Principle. The answer depends on what is meant by the "absence" of the variable. In some cases, the absence of a variable actually refers to the presence of a clear causal condition. For example, a Boolean analyst might code a variable for religion using two values: Protestant (i.e., P) and Catholic (i.e., p). In this case, one can argue that the absence of being Protestant (i.e., being Catholic) is a positive cause of the outcome. However, if the variable values correspond to simply Protestant and non-Protestant, there is no clear causal condition associated with the absence of the variable. In this case, where the absence of a variable is undertheorized and does not correspond to a clear positive category, the Possibility Principle cannot be easily applied.

To this point, we have considered Boolean theories that employ dichotomous independent variables. To consider how the Possibility

---

[11] Boolean algebra is a method of both theory formulation and theory testing. With theory formulation, the technique is used with an initial set of cases to arrive at a set of hypotheses. These hypotheses may then be evaluated with a broader array of cases during a subsequent phase of more explicit theory testing (Ragin 1987). Much the same is true of large-N, statistical research in practice: analysts conduct early tests to explore relationships among variables before arriving at a final theory that is formally tested.

Principle works with continuous independent variables, let us imagine a theory in which four independent variables are jointly sufficient for the positive outcome of interest. Further, let us assume that these variables are coded from zero to one where values close to zero mean that a positive factor is absent.

How would the analyst differentiate negative cases from irrelevant cases in this kind of design? Drawing on Ragin's (2000) work on fuzzy-set analysis, we can formulate a general rule. If one is testing to determine whether a series of variables coded from zero to one are jointly sufficient for an outcome, then one should apply the AND-to-OR replacement rule. In fuzzy-set analysis, OR is implemented by taking the maximum value of the independent variables. For example, if the variable scores for a given case are .17, .33, .33, and .67, then the case receives an overall score of .67, since this is the highest value of the independent variables. In short, there is no problem in applying the AND-to-OR rule with continuous variables: OR is defined as the maximum. Overall, the rule for continuous independent variables can be stated as follows:

> All cases whose maximum of the positively related independent variables is equal to or above the selection threshold should be included in the set of negative cases. Cases whose maximum does not meet the threshold are irrelevant.

The analyst must decide and justify the exact threshold or cutoff point at which the outcome is considered possible. One should set this threshold level using existing theory and evidence. Under some circumstances, the analyst may be better served by setting the threshold at a higher or lower level. For example, if the analyst sets the threshold safely below the estimated true threshold, he or she will define a larger set of negative cases and a smaller set of irrelevant cases. By contrast, if the threshold is set at a high level, the converse is true. Depending on the research design and one's confidence in the initial theory, greater risk may be associated with defining the size of one of these two zones as larger or smaller, and this risk should represent an important consideration when selecting a threshold.

We can again use Skocpol's *States and Social Revolutions* as a concrete example of this rule. To develop and test her theory, Skocpol considers three positive cases of social revolution (France 1787–1800, Russia 1917–1921, and China 1911–1949) and five negative cases

TABLE 7.2
Fuzzy-Set Codes for Skocpol's Variables

Country	State Breakdown	Peasant Revolt	Maximum Value	Positive/ Negative
France 1787–1800	1.00	1.00	1.00	Positive
Russia 1917–1921	1.00	1.00	1.00	Positive
China 1911–1949	1.00	0.75	1.00	Positive
England 1640–1689	1.00	0.00	1.00	Negative
Russia 1905–1907	0.50	1.00	1.00	Negative
Germany 1848–1850	0.25	0.50	0.50	Negative
Prussia 1807–1814	0.75	0.50	0.75	Negative
Japan 1868–1873	0.75	0.00	0.75	Negative

(England 1640–1689, Russia 1905–1907, Germany 1848–1850, Prussia 1807–1814, and Japan 1868–1873). In chapter 9 we summarize and evaluate her argument by coding the two main variables using fuzzy sets (see table 7.2). In the table, the first two columns (after the country column) report the fuzzy-set values for the two independent variables—state breakdown and peasant revolt. Since Skocpol is interested in whether the combination of these two variables is sufficient for social revolution, we adopt the rule listed above and focus on the maximum value of the two variables to determine whether her cases are indeed relevant. This maximum value is reported in the third column; the final column states whether the case is positive (i.e., social revolution is present) or negative (i.e., social revolution is absent).

We believe that Skocpol implicitly used the Possibility Principle in identifying her negative cases. The AND-to-OR replacement rule gives us the following: Possible Social Revolution = state breakdown OR peasant revolt. With respect to Skocpol's work, this proposition means that the negative cases should include all observations where either (or both) a state breakdown or a peasant revolt is present. As the third column ("maximum value") in table 7.2 suggests, at least one of the two major variables is significantly present in all five of the negative cases. If we assume a threshold of at least .50 as a basis for retaining cases, then all five of the negative cases are relevant following the rule introduced above. More generally, this interpretation means that relevant negative cases include all those country periods when a causal factor is as much present as absent.[12]

SCOPE CONDITIONS AND THE POSSIBILITY PRINCIPLE

In this section, we consider scope conditions as an alternative method through which researchers may exclude cases as irrelevant. Whereas the Possibility Principle excludes cases where the outcome is not theoretically possible, scope conditions exclude cases where theory suggests that causal patterns are not homogeneous. Here we spell out the implications of these different modes of case selection. We also consider several examples in which researchers purport to exclude cases through scope conditions, but in fact appear to be implicitly using the Possibility Principle.

What Are Scope Conditions?

Scope conditions refer to the parameters within which a given theory is expected to be valid (Walker and Cohen 1985; Cohen 1989). The need for scope conditions grows out of the fact that social scientists rarely formulate universal propositions that hold across all times and places; rather, they formulate conditional propositions that apply to specific contexts.[13] Cases that do not meet the scope conditions of a given theory are routinely considered irrelevant and are not used to evaluate that theory.

Typically, the methodological justification for imposing scope conditions involves the need to meet the standard of unit homogeneity (e.g., George and Bennett 2005; Bartels 1996; Collier and Mahoney

---

[12]Skocpol's description of her case selection is also consistent with the Possibility Principle: "I shall invoke negative cases for the purpose of validating various particular parts of the causal argument. In doing so, I shall always construct contrasts that maximize the similarities of the negative case(s) to the positive case(s) in every apparently relevant respect except the causal sequence that the contrast is supposed to validate" (1979, 37). This passage suggests that Skocpol selected negative cases that resembled positive cases in terms of certain causal factors but not others, which is consistent with the guidelines above.

[13]Ideally, researchers use scope conditions to identify general parameters that could exist in many times and places, not scope conditions that identity specific times and places themselves (Walker and Cohen 1985, 291; Kiser 1996, 257).

1996; Ragin 2000, 61–62; Zelditch 1971, 272–88).[14] Units are homogeneous when a given change on an independent variable is expected to have the same average net effect on the dependent variable across these units (cf. King, Keohane, and Verba 1994, 91–93). Cases that fall outside of scope conditions do not meet the demands of unit homogeneity and, in many kinds of research, are not considered relevant for testing the theory at hand.

Unit homogeneity is always a theoretical assumption, and thus scope conditions—like the Possibility Principle—are theory laden. Although one may have good reasons for believing that certain scope conditions specify a domain of causal homogeneity, it is difficult to know for certain without actually examining cases outside this domain. If the theory underlying the scope conditions is weak, the researcher may inappropriately exclude certain homogeneous cases or inappropriately include certain cases that introduce unrecognized heterogeneity into the population. In turn, these failures can seriously jeopardize one's findings.[15]

Relationship to the Possibility Principle

The kinds of cases that are excluded using scope conditions and the Possibility Principle are not symmetrical. Scope conditions are designed to exclude any case—positive or negative—that does not meet the standard of causal homogeneity. By contrast, the Possibility Principle is designed to exclude negative cases that fall within scope conditions but that nevertheless provide little useful information for causal inference.

The relationship between scope conditions and the Possibility Principle can be more formally specified with Boolean notation. Let us assume that an analyst has a theory in which three independent variables (A, B, C) are understood to be jointly sufficient for an outcome

[14]This concern is implicit in Walker and Cohen (1985) and Kiser (1996). These analysts mostly justify scope conditions on practical grounds, in particular the failure of theories to apply to all times and places. They do not link the need for scope conditions with possibility ideas.

[15]One might argue that the Possibility Principle offers a less theory-laden basis for excluding cases than scope conditions. The theory underpinning the Possibility Principle is evaluated against the positive and negative cases that are selected. In this sense, there is a check on the validity of the theory underlying the Possibility Principle, even if this check is based on cases that were selected in light of the theory itself. By contrast, a theory of causal homogeneity usually is not tested; rather, it is an untested assumption that analysts accept on theoretical or practical grounds alone.

(one could assume any Boolean model here). To select cases to test this theory, the analyst applies the AND-to-OR replacement rule of the Possibility Principle and adds a separate term Z to represent scope conditions as follows:

$$\text{Relevant Observation} = Z \text{ AND } (A \text{ OR } B \text{ OR } C). \qquad (7.3)$$

The scope conditions (term Z) act as an eliminatory variable in the same way as discussed above for the Rule of Exclusion. That is, the absence of Z is sufficient to declare an observation to be irrelevant. To specify this idea, the logical AND is used to link the eliminatory variable with the core Boolean model. In this sense, the Rule of Exclusion and scope conditions are built around AND, whereas the Rule of Inclusion draws on OR.

In practice, researchers are not explicit about whether they exclude cases using scope conditions or the Possibility Principle. However, because these two techniques approach positive and negative cases differently, we can formulate a simple diagnostic rule:

If *only* negative cases are excluded, then it is likely that the Possibility Principle is being used. If positive and negative cases are excluded, then it is likely that scope conditions are being used.

For example, in her study of social revolutions, we know that Skocpol uses scope conditions because she excludes positive cases of social revolution like Cuba 1959. If she were exclusively using the Possibility Principle, she would have no basis for declaring positive cases where social revolution is obviously possible as irrelevant to her theory.

Scope Conditions or the Possibility Principle? Examples from the Literature

The extent to which cases are excluded as irrelevant through scope conditions versus the Possibility Principle will vary. However, because scope conditions are widely accepted as legitimate in social science research, whereas the Possibility Principle has not been formally discussed, analysts may state that they are excluding cases through scope conditions when they are in fact applying the Possibility Principle.

A good example of this tendency comes from theories of welfare state development. This research has shown that the chances of having a welfare state among poor countries are approximately zero. For example, Hicks (1999) finds that poverty is sufficient for the absence of a welfare state (see also Huber and Stephens 2001, 370–71). This empirical finding is important in its own right. It also has clear implications for scholars who seek to explain welfare state development: the less-developed countries are not useful. Their inclusion in the population hinders our ability to understand why some wealthier countries develop welfare states but others do not. For example, whereas left-leaning governments are related to welfare state development among wealthy countries, there is a much weaker relationship between this variable and welfare state development among all countries. Inclusion of the poor countries distorts results in ways that inhibit substantive understanding of welfare state development.

To avoid these problems, many analysts of welfare states include only OECD countries (see Amenta 2003 for a recent review). Typically, they justify the exclusion of poorer countries through the use of scope conditions. However, they exclude *only* negative cases, and we believe that they are really employing the Possibility Principle, not scope conditions. In particular, they use the Rule of Exclusion to eliminate countries that possess a condition sufficient for the absence of welfare state development—namely, poverty. Indeed, the finding that economic wealth is related to welfare state development among all countries but not among rich countries is what we would expect if all cases are homogeneous (i.e., if scope conditions do not apply).[16]

The failure of analysts to be explicit about their use of the Possibility Principle also introduces confusion into case selection debates surrounding the literature that seeks to explain the spectacular growth rates of certain East Asian countries since the 1960s. In this field, scholars almost always focus on Korea and Taiwan as positive cases, and sometimes Hong Kong and Singapore as well. These successful cases are often contrasted with less successful developers in Latin America, especially Brazil and Mexico. Overall, the negative cases used to test this theory are not representative of all countries in the world, but rather tend to be wealthier nations. One might therefore argue that case selection is systematically biased and that different

[16]Why is this true? Because wealth is correlated with the dependent variable of interest (welfare state development), and a selection strategy that chooses only wealthy countries excludes many negative cases without welfare states. In this context, independent variables other than economic prosperity are likely to appear as especially important despite the existence of causal homogeneity (Collier and Mahoney 1996).

results would appear if a more representative sample of cases was selected. For example, Geddes (2003, 93–105) argues that scholars of the new industrialized countries (NICs) who select only cases with high levels of economic development mischaracterize the effects of labor repression on growth.

Here we use the Possibility Principle to explore the argument that the literature on the NICs inappropriately restricts or excludes poor or very underdeveloped economies. Although the theories that animate this literature are varied, several prominent analysts argue that the ability of countries to move from import-substitution industrialization (ISI) policies to export-oriented industrialization (EOI) policies before heavy industry was established produced the extremely high growth rates (e.g., Gereffi and Wyman 1990; Haggard 1990). In this theory, the formula for success is the combination of early ISI policies (normally before the 1960s) to achieve light industrialization and subsequently the adoption of EOI policies to move toward heavy industrialization. Sequence and timing are important, since EOI policies without the early ISI policies are not believed to produce the economic development of interest.

According to the Possibility Principle, only cases in which exceptional growth is possible should be included when testing this theory. When the Rule of Inclusion is formally applied, the analyst selects those cases that adopt ISI policies during the light phase of industrialization as candidates for exceptional growth. Exceptional growth is considered impossible in countries that lack this condition as of the 1960s. Usually, countries without ISI by this time are characterized by nonindustrial forms of commodity exportation.

The more developed nations of Latin America such as Brazil and Mexico are appropriate negative cases given that they engaged in ISI policies beginning in the 1930s and 1940s. However, most other countries of Latin America are irrelevant cases for the theory, since they were still oriented toward basic commodity exportation well into the 1960s. In fact, Argentina and Chile are the only other examples of countries within Latin America that made clear-cut early moves toward ISI and could therefore be considered definitely relevant. Outside of Latin America, there are very few countries that were characterized by ISI before the 1960s. For example, nearly all of sub-Saharan Africa would be excluded, as would most of South Asia. On the other hand, some countries—perhaps several in the Middle East such as Turkey, Syria, and Iraq—might be argued to have engaged in ISI during this period, and thus could be included as negative cases (Waldner 1999).

In short, the small number of cases evaluated in this literature appears to come close to the full population of cases for which the theory is relevant. Hence, we believe that Geddes (2003) is mistaken to characterize this literature as inappropriately restricting the scope of analysis. Given the actual theory under investigation in much of this literature, exceptional growth is impossible in most countries, and hence the vast majority of potential negative cases can legitimately be excluded.

A GEOMETRIC INTERPRETATION OF THE POSSIBILITY PRINCIPLE

Many of the fundamental case selection issues raised by the Possibility Principle can be illustrated through a geometric interpretation that situates negative cases in relationship to other types of cases. Figure 7.2 offers this geometric interpretation. The cube in the figure is constituted by three parameters: $X_1, X_2,$ and Y. The representation assumes that the theory under investigation takes the form of Skocpol's argument; that is, two independent variables that are individually necessary and jointly sufficient for the dependent variable. Furthermore, it assumes that there are no eliminatory variables that can be applied in conjunction with the Rule of Exclusion. To add substantive content to the representation, the two X-axes are labeled state breakdown and peasant revolt, while the vertical Y-axis is social revolution. All axes are standardized into the [0,1] interval. The variables can thus be interpreted as fuzzy-set membership scores or can be considered regular variables that have undergone scale transformations to range from zero to one.

The cube is divided into eight zones that dichotomize variables and we draw separation lines at the .5 value. This cutoff line is adopted here for illustrative purposes; in real research, the decision about where to separate one zone from another must be driven by substantive and theoretical considerations. Furthermore, whereas the cube draws a sharp and clear separation line between the zones, the actual cutoff points from one zone to another will rarely be so stark. Rather, there will typically be a gray area at the boundary between any two zones.

For our purposes, we are interested in five kinds of cases that occupy these eight zones: (1) positive, (2) negative, (3) irrelevant, (4) impossible-but-happens, and (5) disconfirming. Exemplary cases of

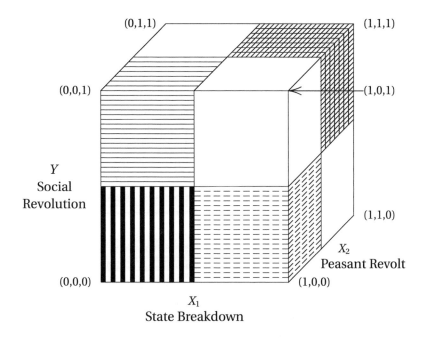

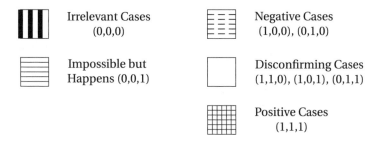

FIGURE 7.2

A geometric interpretation of the Possibility Principle: *States and Social Revolutions*

these types can be found near the corners of the cube. By contrast, as cases approach the center of the cube on one or more dimensions, they enter into the gray zone, and their membership in a given category becomes more ambiguous.

The prototypical *positive cases* are those where the relevant causes (the two X dimensions in the figure) and the outcome of interest (the Y dimension) are present. These observations are located in the

199

right back top zone near the (1,1,1) corner, where all the variables—independent and dependent—have values greater than .50. In the case of Skocpol's theory, the successful revolution cases of France, Russia, and China would be found in this zone.

According to the Possibility Principle, one should select as *negative cases* only those observations where at least one independent variable predicts the outcome. Accordingly, prototypical negative cases are found in the right front bottom and the left back bottom corners (the latter is not visible in figure 7.2), the two zones where one independent variable has a value greater than .5, while the other independent variable and the dependent variable have values less than .5. In Skocpol's theory, the negative cases of Japan and England would occupy the right front bottom corner (where state breakdown is present, but peasant revolts and social revolution are absent), while Russia 1905 and Germany would fall into the left back bottom corner (where peasant revolts are present, but state breakdown and social revolution are absent).

The Possibility Principle states that the *irrelevant cases* are those with low values on all the independent variables; that is, where the $\max(X_i)$ is near zero. If the theory is correct, then values for Y should also be near zero for all these observations. In practice, this means that all irrelevant cases will lie near the origin [i.e., the (0,0,0) point]. Accordingly, we can define the threshold that separates the negative from the irrelevant cases as those that lie within Euclidean distance z from the origin.[17] All other observations beyond this distance should be included in the analysis as relevant. We thus have an important geometric version of the Possibility Principle:

The irrelevant cases are those near the origin in the N-dimensional space of the positively related independent variables.

In the figure, the *impossible-but-happens cases* are those where Y has value greater than .5 (i.e., Y occurs), but both X_1 and X_2 have values less than .5 (i.e., are absent). These cases appear in the left front top zone near the (0,0,1) corner. In the Skocpol example, these would be cases where both state breakdown and peasant revolt are absent, but social revolution nevertheless takes place.

There are two types of *disconfirming cases* for the kind of theory we are considering here. One type includes any observations in which Y

---

[17]The Euclidean distance rule actually generates a sphere around the origin. By contrast, the implementation of the maximum in conjunction with OR produces a cube. However, the spirit of the Euclidean distance and maximum rules is the same.

does not occur (i.e., is closer to zero than to one) when it should (i.e., when X_1 and X_2 are both closer to one), i.e., sufficiency hypotheses. These cases are found in the right back bottom zone near the (1,1,0) corner. These disconfirming observations would initially be selected as negative cases because they have a positive value on at least one independent variable. They would then be classified as disconfirming once it became apparent that their values across independent variables predict the outcome, even though it does not occur. In Skocpol's theory, for example, disconfirming observations would be cases where both state breakdown and peasant revolt are present but social revolution is absent. In effect, cases in this region disconfirm the hypothesis of joint sufficiency.

The other kind of disconfirming case contradicts the hypothesis that each independent variable is individually necessary for the outcome. These cases have a positive value on the outcome (i.e., greater than .5), but only one of the two independent variables is present. We find these observations in the right front top zone near the (1,0,1) corner and the left back top zone near the (0,1,1) corner.

The cube provides thus a nice visual summary of disconfirming observations for necessary or sufficient condition hypotheses. Necessary condition hypotheses are disconfirmed by selecting on the dependent variable, which in the cube are observations in the top half $(Y > .5)$. Sufficient condition hypotheses are disconfirmed when the outcome does not happen, i.e., bottom half of the cube $(Y < .5)$.

The geometric interpretation is instructive for thinking about the distribution of cases in qualitative research. In terms of figure 7.2, very few cases will be situated in the top of the cube, because analysts tend to study outcomes that are rare. Within the bottom half of the cube, where most cases are located, the irrelevant space may be the single most populated area. This is true insofar as the causes of interest in qualitative research are usually not present in most cases. Likewise, assuming that one is working with a good theory, very few or no cases will fall into the disconfirming zone, leaving the other cases in the bottom half within the negative observation zone.

This geometric interpretation of the Possibility Principle offers a solution to an important problem that arises in fuzzy-set analysis. The problem involves what to do with cases that are near the origin (i.e., cases near the (0,0,0) corner). As Ragin notes (2000, 250–51), when testing whether variables are causally sufficient for an outcome, observations with a zero for all the independent variables will always satisfy causal sufficiency and thus artificially inflate the number of cases where the theory works (this dilemma is the Raven Paradox).[18] The Possibility Principle solves this problem by eliminating all of these cases with the exception of any impossible-but-happens cases. Ragin advises that one should not include cases with zero values across all independent variables when testing theories of causal sufficiency: the Possibility Principle provides a coherent theoretical rationale for excluding these problematic cases.

Figure 7.2 also allows us to think systematically about the trade-offs that arise in qualitative research. We can do this most easily by considering the implications of expanding or shrinking the cutoff points between zones. Currently the figure separates all zones at the .5 level, but this decision was made for illustrative purposes, and researchers could have good theoretical reasons for expanding one zone at the expense of another. If the threshold for the presence of the outcome was lowered from .50 to .25 (e.g., from social revolution to political revolution), the size of the positive case area would increase, while the size of the negative case zone would decrease. With a theory like Skocpol's, this move would help the analyst avoid disconfirming observations (because this zone would be reduced in size), but it would also increase the likelihood of encountering an impossible-but-happens case (because this zone is enlarged). Inevitably, to increase the size of one zone is to reduce one risk but increase another kind of risk.

These trade-offs underscore the importance of making substantively and theoretically informed choices about where to draw the line when including or excluding cases vis-à-vis a given zone. The issue is not only where to draw the line for the dependent variable. Rather, different thresholds on independent variables can shrink or expand the size of any given zone, with major implications for theory testing. Qualitative researchers are often especially interested in cases with notably high or low scores on independent variables, because these cases tend to be located in the corners of the cube, where an observation is squarely situated in a particular zone. Hence, the geometric interpretation of the Possibility Principle suggests good methodological reasons why qualitative researchers might focus on cases with extreme values on explanatory variables as well as on the dependent variable.

[18]Smithson (1987) discusses other more technical problems of fuzzy-set analyses when membership scores are zero or near zero.

TESTING THEORY WITH THE POSSIBILITY PRINCIPLE

To illustrate concretely the value added of explicitly applying the Possibility Principle, we consider in this section how the principle could be used to retest Skocpol's *States and Social Revolutions*. We begin by noting that previous tests of this argument have lacked a clear rationale for choosing negative cases. We then apply the Possibility Principle within Skocpol's scope conditions to identify what may be the full set of observations relevant to testing the theory. Finally, we assess Skocpol's argument in light of these negative cases.

Previous Tests of Skocpol's Theory

Critics have raised various objections to Skocpol's argument over the years, but we believe that no analyst has ever retested her theory using evidence from new cases that are relevant for the theory. Rather, when scholars have attempted to retest Skocpol's argument, they have drawn on cases that are irrelevant or out of her scope.

Many scholars have explored Skocpol's argument in light of Third World countries. In some cases, these scholars use evidence from the new cases to directly test Skocpol's theory. For example, Geddes (2003, 106–14) draws on evidence from nine Latin America countries to show that Skocpol's specific arguments about international warfare and state breakdown are not supported.[19] Other scholars use Skocpol's work to build their own theories of social revolution, which may then be tested in conjunction with implicit applications of the Possibility Principle. For example, Foran's (1997) Boolean analysis of social revolution selects as negative cases only country-periods that have a positive value on at least one of his five major independent variables. Goodwin (2001) likewise selects as negative cases only country-periods where at least one key independent variable of his theory is present. More generally, scholars of social revolution in the Third World rarely if ever focus on negative cases where social revolution is clearly impossible, such as modern Costa Rica.

---

[19]Geddes uses correlational analysis to test Skocpol's argument about international pressure and revolution. She also briefly considers necessary condition causation. However, chapter 9 shows that Skocpol's claim involves equifinality in the context of a two-level model, for which Geddes tests are not appropriate.

Many analysts recognize that Skocpol's theory cannot be directly tested in light of Third World countries because these cases clearly violate her scope conditions. Indeed, Skocpol's scope is limited to politically ambitious agrarian states that have not experienced colonial domination (1979, 33–42, 287–90). She explicitly excludes cases in which the possibilities for revolution have been shaped by the legacies of colonialism, dependence in the international economy, and the rise of modern militaries differentiated from dominant classes. Hence, nearly all modern Third World countries are excluded by Skocpol's scope statement.

Selecting the Negative Cases

The first step in retesting Skocpol's argument involves identifying cases that fall within her scope. In addition to the cases analyzed in *States and Social Revolutions*, we believe that the following nine states meet Skocpol's scope conditions: the Austrian Empire (1804–1866) and Austria-Hungary (1867–1918), the Dutch Republic (1579–1795), Mughal India (1556–1857), Spain (1492–1823), Portugal (1641–1822), Sweden (1523–1814), the Polish-Lithuanian Commonwealth (1569–1795), and the Ottoman Empire (1520–1922). Although we cannot claim that these nine cases represent all states relevant to Skocpol's theory, we can say with some confidence that these cases cannot be excluded as irrelevant on the grounds of falling outside of Skocpol's scope conditions.

Here we pose the following question: what specific periods in the histories of these nine new cases are relevant for testing her theory? To answer, we apply the Possibility Principle by considering a case as relevant if it has a positive value on at least one of Skocpol's two main causes (i.e., state breakdown and peasant revolt). Although we examine nine states, our actual unit of analysis is the state-period, in that we are looking for specific periods of time in the histories of these states that are relevant for testing Skocpol's theory. In terms of the outcome of social revolution, all of these cases are negative—i.e., none experienced an event transformative enough to meet Skocpol's definition of social revolution. Hence, our efforts focus on differentiating the negative state-periods from the irrelevant state-periods.

For the state breakdown variable, we consider periods relevant when international wars, state-elite conflict, or agrarian backwardness fostered large-scale political instability and the collapse of reigning governmental and bureaucratic structures. For the peasant revolt variable, we include cases where peasant rebellions against landlords and state agents encompassed broad regions of the state.[20]

As table 7.2 suggests, we conclude that the following state-periods are relevant negative cases for testing Skocpol's theory: mid-nineteenth century Austria, early twentieth century Austria-Hungary, late seventeenth and early eighteenth century India, early nineteenth century Ottoman Empire, eighteenth century Poland-Lithuania, early nineteenth century Portugal, mid- to late-seventeenth and early nineteenth century Spain, and early eighteenth century Sweden. Although none of the nine original states are eliminated as completely irrelevant, the Possibility Principle greatly reduces the range of cases that are considered relevant—most periods of the histories of these states are simply irrelevant to Skocpol's theory. When a period is relevant, it corresponds to a situation of political instability, given that it was selected precisely because of the presence of state crisis or peasant revolt. Said differently, all periods of political stability are irrelevant.

Because only situations of political instability are selected, one might argue that the Possibility Principle leads to truncation on the dependent variable by restricting its range of variation. However, the alternative would be to much more severely jeopardize valid inferences by including a nearly infinite number of negative case observations. For example, every year of nonrevolution in Spain from the late fifteenth century to the early nineteenth century would become negative case. This huge number of negative cases would make it inevitable that Skocpol finds a strong association between her causal factors and revolution. By contrast, the Possibility Principle focuses attention only on cases where social revolution was possible, avoiding all negative cases that are bound to confirm Skocpol's theory.

---

[20] Because we are not experts on most of these cases, it is possible that we have overlooked specific time periods when a causal variable was present, especially given the sparse data on peasant revolts. Thus, we emphasize that this exercise does not constitute the final word concerning the set of cases relevant to testing Skocpol's theory. Furthermore, it is likely that additional relevant negative cases could be generated by evaluating new time periods for the original cases analyzed in *States and Social Revolutions*. For example, given that peasant revolts were common in late eighteenth century Russia, a broader array of country-years than 1905 and 1917 are almost certainly relevant.

TABLE 7.3

Negative Cases for Skocpol's Theory

Country	State Breakdown	Peasant Revolt
Austrian Empire	1848–52: Constitutional reform of state takes place amid fears of Europe-wide war. By 1852, however, constitutional reform is rolled back and neoabsolutist rule reinstated.	Not present: In 1848, in response to peasant mobilizations, the government abolishes feudal duties, thereby pacifying peasant revolts.
Austria-Hungary	Early 20th century: Intense military pressures during World War I. Loss in war leads to allied occupation and dissolution of the empire.	Not present: Dissolution of feudal system in 1848 quells potential for peasant revolt.
Dutch Republic	Late 18th century: Nearly constant warfare with Spain and other powers occurs throughout 16th and 17th centuries, but not until 18th-century conflict with France is the Dutch Republic fully defeated. The Batavian Republic is established under French control in 1795, followed by the Kingdom of the Netherlands in 1806.	Not present: Dutch peasantry is free from feudal bonds and faces only weak seigneurial control over land. Peasants are highly individualized. Some peasant participation in revolts of 1672.
India	Early 18th century: The empire gradually dissolves in the face of inefficient tax system and influence from the British East India Company. Regional powers assert their autonomy and undercut the influence of the Mughal empire throughout the region.	1669–72: Peasant revolts are generally local and infrequent, in part owing to social control embodied in caste system. There are fairly major peasant revolts in Matathura and the Punjab in 1669–72 that are brutally defeated.
Ottoman Empire	Early 19th century: Despite instability in early 17th century, political coherence is maintained until wars with Russia and Egypt (Muhammad Ali) nearly destroy the empire and lead to efforts at massive state reform in the early 19th century.	Not present: Ottomans are effective at subduing class organization. In addition, peasants lack solidarity to lead sustained and coordinated revolts. However, occupied territories do rebel against state centralization.

Poland-Lithuania	Mid-18th Century: Nearly constant wars with Sweden, Russia, Austria, Brandenburg, and the Ottoman empire throughout 17th and early 18th centuries form background to civil war and eventually the partition of the commonwealth into occupied territories.	18th Century: Feudal economy yields frequent peasant revolts in early sixteenth century. Revolts reemerge again in pockets in 1711, the 1750s, and 1769.
Portugal	Early 19th century: Despite a history of nearly continuous warfare, the Portuguese monarchy persists until consecutive French invasions lead to the spread of liberalism, culminating in the Constitution of 1822, which installed a constitutional government.	Not present: Peasants confined to feudal-like conditions, but major revolts reported only in 1637 and 1846.
Spain	Early 19th century: Like Portugal, Spain was involved in countless wars throughout its history, but not until the Napoleonic invasions and the promulgation of a liberal constitution in 1812 did the monarchy fall (only to be restored in 1814, removed again from 1820–23, and then restored yet again by the French).	Mid-late 17th century: Peasants face feudal conditions. Major peasant revolts occur in 1640 and especially 1688–89.
Sweden	Early 18th century: Involved in nearly constant wars in seventeenth century, including the Thirty Years War (1618–48), the Northern War (1655–60), and the Great Northern War (1700–21). Military defeats and economic crises lead to a weakening of the monarchy and the establishment of a constitutional government in 1718.	Not present: Absence of feudalism and repressive labor combined with substantial political rights for peasantry undercuts potential for large-scale rural rebellions.

Testing the Theory

Skocpol's full theory of social revolution has a complex two-level structure, and a complete test of the theory would consider causal claims at both levels (see chapter 9). Here we evaluate only her core argument that state breakdown and peasant revolt are individually necessary and jointly sufficient for a social revolution.

The evidence from the additional relevant cases in table 7.2 is consistent with Skocpol's theory, with the exception of the Polish-Lithuanian Commonwealth in the mid-eighteenth century. Outside of this case, no territory simultaneously features state breakdown and peasant revolt. All of the territories had at least one major state breakdown, but many of them never witnessed large-scale peasant revolts. Hence, we find substantial support for Skocpol's theory from a consideration of several cases not originally analyzed by Skocpol.

The seemingly disconfirming case of mid-eighteenth century Poland-Lithuania corresponds with the partition and eventually obliteration of this commonwealth by Russia, Prussia, and Austria. After the first partition was initiated by Russia in 1772, radical reformers in Poland moved to adopt a progressive constitution, and events unfolded in a manner that suggested a social revolution could be on the horizon. However, the threat of revolution caused the Polish nobility to call in occupation forces, and Russia, Prussia, and Austria dissolved the commonwealth by 1795. Thus, instead of social revolution, Poland-Lithuania experienced a loss of sovereignty. The extent to which this outcome should be seen as a disconfirmation of Skocpol's theory could be debated, though we believe it is difficult to hold Skocpol too accountable for the absence of social revolution in a political entity that ceased to exist.

Negative Case Selection and Causal Inference

One might legitimately raise the "so what" question: even though Skocpol did not include the whole population of negative cases, the addition of these cases really does not change how we view her theory since there are no unambiguously disconfirming observations. Yet, it is only because of this kind of analysis that we can say that a survey of all the negative cases produces no clearly disconfirming cases. Certainly others, such as Geddes (1990, 2003), have proposed that the inclusion of a broader range of cases casts doubt on Skocpol's theory. By contrast, our survey finds no evidence that Skocpol selected only negative cases where her theory works; in fact, the inclusion of additional relevant cases may strengthen her argument.

However, our survey suggests at least one important respect in which Skocpol's theory should be viewed in a new light. Of Skocpol's two main causal factors, it is fair to say that most readers have focused attention on the state breakdown variable. For example, students of Skocpol who have developed their own major theories of social revolution have zeroed in on this variable (Goldstone 1990; Goodwin 2001). Yet our results quite clearly suggest that, empirically speaking, the peasant revolt variable is the causally more important one.

Of the negative cases, the state breakdown variable is significantly more common than the peasant revolt variable. In fact, state breakdown appears in all of the negative cases that we analyze here as well as all of Skocpol's original negative cases, except Germany in 1848. By contrast, peasant revolt is absent from most of our new negative cases as well as from Japan and England in Skocpol's original analysis. Precisely because it is more difficult for peasants to stage large scale revolts than for states to experience major crises, it is appropriate to view peasant revolts as the more important cause. While this might seem counterintuitive, it does make intuitive sense. For example, if a gas leak results in an explosion in the house of a smoker, one is inclined to think that the thousands of cigarettes that have been smoked are less important than the rare gas leak (see Honoré and Hart 1958 for an extensive analysis of this point). Alternatively, one can make the same point by thinking in terms of correlations. The correlation between state crisis and social revolution is much lower than that for peasant revolt and social revolution. If we include Skocpol's original cases with our new cases, there are thirteen times when state breakdown occurs without social revolution but only six peasant revolts that do not lead to social revolutions.

CONCLUSION

Qualitative researchers who study events such as revolutions, welfare state development, genocide, and sustained economic growth generally do not analyze negative cases where the outcome of interest is impossible. Rather, they tend to focus on negative cases where the outcome has a real possibility of occurring. In this chapter, we have made explicit and formalized this common research practice. In doing so, we have created a new set of rules to guide case selection.

We have shown how the Possibility Principle addresses fundamental but rarely discussed issues entailed in defining a relevant population of cases. The definition of the relevant population can affect findings about the significance, strength, and even direction of hypothesized causal relationships. The relevant population therefore should be carefully defined before one turns to specific techniques of case sampling. Regardless of the sampling procedure, when irrelevant cases are included in one's understanding of the population, one will overrepresent observations with a zero value on the dependent variable. Thus, our discussion has called attention to ways of defining the population that generate *too many* negative cases, whereas most of the literature on case selection has focused on procedures that generate error through an insufficient number of negative cases.

More generally, the Possibility Principle offers a powerful tool for thinking about case selection. An analysis of this principle sharpens, for example, our understanding of how scholars use scope statements, and it provides a basis for understanding the specific logic that scholars follow when they exclude only negative cases from tests of their theories. Likewise, by representing the topology of the Possibility Principle, one can see the overall geography of case selection, including the distinction between positive, negative, irrelevant, impossible-but-happens, and disconfirming cases.

We need the Possibility Principle because scholars often have problems with the negative pole of concepts. Nonevents such as nonwar and nonrevolution are hard to identify. As we saw in chapter 2, the positive pole is the focus of attention, the negative pole is often only the absence of some or all of the secondary-level characteristics. The Possibility Principle permits one to identify a plausible set of negative pole cases to go with the positive ones. Without the negative cases we cannot make valid causal inferences and test theories.

Just as Lewis Carroll's King had trouble seeing Nobody on the road, scholars have struggled to identify nonwar, nonrevolution, and the like. The Possibility Principle together with a theory of the positive outcome allow analysts to identify the full range of negative cases relevant to testing their causal theories.

Concepts and Choosing Populations

WITH J. JOSEPH HEWITT

IN THIS CHAPTER we explore how to apply the Possibility Principle to select *populations* and not just negative cases. In the previous chapter we had a given set of positive cases and used the Possibility Principle to select just the negative ones. The Possibility Principle in the large-N conflict literature selects all cases positive and negative. So it is really a question of population selection, not just negative case selection. The main purpose of the Possibility Principle is still to eliminate the irrelevant observations, but in addition it is involved in the selection of the positive ones as well.

Because the Possibility Principle selects the population it thus influences the inclusion of the positive cases. Hence we have the potential for the impossible happening. Recall in figure 7.1 that there is a boundary between the positive cases and the irrelevant ones. Since the Possibility Principle is now selecting positive observations it runs the risk in practice of not drawing that boundary line very well. Hence, one ends up excluding positive observations from the population.

There is thus a fundamental difference between the way the Possibility Principle is used in the previous chapter and this one. In the case of Skocpol we have the positive cases as defined by the concept of social revolution plus the negative cases determined by the Possibility Principle. In this chapter, we *first* use the Possibility Principle to determine the population and *then* use the positive observations that are a subset of that population. In the first procedure (e.g., Skocpol) the impossible cannot happen because the population is the union of the positive and negative cases, hence all positive cases are included. In the second, the impossible can happen because the positive cases are a subset of the population determined by the Possibility Principle. That is the reason why this chapter title refers to "choosing populations": the Possibility Principle is used to select the population of both positive and negative cases.

A central dilemma in quantitative conflict research involves the elmination of irrelevant cases. Here we reframe the use of the Possibility Principle in terms of elminating the irrelevant observations as opposed to selecting the negative ones. The population consists of all relevant—positive and negative—observations as defined by the Possibility Principle.

In the international conflict literature many (e.g., Russett and Oneal 2000) have claimed that one should not include all dyads, but only "politically relevant" ones. In contrast, the "all-dyad" design says there are no irrelevant cases within the spatio-temporal scope of the study. The Possibility Principle underlies many of the arguments that researchers have used when choosing politically relevant dyads as their population. Very frequently the author uses "possibility language" to justify the exclusion of dyads such as Burma-Belgium. Usually the argument claims that these dyads should be excluded because a dispute or war "was not possible." We propose that the Possibility Principle systematizes an informal principle used by many conflict scholars. Once the principle is made explicit, we can begin to investigate the theoretical and empirical issues surrounding the use of politically relevant dyads.

The use of politically relevant dyads relies, more or less explicitly, on Most and Starr's (1989) opportunity and willingness framework. As the Possibility Principle stresses, one needs a theory of the positive occurrence of the dependent variable in order to choose the population. In practice, and usually in theory, only the opportunity part of the framework is applied to generate politically relevant dyads. There is important work, notably Maoz (1996) and Lemke (1995), that elaborates on the opportunity idea in relationship to politically relevant dyads. We argue that this work is useful but must be complimented by equivalent analyses and measures using willingness. The Possibility Principle makes it clear that if we are to apply the opportunity and willingness framework we need to think about willingness as well as opportunity.

The last two chapters have shown how concept choice has important implications for causal inference. In chapter 6 we saw that concept structure had important impacts on extension which then produced correlations with common dependent variables. In the previous chapter, we saw that a complete set of negative cases flipped the relative importance traditionally attributed to Skocpol's two independent variables. Here we shall see that population selection influences causal inferences scholars make because a variable used to select the population is then also included in the basic-level statistical analyses. For example, politically relevant dyads are defined in part by the major power status of a country. This same major power variable is then frequently included in the statistical analysis. Hence the same factor has an impact via population selection and via its inclusion in the statistical model. Thus using a variable in constituting the population and at the same time in statistical analyses means that we must keep both these uses in mind when evaluating its causal impact. Thus to use the Possibility Principle means one must be very aware of how variables used to select the population interact with the basic-level causal model.

THE POSSIBILITY PRINCIPLE AND THE OPPORTUNITY AND WILLINGNESS FRAMEWORK

The Possibility Principle of population selection has the basic form:

> Choose as cases those where the outcome of interest was possible.

As we saw in the last chapter the operational rule is as follows:

> Cases are included if at least one or a small number of independent variables predict the occurrence of the outcome of interest.

In the context of this chapter, the key thing to remember is that we might miss some of the observations that actually occurred, since we might overlook some independent variables that cause occurrence. This is when the impossible happens.

We think that something like the Possibility Principle underlies the arguments for the use of politically relevant dyads. In particular, possibility language is used almost without exception. It is worth quoting Lemke and Reed at length to get a feel for this:

> In addition to the time-saving device [politically] relevant dyads represent, many proponents of their use argue there are fundamental reasons for restricting analysis to relevant dyads. Weede (1976, 396) claims we should restrict analysis to relevant dyads because "only in this relatively small subset of dyads is there a possibility for irreconcilable conflicts of interest to arise and create a substantial risk of war." Cohen (1994, 214)

echoes this sentiment: "The absence of war in relations between Israel and Canada is irrelevant. For the absence of war between states to be of any significance three prerequisites are needed: motive, means and opportunity.... States that have no access to and very little business with each other are not candidates for conflict." Similarly, Maoz and Russett (1993, 627) suggest analysis of all dyads is inappropriate because "the vast majority are nearly irrelevant. The countries comprising them were too far apart and too weak militarily, with few serious interests potentially in conflict, for them plausibly to engage in any militarized diplomatic dispute." Subsequently, Oneal and Russett (1997, 273) justify their analysis of relevant dyads because doing so "excludes dyads that, in the great majority of cases, had no reasonable opportunity to engage in armed conflict." The strongest statement along these lines is Lemke's (1995, 29) claim that relevant dyads matter because they comprise the correct referent group, and thus function as a true control group, against which war dyads are compared. The reason the set of relevant dyads is the correct referent group for war dyads is that it is only the relevant dyads that might have had a war.[1] (Lemke and Reed 2001, 128)

Figure 8.1 shows the by now familiar three-level structure of the political relevance concept. Notice that we have two secondary-level variables, opportunity and willingness. Formally similar to Skocpol, we have two necessary conditions which define the broad outlines of possibility for international military conflict. In the model opportunity and willingness are connected by a logical AND: "[states] will adopt a given policy alternative if, and only if, they have both the 'willingness' and the 'opportunity' to do so" (Most and Starr 1984, 393). Because we are interested in the population of cases where militarized conflict is only possible we replace the AND with an OR: all we need is opportunity or willingness. Here we have one more concrete use of the AND-to-OR replacement rule, and its application in a large-N quantitative setting.

The opportunity and willingness variables are too general to be included per se in statistical analyses of conflict. As a result, researchers have used a variety of indicators designed to tap into the various

[1] Huth and Allee provide another example: "We believe that there are several advantages to analyzing a data set of territorial disputes. First, by requiring that a territorial disagreement exists to begin with, we minimize problems of irrelevant "no-conflict" observations. Our data set consists of cases in which the use of diplomatic or military activity to advance one's claim is always a possibility" (2002, 756).

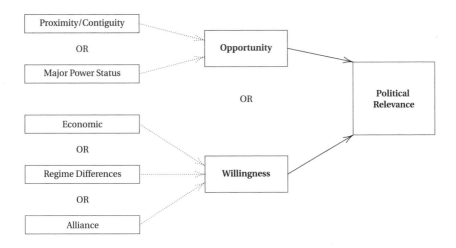

FIGURE 8.1
Politically relevant dyads: Opportunity, willingness, and substitutability.

dimensions of these overarching concepts. In terms of the three-level framework, we need to move down to the indicator level to operationalize the model. Almost all the work using the opportunity and willingness framework to choose cases has focused on the opportunity part. Here the standard indicator variables are (1) geographic contiguity and (2) major power status. While there has been work that elaborates in more detail on opportunity (e.g., Lemke 1995; Maoz 1996) these two indicators remain dominant.

The Possibility Principle states that one should choose cases based on variables which are *positively* associated with the dependent variable. If one examines key articles such as Bremer (1992), two variables always highly correlated with conflict are exactly contiguity and major power status. Clearly these two variables stand out in terms of their association with war and militarized dispute. Both contiguity and major power status tap the ability and capability of states to interact militarily. Thus there is a theoretical coherence between the specific indicators chosen and the larger opportunity and willingness framework used to justify and defend politically relevant dyads as an appropriate population of cases.

However, a rigorous and systematic application of the Possibility Principle means we need to include the secondary-level dimension of willingness. Most and Starr put these two factors on equal terms, and

Cioffi-Revilla and Starr (2003; see also Cioffi-Revilla 1998) weight both opportunity and willingness variables equally in their formal model. Hence, application of both the Possibility Principle and the opportunity and willingness frameworks implies that we should choose cases that score high on opportunity OR willingness.

Using willingness compliments the opportunity approach to politically relevant dyads. In the last Gulf War (2003), we have dyads like Poland-Iraq which do not fall under the opportunity definition of political relevance. Poland does not have the opportunity, but it does have the willingness to fight. Clearly, having a major power ally can solve the opportunity problem. Based solely on opportunity, many of the "impossible but happens" disputes involve this sort of situation, multilateral disputes where a major power aids officially or unofficially the minor power. For example, Morocco was involved in militarized disputes with Zaire in the late 1970s. This was because U.S. aircraft transported Moroccan troops to fight in Zaire. Likewise, the Soviets helped the Cubans get involved in Angola.

Hence a complete application of the Possibility Principle and the opportunity and willingness framework means we should include cases that have either opportunity OR willingness. The use of opportunity only to choose populations is thus radically incomplete. In fact, researchers have chosen populations that are in fact *too small*. Scholars have used opportunity to conceptualize politically relevant dyads to avoid including too many irrelevant cases. However, they have failed to include those states who are willing. Thus populations based just on opportunity are too small.

It is important to note that the concepts of opportunity and willingness differ in terms of their inherent inclusiveness. Opportunity is a relatively restrictive concept. In its widely accepted operationalization (see figure 8.1), only 14 percent of the total population of dyad-years share a border or include at least one major power. Willingness, on the other hand, has the potential for being more encompassing because it makes no requirements about geographic proximity or inclusion of a major power. A dyad qualifies under willingness when the pair of states possess an attribute that indicates the presence of an interest or issue that could give rise to a militarized conflict. We expect far more dyads to qualify under willingness than opportunity.

In terms of figure 8.1, scholars have ignored half of the OR. The next subsection deals with rectifying this state of affairs. We need to develop good indicators of willingness to go with those already existing for opportunity. We need to balance the concerns of eliminating the irrelevant dyads with the need to include dyads where the willingness for conflict exists.

Indicators of Willingness and the Possibility Principle

Before examining a number of different approaches for defining politically relevant dyads based on willingness, we offer some criteria for evaluating the different indicators. One basic criterion for evaluating indicators for choosing politically relevant dyads is how many dyads they include. The basic intuition behind the politically relevant approach is that many dyads are irrelevant. For example, an all-dyad design generates about 650,000 dyads (1816–2000) while approximately 90,000 qualify for relevance based solely on opportunity, an indication of the vast number of dyads that are seemingly irrelevant due to the absence of opportunity for conflict. Thus,

> Indicators of political relevance—opportunity or willingness—must not be too inclusive.

The basic idea is that very inclusive measures will include many politically irrelevant dyads. Moreover, given the research costs for assembling data for large populations of dyads, the pragmatic value of limiting the cases for selection would be undermined by an approach that was overly inclusive.

Another basic criterion for evaluating options for choosing politically relevant dyads uses the following basic rule:

> For any given indicator of political relevance, the more it reduces the number of cases where the impossible happens the better.

Or, as Kenneth Boulding might have put it, if a dispute happened, then it was possible. The indicator should do well at selecting those dyads that actually had a militarized dispute. The argument for the political relevance approach hinges on the notion that the likelihood of conflict between politically irrelevant dyads is vanishingly small because opportunity and willingness for conflict are absent. As such, the face validity for any indicator purporting to measure political relevance depends on how well it captures most of the dispute dyads.

Obviously, the all-dyad design is perfectly effective at avoiding the when the impossible happens problem, but it also captures many irrelevant dyads. Thus, we must be sensitive to both criteria. The best methods are those that are effective at accounting for positive cases while not being overly inclusive.

We begin our evaluation of alternative procedures for choosing the population of politically relevant dyads based on willingness with the τ_b measure. Since we use the measure in a somewhat different manner than usual, some brief comments are in order first about some adjustments we must make before proceeding.

Bueno de Mesquita's (1981) τ_b measure is computed by comparing the type of alliance commitment that each of the dyad partners has with each of the states in the dyad's relevant geographic region. When the two states in the dyad come from the same geographic region, determination of the relevant region is straightforward. When the two states come from different regions, clear rules are needed for determining which of the two states' regions will form the basis for the calculation. For directed dyads, Bueno de Mesquita (1981, 94–98) gave clear rules that identified the relevant region based on the identity of the potential initiator and target in the directed dyad. Since we use nondirected dyads in this study, we offer a slight modification to those rules. The modification is necessary for any case in which, for two states i and j, the relevant region for directed dyad i-j is different than for directed dyad j-i. In those cases, we identify the region of the state with a lower capabilities score as the relevant region based on the logic that the stronger state is more likely to have the ability to project its force to the region of the weaker state (not vice versa), thereby making the alliance commitments with states in the latter's region more relevant for the τ_b calculation.

We use the EUGene software (Bennett and Stam 2000) to generate raw, uncorrected τ_b scores for all dyad-years. Using the τ_b measure, our objective is to divide dyad-years into two classifications—those dyads with essentially similar alliance commitments and those that have essentially dissimilar sets of commitments. We posit that the willingness to pursue militarized disputes is present in the latter, but not in the former. Dichotomizing the scale at the zero point in the raw τ_b data, however, does not properly capture what we intend. The true zero point corresponds to a hypothetical dyad in which both states have elected not to make any alliance commitments whatsoever with any other states in the relevant region.[2] In such a dyad, it is impossible

---

[2]This implies that virtually all uses of τ_b—and S—are flawed. Essentially, scholars have treated them as having an *interval* scale when they really have a *ratio* scale. Both τ_b and S (Signorino and Ritter 1999) have true zeros, and hence are ratio variables. However,

to say whether the states' preferences about security commitments are essentially similar or dissimilar because, in fact, there are zero commitments upon which to make a comparison. Thus, the τ_b value for this hypothetical dyad represents the true zero point on the scale, but due to the mathematical properties of the τ_b measure the computed value for such a dyad will usually not equal zero.[3]

The value of τ_b for the hypothetical dyad described above is the *true zero* of the τ_b measure. The true zero depends on the number of states in the relevant region. For small regional systems, the true zero, i.e., the value of τ_b for the hypothetical pair of unaligned states, will be substantially different from that for the same dyad in a larger system. In particular, the true zero τ_b is a negative number and increases asymptotically toward zero as system size increases. Thus, the true zero τ_b differs across regional systems of different sizes. We compute the true zero for each regional system size and then standardize the raw τ_b scores generated by EUGene so that zero on the transformed scale will correspond to the true zero τ_b.[4]

With the corrected and standardized τ_b, we can proceed to identify dyads with essentially similar or dissimilar preferences about security commitments. Negative values will indicate dyads with willingness to pursue militarized disputes. Table 8.1 presents the results of identifying politically relevant dyads based on the correct τ_b. For comparative purposes, the first line of the table indicates how the definition of political relevance based on opportunity performs. A total of 90,065 dyads

---

this zero value depends on the system size. Unless corrected, as described below, these variables are *not* comparable across years when the system sizes differ. Since very few if any large-N studies have constant system sizes, the use of τ_b and S as generated by EUGene is incorrect.

[3]We are grateful to Bruce Bueno de Mesquita for bringing this property of the τ_b measure to our attention and for his guidance in our formulation of a procedure to identify the proper threshold for τ_b. We note that a similar set of challenges exist for Signorino and Ritter's (1999) alternative measure for alliance similarity, S, because the zero point for that measure also depends on system size. A procedure for standardizing S has not yet been established.

[4]The specific form of the transformation is as follows: for values of $\tau_b \leq$ true zero (denoted b), the standardized τ_b equals $(\tau_b + |b - 0| / 1 - |b - 0|)$. For values of τ_b greater than the true zero, the standardized τ_b equals $(\tau_b + |b - 0| / 1 + |b - 0|)$. It can be seen that the transformation preserves -1 and $+1$ as the scale's minimum and maximum. The true zero converts to zero in the transformation and the units are the same size on the left and right size of zero. Consider an example in which the true zero τ_b for a hypothetical system is -0.35. If the raw τ_b value for a particular dyad is -0.5, this transforms to $(-0.5 + 0.35)/(0.65) = -0.23$.

TABLE 8.1

Comparing Willingness to Opportunity for Defining
Political Relevance: τ_b

Definition of Political Relevance	Total Dyads (%)*	Total Disputes (%)
Opportunity	90,065 (14%)	2,645 (88%)
Willingness		
τ_b, optimal level (< -0.037)	277,874 (42%)	1,257 (42%)
$\tau_b < 0$	435,837 (66%)	1,684 (56%)

*Based on a total base population of 655,545 dyad-years

qualify for political relevance based on the opportunity variant of the definition. Of the total qualifying dyads, 2,645 experienced militarized disputes. These opportunity relevant disputes comprise 88 percent of the total population of disputes in our population (N=3,003). Although the opportunity approach is effective at capturing disputes, it remains an incomplete application of Most and Starr's (1989) framework.

As table 8.1 indicates, τ_b does a relatively poorer job of picking out politically relevant dyads. The $\tau_b<0$ line in the table presents the results when political relevance based on willingness is set such that dyads with strictly negative values of τ_b are considered relevant. A total of 435,837 dyads (66 percent of all dyads) qualify for relevance under this approach; 1,684 of them experience disputes (56 percent of all disputes). By our evaluation criteria, the τ_b method performs poorly because it is not effective at selecting disputes despite being highly inclusive. We experimented by moving the τ_b threshold in 1 percent increments of a full standard deviation for the distribution of all τ_b scores to identify the level of τ_b that minimizes the ratio of identified dyad-years to dispute dyads. We found that a τ_b set at –0.037 (approximately 12 percent of a standard deviation below 0) minimizes the ratio. However, even this optimal level of τ_b does not produce appreciably better results than a threshold of zero. This level of τ_b accounts for only 42 percent of all disputes, which is substantially less than when the threshold is set at zero. Reductions in the inclusiveness of this method do not improve its effectiveness because doing so causes it to miss many more dispute dyads. Moving the threshold from 0 to –0.037 removes more than 150,000 dyads from the population, reflecting the fact that the number of qualifying dyads changes sharply within a very narrow band around the zero point.

In summary, the τ_b procedure for identifying willingness dyads fails on both of our criteria for a good empirical measure of willingness as a means to select politically relevant dyads. A threshold value of zero for τ_b includes most of the total population of dyads (about two-thirds of the population), but accounts for only about half of all disputes. More restrictive methods are successful at reducing inclusiveness, but doing so comes at the cost of identifying substantially fewer disputes. In all, by both criteria we offer for assessing selection procedures, the τ_b procedure has significant weaknesses.

In principle, the τ_b procedure fits the theoretical bill for choosing politically relevant dyads based on willingness. However, as we have just seen, in practice it does not seem to work well. However, we can apply the Possibility Principle via what we call the issue-based approach to defining willingness. Recall that the Possibility Principle states that we should choose cases in which there is a possibility of militarized conflict. In the context of willingness this can be interpreted as selecting those dyads in which the issues over which states commonly fight are present. We would say, for example, that a territorial dispute could very well provide the occasion for a militarized dispute. Although the vast majority of territorial disputes do not result in militarized conflict (Goertz and Diehl 1992), it is still true that the path to many armed conflicts winds through disputes over territory (Vasquez 1993). The Possibility Principle prescribes that we use what we know to be commonly associated with disputes and wars to define the relevant cases. So we need to identify the issues that are commonly associated with militarized foreign policies. Reviewing the literature, including COW coding rules for disputes, we suggest the following short list: (1) territory, (2) regime type, and (3) trade and commerce.

Starting with territory, we note that the criteria for opportunity dyads is based partially on contiguity. For territory, there is a significant overlap between dyads made relevant via opportunity and dyads made relevant via willingness. One can find some isolated cases, e.g., Peru-Ecuador and Latin America in general, where territory is an interest motivating countries to overcome opportunity problems (because the disputed territory is very hard to reach). Our interest in this chapter is willingness as separate from opportunity as usually operationalized so we ignore territory for practical not theoretical reasons.

TABLE 8.2

Comparing Willingness to Opportunity for Defining Political Relevance:
Regime Type and Trade

Definition of Political Relevance	Total Dyads (%)[a]	Total Disputes (%)
Opportunity	90,065 (14%)	2,645 (88%)
Willingness—mixed regime	239,383 (37%)	1,231 (41%)
Opportunity	61,640 (11%)	1,794 (87%)
Willingness		
Significant trade[a]	248,528 (45%)	1,597 (78%)
Nonzero trade[a]	327,868 (59%)	1,697 (82%)

[a] Due to fragmentary data, dyad-years from the periods 1914–19 and 1939–47
have been removed; "significant trade" is trade flows greater than $1 million

According to the COW coding for the disputed issue in MIDs, regime type is a common source of conflict between states. Western history is full of conflicts that arise over the type of government or ideology of the regime in power. In Central America it was liberal versus conservatives, in Europe it was monarchy versus democracy, after World War II it was communism versus democracy and capitalism. Unfortunately, we do not have data coded along these fault lines, but as a first cut we can consider democracy versus authoritarian regimes as having the willingness to fight based over regime differences. Here we can operationally define willingness as significant differences in regime type according to the polity IV data set (Marshall and Jaggers 2002). Any dyad consisting of a coherent autocracy (with a polity score less than or equal to −5) and a coherent democracy (with a score greater than or equal to 5) will be defined as a mixed regime dyad in which the potential for conflict willingness exists.[5]

Table 8.2 shows what happens when we define willingness in terms of difference in regime type. In comparison with the opportunity definition of political relevance it does not do too well: it captures just 41 percent of all dyadic disputes. At the same time, the mixed regime procedure performs much better than the τ_b procedure in terms of

[5] We do not use the ΔJG measure of democracy proposed in chapter 4 because we want to stay within the norms of measurement common in the large-N conflict literature.

inclusiveness with just 37 percent of the total population qualifying for relevance. In this respect, by accounting for roughly the same number of disputes with a less inclusive population, the mixed regime method performs better than the τ_b method.

Economic, trade, and finance issues have a long positive association with conflict. By that, we do not mean to enter the trade and conflict debate by claiming liberal arguments about the pacifying effects of trade are unfounded. The Possibility Principle is completely consistent with the many published findings that dyadic trade interdependence produces peace.[6] The Possibility Principle says that one should choose issues that have been associated with military conflict. Certainly if one looks at wars based on Holsti's (1991) coding one sees that economic issues are present. Similarly, a significant minority of militarized disputes have involved economic matters including disputes regarding natural resources, water rights, fishing rights, finance, and debt.

Concretely we use trade data to indicate economic willingness. The presence of a trade relationship creates the possibility of conflict (not necessarily a strongly positive likelihood of conflict). Again, we also see a potential overlap with opportunity. A state that has the capacity to conduct trade with another state probably also has the capacity to mobilize its navy against that state. If access to air and sea transportation permits commerce, it is probable that the states can utilize the same resources for military purposes. The Netherlands has plenty of opportunities for disputes in the nineteenth century because of its trade with Latin America. Its opportunities in some ways are not really different from those of Great Britain. Nearer the present, the Iran-Iraq war produced many disputes because many countries with oil interests in the Persian Gulf region became entangled in the war when their ships came under militarized attack.

Table 8.2 also presents the results of an analysis based on defining relevant dyads as those that involve states with any amount of trade. Since trade data are not readily available for the entire 1816–2000 period, we utilize data from Oneal and Russett (2001) to cover the 1885–1938 period and data from Gleditch (2002) for the 1948–2000 period. Due to the restricted time period (and many missing observations), the number of valid observations in the all-dyad population shrinks to 556,589. Despite these data limitations, table 8.2 shows that

[6]For a survey of some of these findings, see Oneal's (2003) response to Gartzke and Li (2003).

trade does significantly better than regime type in identifying dyads that had disputes. The trade procedure for defining willingness relevance (dyads with a nonzero value for trade flow) picks up 82 percent of all disputes. This compares favorably with opportunity relevance, which covers a slightly higher percentage (87 percent) of dyadic disputes. The downside is that trade relevance uses significantly more dyads to achieve this result (59 percent of all dyads as compared with 37 percent for the mixed regime procedure).

As we did with τ_b, we experimented with more restrictive thresholds by requiring incrementally larger amounts of trade to qualify for relevance. We found that increasing the threshold from zero to just $1 million (1990 constant dollars) removed approximately 25 percent of the dyads from the set of qualifying dyads. Barring dyads with only token amounts of trade improves the effectiveness of the method drastically because the number of qualifying dyads decreases significantly, while the number of "impossible" disputes increases only slightly. In table 8.2, we note the results for a trade threshold at $1 million. Compared to the mixed regime method, this latter trade method performs better because it identifies significantly more disputes (78 percent of all disputes compared to 41 percent for the mixed regime method) with a comparably sized population of relevant dyads (45 percent of all dyads compared to 37 percent for the mixed regime method).

Finally, to complete the application of the logic of the Possibility Principle, we examine the union of two sets of dyads—those that qualify for relevance through opportunity and those that qualify through willingness. The complete application of the principle should involve a selection of all cases with opportunity OR willingness. We take the standard definition of opportunity and use some of the more viable candidates for willingness discussed above to examine empirically the populations of cases generated. To carry out this analysis, we work with the slightly smaller base population that has valid observations for trade.

Table 8.3 shows how the various combinations of populations account for dyadic disputes. Glancing at the table, two procedures stand out as being particularly effective at capturing disputes left unaccounted for by the strict opportunity approach—trade and mixed regime dyads. Both procedures capture more than 90 percent of the dispute dyads with a modestly sized population of relevant dyads (slightly more than 250,000 in each procedure). These procedures are far more efficient than a procedure that combines opportunity dyads with negative τ_b dyads. Under that procedure, 75 percent of all

TABLE 8.3

Politically Relevant Dyads: Opportunity OR Willingness

Definition of Political Relevance	Total Dyads (%)	Total Disputes (%)	Impossible
Opportunity	61,640 (11%)	1,794 (87%)	266
Opportunity OR τ_b[a]	417,797 (75%)	1,968 (96%)	92
Opportunity OR mixed regime	253,407 (46%)	1,920 (93%)	140
Opportunity OR trade[b]	257,020 (46%)	1,966 (95%)	94
Opportunity OR mixed regime OR trade	368,581 (66%)	2,003 (97%)	57

Base population: 1885–2000; $N = 556,589$; 2,060 total disputes

[a]Dyads with τ_b less than 0 qualify for relevance

[b]Dyads with trade flow greater than $1 million qualify for relevance

dyads qualify as relevant, but the number of dispute dyads is not appreciably greater. Combining mixed regime dyads and trading dyads with opportunity dyads produces a smaller population that captures more disputes. By the criteria we offered for evaluating procedures, we conclude that this procedure is better than the procedure based on opportunity or τ_b.[7]

In the end, of the three procedures we consider for identifying dyads with the willingness for conflict, mixed regime and trading dyads distinguish themselves as most effective. These procedures are not overly inclusive and still account for a sizable portion of dispute dyads that are left unaccounted for by the strict opportunity approach. The population of dyads that qualify for opportunity, mixed regime, or trade accounts for 97 percent of all dyadic disputes and, at the same time, excludes more than one-third of the total number of dyads from the population of politically relevant dyads.

[7]Although we do not report it in table 8.6 below, a procedure that combines all four sets of dyads (opportunity, mixed regime, significant trade, and negative τ_b) does not perform effectively compared to the procedure based on opportunity, mixed regime, and significant trade. Such a procedure identifies 135,000 more dyads as relevant, but identifies only 34 more disputes.

In all, it probably comes as no surprise that it is more difficult operationally to define politically relevant dyads based on willingness than on opportunity. Theoretically, both approaches have equal validity, but willingness is harder to put into empirical practice. At the same time, if opportunity and willingness (defined by mixed regimes or trade) are absent for a particular dyad, then a strong case can be made that such a dyad is irrelevant. From this point of view, approximately one-third of all dyads (approximately 190,000) seem completely irrelevant, with just 57 impossible-but-happens disputes occurring with this population.

POPULATION CHOICE AND CAUSAL INFERENCE

The last chapter illustrated how the Raven Paradox interacts with issues similar to politically relevance to dramatically increase the N of a study, potentially with many irrelevant cases. While it is common knowledge that increasing the N of a study is a way to get more significant results, the Raven Paradox increases in N in a particular way. One can legitimately increase the N, for example something King, Keohane, and Verba (1994) recommend, but increasing the N via politically irrelevant dyads is dubious at best.

Beyond merely increasing the N, the inclusion of politically irrelevant dyads can significantly influence causal inference. Not only the strength of the causal relationship can vary but even the direction of the relationship can change. Statistical inference hinges crucially on the nature of the negative or control population. It is only the comparison of the positive with the negative cases that determines the significance and the sign of the relationship. Any major change to the negative population can thus lead to radical revision of causal inferences.

One long-standing debate regards the impact of power (a)symmetry on conflict (see Lemke and Kugler 2000 for a survey). One side argues that power symmetry encourages disputes because both sides can reasonably expect to prevail; power asymmetry discourages actual military conflict because the weaker side will make concessions to avoid a war it will most likely lose. In opposition, some scholars propose that countries will take advantage of power superiorities to initiate wars they are likely to win (the recent 2003 Gulf War would be a good example of this). More directly relevant are the results of

TABLE 8.4

Population Selection and Causal Inference: Capability Ratios

	No MID	MID	Total	Odds Ratio
All Dyads N=655,545				
Preponderance %	.996	.004		1.25
N	459,878	1,954	461,832	
Parity %	.995	.005		
N	192,664	1,049	193,713	
Opportunity Relevant Dyads N=90,065				
Preponderance %	.977	.023		2.75
N	74,157	1,763	75,920	
Parity %	.938	.062		
N	13,263	882	14,145	

Preponderance is defined as 300% or more capability

Lemke and Reed when they contrast an all-dyad research design with a politically relevant one. Quite notably the sign for the power variable flips from positive to negative. They do not discuss this much, but it is very directly related to how one chooses the population of cases.

As shown in table 8.4, what determines to a large degree the sign of the relationship between power symmetry and dispute initiation is the proportion of cases in the negative, "No MID," column. Since the number of MIDs is basically fixed[8] depending on how we choose the population of cases—all dyads versus politically relevant dyads— this percentage can move. If the percentage is *higher* than that in the positive outcome column then the sign of the relationship will be negative since compared with the control group conflict is less common among symmetric dyads. If for the other negative group the percentage happens to be *lower* then the sign of the relationship will be positive.

Table 8.4 illustrates what can happen when choosing different control groups. In the case of all dyads the odds are only slightly greater

[8] It would be constant if the concept of a politically relevant dyad did not produce any impossible-but-happens cases.

TABLE 8.5
Population Selection and Causal Inference: Military Alliances

	No MID	MID	Total	Odds Ratio
All Dyads N=655,545				
Nonallied %	.996	.04		2.60
N	609,098	2,453	611,551	
Allied %	.987	.103		
N	43,444	550	43,994	
Opportunity Relevant Dyads N=90,065				
Nonallied %	.972	.028		1.21
N	73,271	505	14,654	
Allied %	.966	.034		
N	14,149	882	14,145	

(odds ratio=1.25) of a MID occurring in the situation of capability parity than in preponderance. In contrast, the odds ratio increases by 100 percent to 2.75 when the control group consists of politically relevant dyads. While both relationships are significant (not surprising given N's of about 500,000 or 75,000) the importance of power parity varies significantly.

It is quite clear why this is happening. The difference between the two control groups lies in noncontiguous minor powers. By including hundreds of thousands of these dyads we increase the number of power parity dyads vis-à-vis the opportunity relevant dyad population. Since these additional dyads are more likely to be of the same power level (since they are all minor powers) we have diluted the effect of power parity by including a large of dyads that have parity, but which are very unlikely to experience a MID.

In the case of capability parity we found stronger relationships in the politically relevant population. This need not necessarily be the case. Take the widely used COW alliance variable and the results in table 8.5. In the set of politically relevant dyads there is almost no relationship (odds ratio=1.21) between alliance and dispute occurrence. In contrast, in the all-dyad population we find an odds ratio over twice as high (2.60).

In summary, the choice of the control group can significantly affect causal inference. For both capability and alliance the sign remains the same, but the importance of the variable shifts significantly. Lemke and Reed's (2001) results are there to remind us that it is quite possible for the sign to change as well. One must keep in mind that the differences between the two populations are significant. The population of noncontiguous minor power dyads *alone*—i.e., non-opportunity relevant dyads—is 600–700 percent larger than that of opportunity relevant dyads. What happens in this group of countries will determine to a large extent the character of the statistical findings.

Interactions between the Possibility Principle and Basic-Level Causal Inferences

It still remains an open question the extent to which choosing a more theoretically appropriate population of opportunity or willingness influences causal inferences in a typical multivariate statistical analysis. Here we have two standards by which to compare the impact of including willingness into the theory of politically relevant dyads. The first is the all-dyad design, the second is the opportunity relevant universe of cases. We can then contrast various operationalizations of political relevance using willingness and/or opportunity to define politically relevant dyads. This is key because as we have emphasized, the Possibility Principle is theory dependent. Often the variables used to define the population also appear in the multivariate analyses. For example, we will include a major power variable in the logit analyses, but we need to keep in mind that major power status is used to define opportunity political relevance.

In short, in this subsection we have two key concerns. The first is the impact of including willingness in defining politically relevant dyads and the second is the impact of including variables used to define the population in statistical analyses of that population. Both of these can produce significant variations in how we evaluate important hypotheses about the causes of international conflict.

Table 8.6 presents the results of estimating a logit model for dispute initiation based on eight different populations of dyads. The model includes seven independent variables (lagged by one year) that are typically included in such analyses. As in chapter 5, for illustration purposes we aim to reproduce models typical both in terms of statistical methodology as well as in terms of substantive variables included.

TABLE 8.6
Politically Relevant Dyad Populations and Causal Inferences

	All Dyads	Opportunity	(a)	(b)	(c)	(d)	(e)	(f)
Democracy	-0.05**	-0.04**	0.11**	-0.05**	-0.05**	-0.03**	-0.05**	-0.04**
	(0.01)	(0.01)	(0.04)	(0.01)	(0.01)	(0.01)	(0.01)	(0.01)
Trade Interdependence	-29.33*	-14.03	-1.01	-18.33	-26.59	-31.02*	-23.10*	-28.69*
	(16.68)	(10.84)	(11.40)	(12.45)	(16.19)	(17.87)	(13.93)	(16.46)
Capability Ratio	-0.28**	-0.30**	-0.36**	-0.28**	-0.29**	-0.28**	-0.27**	-0.28**
	(0.03)	(0.03)	(0.04)	(0.04)	(0.03)	(0.03)	(0.03)	(0.03)
Allies	-0.11	-0.19*	-0.36*	-0.10	-0.15	-0.20	-0.16	-0.16
	(0.12)	(0.11)	(0.20)	(0.13)	(0.13)	(0.12)	(0.12)	(0.12)
Major Powers	2.09**	0.70**	2.74**	1.77**	2.01**	1.89**	1.77**	1.96**
	(0.16)	(0.12)	(0.20)	(0.15)	(0.16)	(0.15)	(0.14)	(0.15)
Log Distance (capital-capital)	-0.47**	-0.11**	-0.62**	-0.36**	-0.44**	-0.40**	-0.35**	-0.43**
	(0.05)	(0.04)	(0.07)	(0.05)	(0.05)	(0.05)	(0.05)	(0.05)
Contiguity	2.47**	1.24**	2.06**	2.25**	2.34**	2.39**	2.27**	2.41**
	(0.16)	(0.13)	(0.19)	(0.15)	(0.16)	(0.15)	(0.14)	(0.15)
Constant	-1.22**	-1.70**	-1.14*	-1.82**	-1.30**	-1.39**	-1.72**	-1.39**
	(0.45)	(0.36)	(0.61)	(0.41)	(0.45)	(0.44)	(0.39)	(0.43)
N	516,191	57,937	198,966	228,965	334,739	235,463	236,978	340,073
Wald χ^2	3752.36	1385.25	1483.15	2657.10	2883.54	2775.44	2980.72	3218.81
p of χ^2	<.001	<.001	<.000	<.001	<.001	<.001	<.001	<.001

(a) mixed regime dyads; (b) dyads with significant trade; (c) mixed regime or trading dyads;
(d) opportunity or mixed regime dyads; (e) opportunity or trading dyads; (f) opportunity or mixed regime or trading dyads
Robust standard errors used
Estimated coefficients for three peace-years spline variables are not reported
*$p < .05$, **$p < .01$, one-tailed test

The relative stability of many of the variables over the various operationalizations of political relevance is, perhaps, surprising. Democracy, capability ratio, major power dyads, logged capital-capital distance, and contiguity each achieve essentially the same level of statistical significance across most populations. At least we see no sign shifts.

The dichotomous variable indicating allied dyad partners is one notable exception. Although the presence of an alliance is associated with the absence of militarized disputes within the opportunity sample, alliances were found to be unrelated to dispute onset in the all-dyad model. Based on our earlier analysis in table 8.5, the difference is likely due to a difference in the negative cases. As we saw, when making comparisons to the control group of unallied dyads, allied dyads appear to be relatively less prone to disputes within the opportunity dyads sample as compared to the all-dyad sample. The finding in the second column of table 8.6 that alliances are a significant inhibitor of disputes may well be related to this attribute of the opportunity population. Looking across other populations, it can be seen that alliances are a significant inhibitor of disputes in only one other population— mixed regime dyads (column a).

A key issue in this section is what happens when the same variable is used to define political relevance and then used in the multivariate analysis. Many of the independent variables are used to define one population or another. These include (1) democracy (i.e., regime type), (2) trade, (3) major powers, and (4) contiguity. For example, major power status is a core part of the definition of opportunity political relevance. Since we use major power status to define relevant dyads we might expect to see this factor be less important in an analysis of opportunity relevance dyads. In fact, this appears to be the case: both the coefficient and the significance levels are much lower in the opportunity relevant population. To appreciate the substantive differences between the coefficient estimates in the two models, consider how a major power dyad compares to a baseline dyad composed of nondemocratic, unallied, noncontiguous minor powers with mean values for all other variables. Using the coefficients from the model based on all dyads, the estimated probability of a dispute for a major power dyad with all of the other attributes of the baseline dyad is more than six times higher than the baseline dyad. In contrast, using coefficients from the model estimated from only the opportunity relevant dyads, a major power dyad is only two times more likely to experience a dispute compared to the baseline. The differences can be traced back to characteristics of the two underlying populations. In the all-dyad population, major powers appear to be particularly prone to militarized conflict in contrast to the vast multitude of largely peaceful noncontiguous minor powers that are also included. In the opportunity relevant design, however, the dispute proclivities of the major powers do not contrast so sharply with the control group and, consequently, the estimated substantive effect of major power status is comparatively smaller.

A similar effect is present for contiguity. In the all-dyad design contiguous dyads contrast sharply with the many noncontiguous pairs in terms of the likelihood of disputes. Consequently, the estimated coefficient for contiguity is largest for the model estimated from the all-dyad design. That contrast is muted in the more restrictive sample defined strictly by opportunity relevance.

We see the same effect with trade. When we look at the trade-only populations the trade variable is not significant at all (column b). We find similar results when looking at the other two willingness-only populations (columns a and c). However, once we have a theoretically complete population of opportunity and willingness dyads trade is significant in all three of these populations.[9]

Consistent with expectations from the vast democratic peace literature, we found that increases in dyadic democracy (measured as the lower democracy score of the dyad partners) reduce the likelihood of a dispute in all but one of our models. The exception is the model based on the population of mixed regime dyads (column a). As emphasized in the previous chapter, one should not use central factors under examination in the case selection procedure. If one is looking at hypotheses regarding the democratic peace peace then the population should not exclusively be determined by regime-type variables. Recall that joint democratic countries are excluded from the population if it is exclusively based on mixed regime types. It would be unreasonable to expect the democratic peace hypothesis to hold in this circumstance. Here we see an extreme example of the interaction between variables used to select populations and basic-level causal analyses.

There is no easily and clear solution to the case selection issue. We hope our analyses have illustrated some of the inferential issues of using all dyads, opportunity, and/or willingness politically relevant

---

[9]As we have seen and discussed in chapter 6 results on trade variables across studies and within studies appear to be quite volatile. Nevertheless, we see a clear bias against these variables when using opportunity-only populations.

dyads. Generally, one must be very careful in using variables that form part of central hypotheses under investigation as part of the conceptualization of politically relevant dyads. If such variables are used to define politically relevant dyads then that must always form part of the interpretation of the statistical results. Conversely, when interpreting the results from an all-dyad design one must keep in mind that the vast majority of dyad-years come from noncontiguous minor powers and what that means for causal inference.

CONCLUSION

Our use of the opportunity and willingness framework to theorize and operationalize the concept of politically relevant dyads has close ties with the formalization of opportunity and willingness along with foreign policy substitutability developed by Cioffi-Revilla and Starr (2003). In fact, this will an important example of two-level theories in chapter 9. Their formalization of opportunity and willingness makes it clear that willingness has the same importance theoretically as does opportunity. In agreement with the Possibility Principle, the opportunity and willingness framework is a theory about positive occurrences. Not surprisingly we can see possibility language being used: "[opportunity for war] means that interaction exists between individuals of one national state and those of another so that it is *possible* for conflict to arise" (Most and Starr 1989, 30).

One of the most interesting aspects of the Cioffi-Revilla and Starr model is how it combines opportunity and willingness with foreign policy substitutability. There are many ways in which countries can have opportunity or willingness, i.e., there is substitutability in achieving opportunity or willingness. Our operationalization of opportunity and willingness has exactly this character. As illustrated in figure 8.1, one can have the opportunity for conflict in two ways (1) physical proximity, i.e., contiguity or (2) major power status. Willingness can be achieved via the various issues that often generate militarized conflict or are a reflection of conflict such as (1) territory, (2) trade, (3) alliance, and (4) regime differences. At this indicator level our model uses the same OR as does the Cioffi-Revilla and Starr model. Our model proposes that these various routes to willingness are substitutable.[10]

[10]Kinsella and Starr (2002) divide many of the standard conflict variables into either the opportunity or willingness class just as we do here.

The various analyses in this chapter make a powerful case for a theoretically complete opportunity and willingness conceptualization of political relevance. While the use opportunity only is too exclusive, the use of all dyads is too inclusive. While the various opportunity and willingness populations have significantly more observations than an opportunity-only one, we have very good theoretical reasons to include these cases. At the same time we have populations that are a lot smaller—i.e., by 150,000–200,000 cases—than an all-dyad design.

The use of concepts to select cases has a variety of very important impacts on causal inference. As the Raven Paradox illustrates, one can easily inflate the number of observations and hence significance levels. Causal strength and direction depend on the distribution of observations in the negative set (and the positive, of course). Because observations are not randomly distributed in the irrelevant set, significance levels and signs can easily vary when irrelevant observations are included. Finally, the use of variables simultaneously to define populations and in basic-level statistical analyses poses major issues of causal interpretation. One must constantly keep in mind how the population is defined when making causal interpretations of statistical results.

The last three chapters have surveyed some of the ways concepts intersect with key issues of case selection. There are many boundary decisions that must be made, decisions about positive concepts, gray zones, negative cases, impossible zones, populations, and finally scope issues. Concepts play a key role in all of these research design decisions.

PART THREE

CONCEPTS IN THEORIES

*

Concepts in Theories: Two-Level Theories

WITH JAMES MAHONEY

> Every one may observe how common it is for names to be
> made use of, instead of the ideas themselves . . . especially if
> the ideas be very complex, and made up of a great collection
> of simple ones. This makes the consideration of *words* and
> *propositions* so necessary a part of the Treatise of Knowledge,
> that it is very hard to speak intelligibly of the one, without
> explaining the other.
> *John Locke*

CONCEPTS PLAY TWO IMPORTANT ROLES in the research enterprise, as constituent parts of theories and as an essential part of case selection. The last few chapters have examined some core aspects of concepts and case selection. It seems appropriate to end this volume with how concepts play a role in theories.

As this volume has stressed throughout, secondary-level dimensions play a key causal part in the larger theoretical, explanatory enterprise. If one takes the standard regression-type model it consists of basic-level concepts. Once we put multilevel concepts into these variables we produce multilevel theories. As a result, we will refer to two-level theories. We call them two- and not three-level *theories* because the third level of concepts deals with measurement and data. This level rarely comes into play in the description of causal mechanisms and explanations at the basic level. In contrast, secondary-level dimensions frequently appear as part of the theoretical framework. For example, the analysis of the liberal peace in chapter 5 shows that two-level theories appear in statistical settings as well. Embedded in the dyadic concepts of democracy and trade dependence are causal hypotheses. The dyadic concepts are then correlated with the basic-level outcome variable of militarized dispute. We suggest that in fact many quantitative as well as qualitative models have two-level theories because of the causal hypotheses embedded in concepts.

Putting multilevel concepts into hypotheses and propositions generates a complex theoretical edifice. Not only do we need to decide how to construct concepts, but now we need to decide how the basic-level concepts are "put together" and structured to form some kind of hypothesis or theory. Of course, by now this is a fairly familiar problem. It is one that the researcher has faced in "aggregating" from the indicator level to the secondary level, and from the secondary level to the basic. Not surprisingly, we will continue to use the same structural principles *between* basic-level concepts, the logical AND and OR.

Just as we can use AND and OR to structure concepts we can use them to model the relationship between independent and dependent variable. As we shall see, many influential scholars have used this methodology for their theories. They have claimed that some factor **X** is a necessary condition for the outcome **Y** (we continue to use boldface fonts for basic-level variables). For example, in Skocpol's theory of social revolution, a continuing example in this book, state crisis is a necessary condition for social revolution. The logical forms used to construct multilevel concepts also apply to the construction of theories using basic-level concepts.

As examples of concepts in theories we will be revisiting some familiar friends, concepts such as social revolution, welfare state, democracy, and others. These concepts appear as key independent and dependent variables in major social theories. While previous chapters have analyzed these concepts in isolation, it is useful to see how these core concepts of politics science and sociology appear when surrounded by other multilevel concepts.

Throughout this volume I have stressed the importance of ontology, substitutability, and causality in building concepts. I have stressed the ontological view most in this volume since it is not generally recognized as an approach to concepts. However, two-level theories can involve causal relationships between levels. We have already seen (chapter 2) that factor analytic approaches see indicators as effects of basic-level causes. Here we explore the converse pattern, how basic-level factors are effects of secondary-level causes. Using Skocpol once again, we show how basic-level factors like state breakdown are produced by some secondary-level causes like international pressure.

In this kind of two-level model we still have basic and secondary levels, but now the causal arrow goes from the secondary level to the basic level. One can think of this relationship between levels in terms of causal mechanisms. The secondary level provides various causal mechanisms for the production of basic-level phenomena.

One *noncausal* relationship between secondary and basic levels takes the form of substitutability. Typically, this refers to different means to attain a given end (e.g., foreign policy substitutability; Most and Starr 1984). Our principle example of this will be Ostrom's theory of common pool resource institutions (1991). For example, an important basic-level factor is the ability to monitor compliance with institution rules. However, depending on the characteristics of the society and the resource itself there are various *means* of achieving successful monitoring. These means do not stand in a causal relationship to monitoring, they are different ways to do it. While the Skocpol model involves equifinality, it is a causal equifinality; in the substitutability model, it is a noncausal equifinality.

The power of the three-level concept framework comes out in how famous scholars have implicitly used this structure. In particular, we shall continue our empirical examination of Skocpol's theory of social revolution because it is a famous study that has been at the center of much methodological debate. We suggest that our analysis provides for the first time a succinct and accurate portrayal of the *structure* of Skocpol's theory. We believe that her work has been influential not only because of her substantive arguments, but also because she constructed a two-level theory.

Using Skocpol as a concrete example also permits us to illustrate the usefulness of fuzzy sets as a methodological tool for dealing with two-level theories. If one's conceptual theory along with the propositions combining concepts all use the logic of AND and OR then fuzzy logic provides a natural and coherent way to operationalize the overall theory. Fuzzy logic is built on the foundation of the logic of AND and OR, as such it translates directly two-level theories into appropriate methods. It is a relatively straightforward matter using fuzzy sets to move from the indicator level to the secondary level to relationships between basic-level variables. In contrast, it is not clear at all how this would work using standard statistical methods (though see Braumoeller 2003). So while we focus on evaluating Skocpol's theory of social revolution the basic methodological tools apply to three-level concepts as well.

We conclude that fuzzy-set methods are very helpful for testing two-level theories because they allow the analyst to think about complex causal patterns in terms of necessary and sufficient conditions. Yet these methods will have problems evaluating two-level theories if one is not clear about the structure of these theories from the onset. For example, a fuzzy-set test that focuses on variables of the secondary level will not generate meaningful results unless the relationship between these variables and basic-level causes are systematically considered. Hence, analysts must consider the overall structure of a two-level theory *before* evaluating it using fuzzy-set techniques.

The Structure of Two-Level Theories

In this section, we describe the common structure of two-level theories, drawing on the concepts of basic level and secondary level. We also review the different logical structures that can exist at the two levels, and the different kinds of relationships that can exist between the secondary and the basic levels.

Basic Level

In a two-level theory, the basic level contains the main causal variables and outcome variable of the theory as a whole. Variables at the basic-level form the building blocks of two-level theories, but there are different logical relationships with which these variables can be put together to form theories. We find that much qualitative and comparative work uses two logical structures at the basic level: (1) a set of causal factors that are individually necessary and jointly sufficient for an outcome; and (2) a set of causal factors that are individually sufficient but not necessary for an outcome. We refer to the first structure as a "conjuncture of necessary causes" to highlight the fact that a combination of necessary conditions are sufficient to produce an outcome. We refer to the second structure using the term "equifinality," which means that there are various conditions that are sufficient to produce the same outcome and hence *multiple paths* to the same end (Ragin 1987). For example, a classic example of equifinality is Barrington Moore's (1966) argument that there are three independent routes to the modern world.

The underlying logical structure of a conjuncture of necessary causes can be specified simply as

$$Y = X * Z. \tag{9.1}$$

In this equation, we have two necessary conditions (X and Z) that are jointly sufficient for Y. We can refer to this basic structure as characterized by AND.

The second logical structure is equifinality. In contrast to equation (9.1), there are no necessary conditions in this structure. Instead, there are multiple paths by which Y can occur:

$$Y = X + Z. \tag{9.2}$$

Equation (9.2) provides this structure where the plus sign designates the logical OR, such that X *or* Z is sufficient for Y. Hence, equifinality is a logical structure characterized by OR.

These two types are not the only options for representing causal structures at the basic level. For example, one could have a basic-level theory that simply focused on individually necessary causes. Likewise, one could easily formulate more complex hybrid structures such as

$$Y = U * X + U * Z. \tag{9.3}$$

In equation (9.3), we have both a necessary condition (i.e., U) and equifinality [i.e., (U AND X) OR (U AND Z)]. For the purposes of this chapter, we will focus our discussion of the basic level on the two canonical causal structures of equifinality and a conjuncture of necessary causes.

Secondary Level

Variables at the secondary level are less central to the core argument and refer to concepts that are less easily remembered and processed. Nevertheless, these variables play a key theoretical role. For example, in theories about democracy, factors such as free elections, civil liberties, and broad suffrage often play a major role, even though they are still secondary compared to the basic-level concept of democracy itself.

As discussed in detail in chapter 2, three relationships can exist between the secondary level and the basic level: causal, ontological, and substitutability. It bears emphasis that none of these relationships is simply one in which the secondary-level variables serve as indicators or measures of the basic-level variables. The role of the secondary-level variables is *not* to operationalize the basic-level variables. Rather, in a two-level theory, the secondary-level variables *always have a causal relationship to the main outcome variable.* Two-level theories are complex precisely because the nature through which secondary-level variables affect the main outcome variable varies depending on how these variables relate to the causal variables at the basic level.

First, there may be a *causal relationship* between secondary-level variables and basic-level variables; in this case, secondary-level variables represent "causes of causes." With a causal relationship between levels, the secondary-level variables affect the main outcome variable by helping to bring into being more temporally proximate causal variables at the basic level. Hence, when a causal relationship exists between levels, one can usefully speak about more remote causes (i.e., secondary-level causes) and more proximate causes (i.e., basic-level causes).

Second, an *ontological relationship* can exist between levels. In this case, the secondary-level variables represent the defining features that constitute the basic-level variables; the secondary-level variables literally *are* the elements that compose the basic-level variables.[1] For example, free elections, civil liberties, and broad suffrage are the ontological secondary-level variables that constitute the basic-level

---

[1] Hall (2003) defines ontology as fundamental assumptions about the nature of causal relationships in the world. By contrast, our understanding of ontology focuses on the way in which secondary-level factors constitute basic-level variables. This constitutive relationship can be modeled with different theoretical or mathematical structures (e.g., equifinality, a conjuncture of necessary conditions), but in each case the assumption is that the secondary-level variables do not cause basic-level causal variables; rather, they describe the ontology or essential make-up of the basic-level causes. Our view of ontology is like Hall's in that we stress that the secondary-level constitutive factors have causal relationships with basic-level outcome variables. A description of the causal mechanisms will almost always invoke secondary-level variables. Our understanding of an ontological relationship is similar to what Wendt (1999) calls constitutive explanation, though we prefer to reserve the label "explanation" for causal relationships. We agree with Wendt that the secondary-level constitutive elements are parts of causal explanations.

variable of democracy. We use the word "ontological" to describe this relationship because it stresses that the issue concerns the essential character, structure, and underlying parts of the phenomenon to which the basic-level concept refers. The secondary-level variables play a key causal role in explaining why the basic-level causal variables have the effects they do. For example, the institutional theory of the democratic peace invokes elections as a key part of the explanation for why democracies do not fight wars with each other. In this theory, the ontological secondary-level variable of elections (which in part defines the basic-level concept of democracy) has a causal impact on the main outcome variable of war.

The logical structure of an ontological relationship can take different forms. Traditionally, most scholars have defined concepts in terms of necessary and sufficient conditions. For example, the classical approach to concepts built around a taxonomical hierarchy, as exemplified by Sartori (1970), treats defining attributes (secondary-level variables) as necessary and sufficient for membership in a concept. With the classical approach, the analyst uses AND to connect the secondary-level variables with the basic-level variable.

To connect the secondary-level variables with the basic-level variable in the family resemblance structure, the analyst uses OR. However, because the family resemblance structure may require that more than one secondary-level variable must be present for membership in the basic level, the strict application of OR will not always be adequate (i.e., the presence of a single secondary-level variable may *not* be sufficient for membership in the basic-level category). Instead, the structure can be better modeled by another version of OR that implements the rule that m of n characteristics must be present. Thus, when considering the ontological family resemblance structure, we propose to implement OR as follows:

$$X = \min(\text{sum}(X_1, X_2, \ldots), 1). \tag{9.4}$$

Equation (9.4) is a fuzzy-set logic implementation of the family resemblance m-of-n rule.[2] When using this implementation, the values of the secondary-level variables are calibrated to reflect the number of attributes that must be present for a case to be a member of the

---

[2]In fuzzy-set logic there are various ways to implement OR; see Smithson 1987 for a discussion.

basic level. For example, if at least two of four possible attributes must be present to be a member, then the values of the secondary level variables should be set to a maximum of .50 (e.g., if the variable is coded dichotomously, its possible values are .00 and .50). Hence, if two secondary-level variables are present, the case would be a member of the family (i.e., the sum of .50 and .50 is 1.00). If only one secondary-level variable is present, the case would be excluded from full membership. We use the expression min(sum X_i, 1) to characterize this procedure for implementing OR.

Finally, we consider a *substitutable relationship* between the secondary and basic levels. In this case, the secondary-level variables are neither causes nor constitutive features of the basic-level causal variables. Rather, each secondary-level variable is a substitutable means to a given basic-level variable. At the basic level is a concept such as "labor incorporation" (Collier and Collier 1991). Substitutability at the secondary level is an analysis of the different ways that labor can be or has been incorporated in different countries. In some countries this incorporation occurred via political parties, while in others it has been done by the state. Cioffi-Revilla (1998) stresses that substitutability is related to redundancy in systems (e.g., Bendor 1985; Landau 1969). Systems are more stable if necessary components have backups and alternative sources. An example is U.S. nuclear deterrence via the triad of air-, land-, and submarine-based weapons. If any one or two legs of the system were to be taken out by attack, there is enough redundancy in the system to give the United States a second strike capability (Cioffi-Revilla 1998).

Two-level theories are thus distinctive and powerful precisely because secondary-level variables are systematically related to basic-level factors. The addition of the secondary-level variables not only adds complexity to the argument developed at the basic level, but also helps analysts empirically substantiate the argument at the basic level. To concretely test the claims at the basic level, analysts must draw on the information at the secondary level, which allows them to move down levels of analysis and examine factors that further elaborate the causal relationship. For example, the examination of an ontological relationship between levels allows the analyst to explore the specific defining properties of the basic-level concepts that actually affect the outcome of interest. In the case of an ontological relationship, the specific properties identified in the secondary level are "mechanisms" that explain why the basic-level variables have the effects they do.

Substitutability is usually pursued when the analyst needs to explore the different ways in which the basic-level process can be fulfilled. Here the basic level taps a factor which is common across cases (e.g., labor incorporation), while the secondary level permits differentiation among cases in the ways in which this can occur (e.g., state or party incorporation of labor). Finally, a causal relationship enables the researcher to deepen the analysis by adding an account of the more temporally removed processes that bring into being the proximate basic-level causes themselves. This approach is highly effective when the basic-level causes are very closely related to the main outcome of interest.

In this discussion, we have emphasized different ways in which secondary-level variables can relate to *causal* variables at the basic level. However, two-level theories that propose an ontological relationship may consider the linkage between secondary-level variables and the main *outcome* variable at the basic level. In doing so, the theory draws on the secondary level to explicate and conceptualize the basic-level outcome variable. When analysts define their outcome variable in terms of secondary-level variables, they are offering an ontological and conceptual account of how secondary-level variables relate to the basic-level outcome variable.

Not only do two-level theories provide a framework for future theorizing, we suggest that they are very useful in understanding existing theories. Many social theorists have implicitly thought in two-level terms. Much of the confusion around some theories, e.g., Skocpol (1979), arises from a failure to appropriately conceptualize levels and relationships between levels. In the next section, we provide some examples of what two-level theories look like in practice.

SUBSTANTIVE EXAMPLES OF TWO-LEVEL THEORIES

In this section, we offer several different examples of two-level theories. Since the concept of a two-level theory is not prominent in the literature (though see Cioffi-Revilla 1998; Cioffi-Revilla and Starr 2003), we must interpret the degree to which the studies in question are two-level theories. In addition, we must uncover the specific two-level theoretical structures of the studies, since they are not explicitly developed. We have tried to focus on clear examples of two-level theories that exhibit some of the different possible theoretical structures. At the same time, we wish to be clear that what follows are our *stylized reconstructions* of authors' works—reconstructions that inevitably simplify sophisticated arguments.

Skocpol's Theory of Social Revolution

We begin with Skocpol's *States and Social Revolutions*, which seeks to explain the onset of social revolution in France, Russia, and China through a comparison with several other cases that did not experience social revolution. Despite all the attention surrounding this work, most analysts have failed to recognize its two-level structure. In figure 9.1, we summarize that structure.

Basic level. At the basic level, *States and Social Revolutions* has the structure of a conjuncture of two necessary causes that are jointly sufficient for the outcome of social revolution. Skocpol summarizes these two basic-level causes as follows:

> I have argued that (1) state organizations susceptible to administrative and military collapse when subjected to intensified pressures from more developed countries from abroad, and (2) agrarian sociopolitical structures that facilitated widespread peasant revolts against landlords were, taken together, the sufficient distinctive causes of social-revolutionary situations commencing in France, 1789, Russia, 1917, and China, 1911. (1979, 154)

These two causes refer to conditions for state breakdown and conditions for peasant revolt, and they can be summarized simply as "state breakdown" and "peasant revolt." Because these variables are at the basic level, most (good) summaries of Skocpol's work have referred to them.

Skocpol is explicit that these two causes are jointly—not individually—sufficient for social revolutions. This is clear from her assertion that the two factors "were, taken together, the sufficient distinctive causes" and from her explicit remarks that state breakdowns would not have led to social revolutions without peasant revolts (1979, 112). Elsewhere she attempts to empirically demonstrate that neither condition is by itself enough to produce social revolutions by examining cases of non–social revolution in which only one of the two conditions was present.

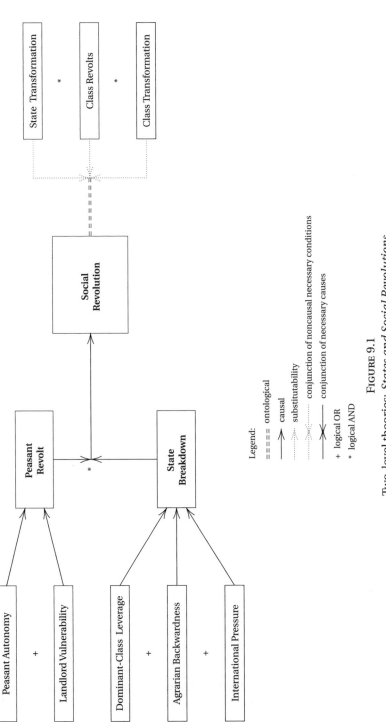

Legend:

===== ontological
→ causal
.... substitutability
.... conjunction of noncausal necessary conditions
———— conjunction of necessary causes
+ logical OR
* logical AND

FIGURE 9.1
Two-level theories: *States and Social Revolutions*

It is harder to find explicit passages in *States and Social Revolutions* where Skocpol states that her key variables are *necessary* for social revolution. But there are passages that strongly hint at the necessary condition character of her two core variables. For example:

> Nevertheless, peasant revolts have been the crucial insurrectionary in-gredient in virtually all actual (i.e., successful) social revolutions to date … Without peasant revolts urban radicalism in predominantly agrarian countries has not in the end been able to accomplish social-revolutionary transformations . . . they [English and German revolutions of 1848] failed as social revolutions in part for want of peasant insurrections against landed upper classes. (1979, 113)

In addition, Skocpol has been widely interpreted as identifying nec-essary causes (e.g., Kiser and Levi 1996, 189–90; Dion 2003) and her work is used by Ragin as a central example of necessary conditions: "Consider the argument that both 'state breakdown' and 'popular in-surrection' are necessary conditions for 'social revolution' " (2000, 219).

The basic-level argument of *States and Social Revolutions* therefore has the formal structure of equation (9.1), which we call a conjuncture of necessary causes. Here we succinctly—and perhaps for the first time in print—state Skocpol's basic theory of social revolutions:

> State breakdown and peasant revolt are individually necessary and jointly sufficient for social revolution.

This proposition is bound by certain scope conditions, such as the presence of an agrarian-bureaucratic state that lacks a significant colo-nial history. Within the scope identified by Skocpol, however, state breakdown and peasant revolt represent a combination of individu-ally necessary and jointly sufficient variables.

Secondary level. At the secondary level, Skocpol focuses on the dif-ferent processes that can produce state breakdown and peasant revolt. In this sense, there is a *causal relationship* between secondary-level variables and basic-level causes. The logical structure of this causal re-lationship is one of equifinality—that is, the secondary-level variables are sufficient but not necessary for either state breakdown or peasant revolt. Formally, to characterize Skocpol's argument in this way, we use OR at the secondary level of the theory. Hence, whereas Skocpol's theory is built around a causal conjuncture of necessary conditions at the basic level, it is characterized by equifinality at the secondary level.

With respect to explaining the basic-level cause of state breakdown, Skocpol focuses her analysis on three secondary-level causes: (1) *international pressure*, which causes crises for regime actors; (2) *dominant-class leverage* within the state, which prevents government leaders from implementing modernizing reforms; and (3) *agrarian backwardness*, which hinders national responses to political crises. With respect to peasant revolt, Skocpol focuses on two secondary-level variables: (1) *peasant autonomy and solidarity*, which facilitate spontaneous collective action by peasants; and (2) *landlord vulnerability*, which allows for class transformation in the countryside.

Skocpol's theory not only relates secondary-level variables to the causal variables of the basic level, but also directly relates secondary-level variables to the outcome variable of social revolution itself. Here, however, the relationship is ontological; we have a theoretical structure of what social revolution *is*—i.e., the defining features of the concept.

In classical fashion, Skocpol defines social revolution using a necessary and sufficient condition structure: "Social revolutions are rapid, basic transformations of a society's state and class structures; and they are accompanied and in part carried through by class-based revolts from below" (1979, 4–5). This definition holds that social revolutions are the combination of three components: (1) class-based revolts from below, (2) rapid and basic transformation of state structures, and (3) rapid and basic transformation of class structures.[3] Skocpol is explicit that if any one of these three attributes is missing, the case in question cannot be considered a social revolution. In this sense, each of the three attributes is *necessary* for social revolution. Skocpol also strongly implies that the simultaneous presence of the three components is *sufficient* for an event to be classified as a social revolution: any case that contains her three components is definitely a social revolution.

Given that Skocpol uses a necessary and sufficient approach to defining the outcome variable, it is appropriate to use AND in specifying the relationship between Skocpol's three definitional components and social revolution. When the two-level structure of the outcome

---

[3]The first component is actually somewhat problematic, given that it may be causally related to the other two, thereby raising questions of endogeneity.

variable is added to the two-level structure of the causal variables, the full argument depicted in figure 9.1 emerges.

We suggest that much of the debate around Skocpol can be traced to confusion about what variables belong to which levels and the structural relationships between levels. Not surprisingly, as we shall see below, this has important ramifications for theory testing.

Other Two-Level Theories

Skocpol is not alone in her use of a two-level theory; in fact, prominent analysts present theories that have the same basic structure of Skocpol's two-level theory (e.g., the exercises to this book provide many examples; see Exercises and Web Site at the end of this volume). However, other analysts have formulated two-level theories that vary from Skocpol's in at least two ways. First, whereas Skocpol primarily explores a causal relationship between levels, other scholars examine substitutability or ontological relationships. Second, whereas Skocpol's theory identifies a set of necessary conditions that are jointly sufficient at the basic level, other scholars examine equifinality at the basic level (i.e., individually sufficient causes).

Common pool resource institutions: Ostrom. An excellent example of a two-level theory that uses a *substitutable* relationship between the secondary and basic level is the work of Ostrom (1991). Ostrom identifies eight conditions[4] that are necessary for her key outcome of "institutional functioning." Of these eight conditions, monitoring and sanctions stand out. In fact, in her APSA presidential address, she selects them for special attention: "Most robust and long-lasting common-pool regimes involve clear mechanisms for monitoring rule conformance and graduated sanctions for enforcing compliance" (Ostrom 1998, 8). Thus, her argument emphasizes necessary conditions that form a conjuncture that is sufficient. In figure 9.2, we have represented this basic-level theory by focusing on how "monitoring" and "sanctions" are individually necessary and jointly sufficient for the outcome of institutional functioning (see Goertz 2003 for an elaboration of this model).

---

[4]These are (1) monitoring, (2) graduated sanctions, (3) clear boundaries and memberships, (4) congruent rules, (5) conflict resolution mechanisms, (6) recognized rights to organize, (7) nested units, and (8) collective-choice arenas (Ostrom 1991, 180).

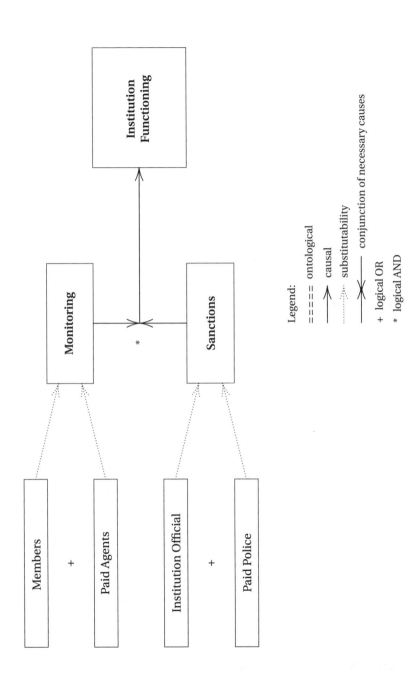

Legend:

= = = = =   ontological

→   causal

⋯⋯ substitutability

✳   conjunction of necessary causes

+ logical OR

* logical AND

FIGURE 9.2

A two-level model of common pool resource institutions

At the secondary level, Ostrom identifies variables that are specific means of sanctioning and monitoring, thereby employing a substitutable relationship between levels. She describes two ways that monitoring can be accomplished, monitoring by an institutional member or monitoring by a paid agent. Clearly, these two types neither cause nor define the basic-level variable of monitoring. Analogously, the basic-level cause of sanctions can be arrived at in one of two ways, sanctions by institutional officials or sanctions by paid police. Again, the relationship here is one equifinality: institutional-official sanctions or paid-police sanctions are alternative paths to sanctions in general.

Here we see a typical example of how the basic level focuses on a factor, e.g., monitoring, common to all successful common pool resource institutions. The secondary level is then an analysis of how different societies with different resource technologies go about implementing a monitoring system. At the basic level the key fact is that someone monitors; the secondary level shows the substitutable ways in which this can occur in different cases. In other words, we have a situation of equifinality in which the secondary-level variables are sufficient for the basic-level variable, as represented by the OR in figure 9.2.

Cioffi-Revilla (1998) and Cioffi-Revilla and Starr (2003) provide a mathematical and probabilistic analysis of a model with the same structure as Ostrom's. Most and Starr introduced the influential notion of foreign policy substitutability [Most and Starr 1984; see also the special issue of the *Journal of Conflict Resolution* 2002 39(1)]. They are also well known for the idea that opportunity and willingness are individually necessary and jointly sufficient for foreign policy action. If one puts opportunity and willingness at the basic level and foreign policy substitutability at the secondary level, one arrives at the model in figure 9.2. Cioffi-Revilla and Starr (2003) formally model this in ways that make clear the tight link with our analysis of two-level models and they do so in a completely probabilistic fashion.

Beyond the Cioffi-Revilla and Starr example, we believe that two-level theories which propose substitutable relationships are reasonably common, particularly in the comparative-historical literature. The exercises that accompany this volume provide numerous other examples; see Exercises and Web Site.

Early modern democracy: Downing. Downing's (1992) *Military Revolution and Political Change* offers a two-level theory of the origins of liberal democracy in early modern Europe (see figure 9.3). At the basic level, Downing identifies two main causes that are individually necessary and jointly sufficient for liberal democracy: (1) medieval constitutionalism—i.e., an institutional heritage that included representative assemblies and other constitutional features; and (2) the absence of military revolution—i.e., little or no domestic mobilization of resources for war-fighting purposes during the sixteenth and seventeenth centuries. In his words: "To put the argument in its barest form, medieval European states had numerous institutions, procedures, and arrangements that, if combined with light amounts of domestic mobilization of human and economic resources for war, provided the basis for democracy in ensuing centuries" (1992, 9).

In the two-level theory, the medieval constitutionalism variable is constituted by four secondary-level variables that literally are "medieval constitutionalism." Thus, according to Downing, medieval constitutionalism is "parliaments controlling taxation and matters of war and peace; local centers of power limiting the strength of the crown; the development of independent judiciaries and the rule of law; and certain basic freedoms and rights enjoyed by large numbers of the population" (1992, 10). As figure 9.3 shows, Downing uses the classical necessary and sufficient approach to concept membership when modeling medieval constitutionalism (as indicated by the AND in the figure). These ontological secondary-level variables enter into the causal analysis because they affect the possibility of democracy. For example, if a country lacks one or more of the defining attributes of medieval constitutionalism (e.g., independent judiciaries), then that country will also lack an essential prerequisite (i.e., necessary condition) for democracy. Hence, ontological secondary-level variables are causally related to the basic level outcome variable.

For the basic-level cause of "absence of military revolution," the relationship with the secondary level is one of equifinality. Four secondary-level variables are alternative causes of the absence of a military revolution. Thus, when faced with heavy warfare, a country can avoid a substantial mobilization of national resources for the military if one or more of the following causes are present: (a) a geography that provides a natural barrier to invading armies, (b) commercial wealth that allows the country to protect itself while mobilizing only a proportion of resources toward war, (c) foreign resource mobilization that takes place when war is conducted primarily outside a country's territory, and (d) alliances that reduce the extent of domestic resources that

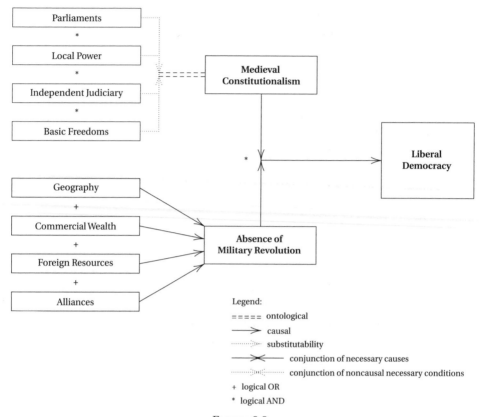

FIGURE 9.3
A two-level model of the early modern roots of liberal democracy

must be mobilized (1992, 78–79, 240). A key aspect of Downing's argument involves exploring the different ways that specific countries avoided a military revolution and stayed on a path leading to democracy.

Welfare state: Hicks, Misra, and Ng. Ragin's (1987; 2000) discussions of qualitative comparative analysis (QCA) and fuzzy-set (fs) analysis are centrally concerned with the following logical structure: substitutability at the basic level and necessary conditions at the secondary level. By contrast, the examples discussed so far tend to have the converse structure: a conjuncture of necessary conditions at the basic level and mostly equifinality at the secondary level. We do not believe that the logical model on which we have focused is more important

254

than the typical fsQCA one, but rather that it needs to be recognized as powerful and common in its own right. In this section, however, we consider the logical structure familiar from fsQCA analyses.

We examine the two-level theory developed in Hicks, Misra, and Nah Ng's (1995) QCA analysis (see figure 9.4). The outcome variable of this study is the creation of welfare states during the crucial period of social provision expansion in the 1920s. This outcome is conceptualized using the family resemblance approach to concepts. Thus, a country is coded as a "welfare state" if it adopts at least three of four classic welfare programs: (1) old age pensions, (2) health insurance, (3) workman's compensation, and (4) unemployment compensation. Here we have an equifinality relationship between secondary-level variables and the outcome variable: no single condition is necessary; there are multiple paths to the welfare state.

At the basic level, the structure of the causal theory is also one of equifinality. The main secondary-level variables are: working-class mobilization, patriarchal state, unitary democracy, catholic government, and liberal government. The QCA results yield a relatively parsimonious model that is consistent with previous theory yet enriches it in other ways. In the final model, there are respectively "three routes to the early consolidation of the welfare state ... (1) a 'Bismarckian' route, (2) a unitary-democratic 'Lib-Lab' [i.e., Liberal-Labor] route, and (3) a Catholic paternalistic unitary-democratic route" (1995, 344). The routes are represented by the following variable summaries: (1) WORK * PATRIARCHY * catholic * unitary-democracy, (2) WORK * UNITARY-DEMOCRACY * catholic, and (3) WORK * PATRIARCHY * CATHOLIC * UNITARY-DEMOCRACY * liberal. In presenting these equations, we follow the standard QCA practice of designating variables that are present with capital letters and those that are absent with lower-case letters.

This QCA analysis thus arrives at substantively important findings. Working-class mobilization is a necessary but not sufficient condition for all causal paths to a welfare state. In the Bismarckian path, working-class mobilization combines with a patriarchal authoritarian regime to produce a welfare state. In the other two routes, welfare states emerge in democracies facing working-class mobilization, either under the support of Liberals or under the support of Catholics in a context of patriarchy. Though scholars have discussed the important role of Liberals in creating welfare states, Hicks and his collaborators suggest that the Catholic path to welfare consolidation was also critical.

255

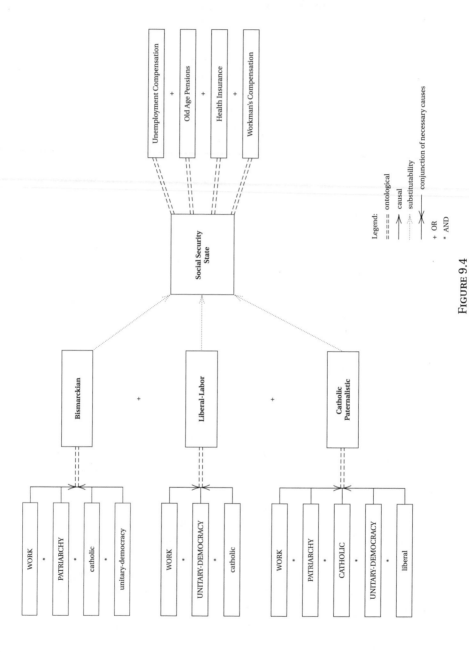

FIGURE 9.4

A two-level model of the development of the social security state

THE FUZZY-SET METHODOLOGY OF TWO-LEVEL THEORIES

Given the complex relationships modeled in two-level theories, how can scholars test the propositions of these theories? In this section, we argue that fuzzy-set analysis is an extremely useful methodology for carrying out this task. The advantages of fuzzy-set analysis for testing two-level theories include enabling researchers to logically analyze necessary and sufficient causation and allowing these researchers to code qualitative variables in light of their specialized knowledge of particular cases.

The application of fuzzy-set analysis can be complicated, even for relatively straightforward causal propositions. When we move to two-level theories, the issues are especially challenging. Thus, rather than offer superficial tests of multiple two-level theories, we choose instead to provide a sustained consideration of one specific two-level theory: Skocpol's *States and Social Revolutions*. We focus on Skocpol's book because it is a well-known study that usefully highlights many of the challenges that arise in using fuzzy-set analysis to test two-level theories. Our goal is ultimately less to offer a definitive test of Skocpol's argument and more to examine the general methodological issues that it raises.

Before beginning, it is worth underlining again that many critics of Skocpol have not adequately understood key elements of her two-level theory. In some cases, the problem has been confusion about levels. For example, in a widely cited critique, Geddes (1990; also Geddes 2003) treats Skocpol's secondary-level variables as if they directly affect the outcome of social revolution itself. For example, she correlates international pressure (a secondary-level variable) directly with the outcome of social revolution. Yet, as we have stressed, one cannot understand the effects of Skocpol's secondary-level variables on social revolution without understanding the equifinality relationship between levels. A weak correlation between international pressure and social revolution is hardly evidence against Skocpol: international pressure does not matter for social revolution as long as there is another secondary-level variable (i.e., dominant class leverage or agrarian backwardness) to take its place. In a subsequent analysis, Geddes (2003, 114–16) treats international pressure as a necessary cause of social revolution. Again, however, our reading is that international pressure is one of several sufficient causes of the basic-level variable of state breakdown.

257

We also observe that many of Skocpol's critics have not correctly represented the causal structure of her theory at the basic level itself. Most commonly, analysts proceed as if Skocpol's theory were modeling correlational causes in which variables are related to one another in a linear pattern (see Goertz 2005 for a contrast of necessary condition models with linear ones). For example, Geddes (1990) frames her discussion of Skocpol in the context of selection bias as conventionally understood in statistical research. Yet, as Dion (2003) has pointed out, these issues of selection bias cannot be meaningfully extended to studies focused on necessary causes. In short, from the previous methodological literature discussing Skocpol's book, we can initially underline two important lessons: (1) confusing basic-level and secondary-level variables grossly distorts any subsequent test of a two-level theory and (2) confusing correlational relationships for those of necessary or sufficient causes grossly distorts any subsequent test of a two-level theory.

Coding the Variables

We begin our evaluation of Skocpol's work by considering how fuzzy sets might be used to code her outcome variable and causal variables at both the basic level and the secondary level.

Outcome variable. Earlier we discussed Skocpol's three-component definition of social revolution, noting that she treats each component as necessary and the combination of the three as sufficient for membership in the category social revolution. Although Skocpol often sees variables as either present or absent, her analysis makes it clear that many cases are neither fully "in" nor fully "out" of a given dimension. On this basis, it is possible to use fuzzy sets to code cases across the three secondary-level variables (see table 9.1).[5] To do this, we adopt a simple five-value coding scheme: .00, .25, .50, .75, 1.00. A more sophisticated approach to coding variables is not easily pursued given the inevitable qualitative distinctions developed in *States and Social Revolutions.*

At least two strategies can be used for aggregating the fuzzy-set scores from the secondary level into overall fuzzy-set scores of social

[5]We have gathered the key passages and evidence for these scores into an index that is available upon request.

TABLE 9.1

Fuzzy-Set Test of Skocpol's Theory: Outcome Variable

Country	Secondary Level			Basic Level	
	Class Revolts	State Transform.	Class Transform.	Social Revolution Minimum	Social Revolution Min(sum X_i,1)
France 1787–1800	1.00	1.00	1.00	1.00	1.00
Russia 1917–1921	1.00	1.00	1.00	1.00	1.00
China 1911–1949	1.00	1.00	1.00	1.00	1.00
England 1640–1689	.00	1.00	.25	.00	.42
Russia 1905–1907	1.00	.00	.00	.00	.33
Germany 1848–1850	.50	.00	.00	.00	.17
Prussia 1807–1814	.00	.25	.50	.00	.25
Japan 1868–1873	.00	1.00	.25	.00	.42

revolution. One possibility is to use the classical approach based on AND as we did above—i.e., social revolution is a product of class-based revolts *and* state transformations *and* class transformations. In fuzzy-set analysis, AND is calculated by taking the *minimum* membership score of each case in the sets that are intersected. Given that all the cases besides France, Russia 1917, and China have a score of .00 for at least one secondary-level component, these cases also receive a score of .00 for social revolution. By contrast, since France, Russia 1917, and China have a score of 1.00 for all secondary-level variables, they also receive a score of 1.00 for social revolution. This procedure of using the minimum leads to a dichotomous coding of social revolution (see table 9.1).

Second, an alternative aggregation procedure involves using the min(sum X_i,1), which as we noted above is appropriate for concepts built around the family resemblance structure. In the case of Skocpol, we implement this procedure by dividing all values for secondary-level variables by 3 and then summing the three variables together to generate a total score for social revolution. For example, the score for Japan is calculated as follows: $0/3 + 1/3 + .25/3 = .42$. Clearly, as table 9.1 shows, the use of the min(sum X_i,1) generates different values than the use of the minimum. In fact, no case has a score of 0.00 when the min(sum X_i,1) is used, since at least one secondary-level variable is partially present for every case.

Using the min(sum X_i,1) as an approach to creating scores for social revolution has two supporting arguments. First, although Skocpol generally characterizes social revolution in a manner consistent with the minimum, her argument also suggests that she uses a family resemblance framework for her three defining attributes. In particular, Skocpol explicitly notes that she selected only "negative" cases that were fairly close to becoming social revolutions, not cases that were maximally distant from the category social revolution. Thus, for example, her nonrevolution cases do not include any instances of political stability and few situations where change did not occur at all. Instead, they all resemble social revolutions to some degree, and they all can be meaningfully seen as overlapping with the category social revolution at least to some extent.

The second reason is that Skocpol's dichotomous coding can also be derived from the family resemblance structure that uses the min(sum X_i,1). Thus, table 9.1 shows that no case other than France, Russia 1917, and China receives a fuzzy-set score above .50. Hence, if these fuzzy-set scores were recoded dichotomously, one would still conclude that only these three countries experienced social revolutions.

Secondary-level causal variables. With regard to the causal variables, we begin with the secondary level, because these variables are causally prior to those at the basic level. Skocpol makes numerous observations about the degree to which each secondary-level cause is present. These observations provide a basis for coding the variables as fuzzy sets, a task which is carried out in table 9.2.[6]

Basic-level causes. In a two-level theory, the values for basic-level causes are derived directly from the values of the secondary-level

[6]The scores in this table reflect an ordinal coding of the cases that was independently carried out for a different purpose (Mahoney 1999).

TABLE 9.2

Fuzzy-Set Test of Skocpol's Theory: Secondary Level

Country	State Breakdown			Peasant Revolt	
	Internal Pressure	Class Leverage	Agrarian Backward	Peasant Autonomy	Landlord Vulnerable
France 1787–1800	.50	.75	1.00	.75	1.00
Russia 1917–1921	1.00	.25	.50	1.00	1.00
China 1911–1949	.75	.75	1.00	.00	.75
England 1640–1689	.50	1.00	.25	.00	.00
Russia 1905–1907	.50	.25	.50	1.00	1.00
Germany 1848–1850	.25	.25	.25	.50	.00
Prussia 1807–1814	.75	.25	.25	.50	.00
Japan 1868–1873	.75	.00	.50	.00	.00

causes. Hence, the methodological task of scoring basic-level causes is straightforward once the secondary-level variables are coded and the structural relationship is identified. In Skocpol's theory, each secondary-level causal variable is individually sufficient for a particular basic-level cause. Thus, we can use OR to determine values for basic-level causes. In fuzzy-set analysis, the use of OR requires taking the *maximum* score of the secondary-level variables. For example, France's scores for the secondary-level variables that cause state breakdown are .50, 1.00, and .75, and thus the case receives a score of 1.00 for state breakdown, since this is the highest score among the intersecting sets. We use this same procedure to arrive at all the scores for state breakdown and peasant revolt in table 9.3.

TABLE 9.3
Fuzzy-Set Test of Skocpol's Theory: Basic Level

Country	State Breakdown	Peasant Revolt	State Breakdown* Peasant Revolt	Social Revolution Minimum	Social Revolution Min(sum X_i,1)
France 1787–1800	1.00	1.00	1.00	1.00	1.00
Russia 1917–1921	1.00	1.00	1.00	1.00	1.00
China 1911–1949	1.00	.75	.75	1.00	1.00
England 1640–1689	1.00	.00	.00	.00	.42
Russia 1905–1907	.50	1.00	.50	.00	.33
Germany 1848–1850	.25	.50	.25	.00	.17
Prussia 1807–1814	.75	.50	.50	.00	.25
Japan 1868–1873	.75	.00	.00	.00	.42

Testing Two-Level Theory with Fuzzy-Set Analysis

This section reanalyses of Skocpol's theory using fuzzy-set methods. Though we are focusing here only on Skocpol's argument, many other two-level arguments with alternative causal structures can also be evaluated with fuzzy-set methods.

Testing joint sufficiency. We begin by testing Skocpol's argument that state breakdown and peasant revolt are jointly sufficient for social revolution. The column for "state breakdown*peasant revolt" in table 9.3 gives the fuzzy-set values for this causal combination. The table also includes columns with the two different scorings for the outcome variable depending on whether the minimum or the min(sum X_i,1) is used. We first offer our best attempt to be faithful to the structure of Skocpol's argument, which entails using the minimum for the outcome.[7] Likewise, since we cannot assume that Skocpol thinks of her variables in terms of continuous fuzzy-set scores, we begin by looking at results for dichotomous codes. This can easily be done in table 9.3 by converting all values of .50 or less to .00, and all values of greater than .50 to 1.00.

In dichotomous terms, Skocpol's theory does quite well with respect to the proposition that state breakdown and peasant revolt are jointly sufficient for social revolution. It predicts accurately all the positive cases of social revolution: France, Russia 1917, and China. That is, all three of these cases have a dichotomous 1.00 in the column for "state breakdown*peasant revolt" and a dichotomous 1.00 for social revolution. For the negative cases, the theory also correctly predicts a .00 (absence of social revolution) for England, Russia 1905, Germany, Prussia, and Japan. These results give us some confidence that our codes of the data are a reasonable approximation of Skocpol's work and that we have correctly represented the structure of her theory.

When dichotomous codes are used, counting hits and misses is fairly straightforward. Once we move to fuzzy-set scores, however, it becomes more difficult to evaluate success and failure. The use of continuous fuzzy-set scores increases the probability that small coding errors will lead one or more cases to violate sufficiency or necessity. Since we have a complex model and only approximate codings for the secondary-level variables, it is quite likely that our test will produce one or more false negatives. Hence, we will consider a case to be consistent with causal sufficiency (or necessity) if its fuzzy-set value on the cause (or outcome) exceeds its score on the outcome (or cause) by no more than one fuzzy membership unit, which in our coding scheme means a difference of no more than .25 (Ragin 2000). For example, we consider the value for Germany of .25 for the joint combination of state breakdown and peasant revolt to be close enough to the outcome value of .00 to be considered a success.

When the minimum is used to construct the outcome variable, the predictions of Skocpol's theory (as reconstructed by us) suggest that we should see higher levels of social revolution in two cases, Russia 1905 and Prussia (i.e., both cases have a fuzzy-set value of .50 for the causal

---

[7]Strictly speaking, for the dichotomous test, either the minimum or the min(sum X_i,1) could be used for the outcome variable, since, as pointed out above, both procedures lead to a dichotomous coding in which only France, Russia 1917, and China are social revolutions.

combination but a value of .00 for social revolution). With Russia, Skocpol argues that the Revolution of 1905 was nearly a full-blown social revolution, and only the abrupt end of international pressures allowed the country to temporarily avoid this fate (1979, 95). Given that this country did experience a social revolution about a decade later, the low value on the outcome for Russia 1905 can perhaps be understood as an early measurement of a variable whose value was soon to increase. As for Prussia, its low value on the outcome reflects the fact that class-based revolts were not an important component of the reforms of 1807–14, leading the case to be coded as zero for social revolution. Again, though, this low value was a temporary situation. By the time of the German reform movement in 1848, the value for the class revolts dimension of social revolution was .50. Hence, Prussia is not successful in the test because Junker landlords were able to keep class-based revolts in check to a surprising degree, though they were not able to sustain this control and the country would soon more closely approximate a social revolution.

While not a miss by our standards, the China case merits discussion. The predicted value is .75 or lower while the outcome is 1.00. A value less than 1.00 is predicted on the outcome because China receives only .75 on the basic-level cause of peasant revolt. Other analysts have previously raised concerns about Skocpol's treatment of peasant revolt in China, suggesting that it is not fully consistent with her theory (e.g., Taylor 1989; Selbin 1993). For her part, Skocpol argues that the Chinese Communist Party created a high level of peasant autonomy and solidarity once the revolution was under way. If these organizational activities are taken into consideration, the Chinese case might be seen as having a 1.00 for the peasant revolt variable.

Looking at the min(sum X_i,1) for social revolution provides an instructive contrast to Skocpol's use of the minimum. The practical effect of using the min(sum X_i,1) is to increase the value of the cases that have a zero with the minimum. Hence, the min(sum X_i,1) makes it easier to find causal sufficiency, since the value of the outcome variable may be increased (but never decreased) compared to the minimum. For example, both Russia 1905 and Prussia are within the neighborhood of causal sufficiency when the min(sum X_i,1) is used for the outcome variable. Russia 1905 has a value of .50 for the combination of state breakdown and peasant revolt, which is only slightly above its score of .33 for the outcome using the min(sum X_i,1). Hence, if the min(sum X_i,1) is used for the outcome variable, an even stronger case can be made that state breakdown and peasant revolt are jointly sufficient.

Testing causal necessity. The previous discussion offered a test of Skocpol's theory about joint sufficiency for the basic-level variables. Here we explore the other central claim of her main theory: state breakdown and peasant revolt are individually necessary for social revolution.

For the state breakdown variable, the data support the argument about causal necessity. All eight cases have scores on the state break-down variable that are greater than or equal to their scores on the outcome within one fuzzy-set unit (i.e., within .25). We find this for both versions of the social revolution variable. This support for causal necessity is not unrelated to the way in which the basic-level causes were constructed from the secondary level. In particular, the maximum was the mode of creating the basic level, which gives the highest possible value for the basic-level variables. This mode of moving across levels makes it easier to support claims of causal necessity, since it produces higher values on the basic-level causes.

The necessity of peasant revolts depends heavily on how the outcome variable is coded. When the minimum is used, necessity is achieved for the non–social revolution cases because they all have a value of zero on the outcome. Hence it is easy to have a larger or equal value on the peasant revolt causal variable!

Once we move to the min(sum X_i,1) for the outcome variable, however, Japan and England are no longer consistent with the argument about causal necessity. This lack of empirical support is driven by the complete absence of peasant revolts combined with a reasonably high fuzzy-set score for social revolution (i.e., .42). We would suggest that Skocpol's selection procedure might have led her to this kind of contradictory case. Skocpol may have selected England and Japan precisely because peasant revolts were totally absent even though the cases resembled social revolutions in certain important respects. This kind of selection procedure in which a case is chosen because it has a very low value on a causal variable but a reasonably high value on the outcome variable is almost certain to violate causal necessity. Again, though, we emphasize that Skocpol most likely prefers to think about the outcome variable in terms of the minimum, not the min(sum X_i,1), and her cases are consistent when that approach is used.

Our analysis provides substantial support for Skocpol's theory, though it also raises some lingering questions about specific cases. Above all, the example shows how challenging it is to confirm a two-level theory that proposes, at the basic level, a set of variables that are individually necessary and jointly sufficient. This is true because an aggregation procedure for moving from secondary-level variables to basic-level causes that makes it more likely to find necessity for individual variables simultaneously makes it more difficult to find sufficiency for a combination of these variables. For example, the maximum will produce high values for the basic-level causes, which in turn will make it easier to find causal necessity when these variables are tested with fuzzy-set methods. At the same time, however, the use of the maximum for constructing basic-level causes will make it more challenging to support claims that these variables are jointly sufficient, since this mode will inflate the value of the causal combination. Concerning the outcome variable, the minimum makes it easier to find causal necessity and more difficult to find causal sufficiency when compared to the min(sum X_i,1).

Our empirical analysis of Skocpol's theory suggests that it is not clear how one might go about testing her explanation with statistical methods (e.g., Geddes 2003). It is a complex, multilevel model constructed using necessary and sufficient conditions, along with equifinality at the secondary level. As Pierson says in the context of the welfare state literature: "Different welfare state configurations are the products of complex conjunctural causation, with multiple factors working together over extended periods of time to generate dramatically different outcomes. There is no theoretical justification for arguing that a 10 percent shift in the value on one variable or another will have a simple direct effect on outcomes" (2000, 809–10). Braumoeller (2003) is a rare example of an attempt to model theories formulated in terms of AND and OR in a way that is faithful to the theory and estimatible using statistical techniques. As our various examples have illustrated, qualitative, comparative theories often are complex and multilevel. Much more needs to be done to understand what are the appropriate empirical (statistical, fuzzy set, or whatever) methods for evaluating such theories.

TWO-LEVEL THEORIES AND THE INTERPRETATION OF FSQCA

The Skocpol example illustrates how important the mode of aggregating secondary-level variables to the basic level can be for testing theoretical claims. The results of the fuzzy-set test depended in part on her use of the maximum for creating the basic-level causes. In this section, we briefly discuss alternative options for aggregating to the basic level. In addition, we assess the benefits of reinterpreting fsQCA results presented at a single level in terms of two levels.

QCA and fuzzy-set analyses generate single-level models where there are multiple paths to the outcome variable. However, conceptualizing these models in terms of two levels can make the interpretation of the results more coherent both formally and theoretically.

A not uncommon situation is when the final results of the fsQCA analysis look like:

$$Y = (A * B * C) + (A * B * D). \tag{9.5}$$

Often it makes much theoretical and empirical sense to think of C and D as substitutes for each other. Accordingly, one arrives at a two-level model such as

$$Y = A * B * E, \tag{9.6}$$

$$E = C + D. \tag{9.7}$$

To reconceptualize QCA results in this fashion, the analyst must identify the concept E for which C and D can substitute. Typically, this will involve moving up the ladder of abstraction to a more general concept. For example, Amenta and Poulsen (1996) show that there are two necessary conditions for New Deal policies such as OAA pensions, voting rights, and absence of patronage politics. To achieve sufficiency, some mechanism for positively pushing reform through government must be present. This can happen in substitutable ways, e.g., "administrative powers" or "democratic or third parties" (see also Amenta et al. 1992). These substitutable means are like variables C and D, while the general idea of a mechanism for achieving reform is like variable E.

The key point is that often we can reinterpret QCA or fuzzy-set analyses in terms of two-level theories, particularly using the substitutability relationship. This is another reason why two-level theories provide a rich set of methodological tools: they can help make sense of the results of single-level models by reinterpreting them as two-level models.

In this chapter, we have given some examples of prominent works that implicitly use two-level models. While we do not pretend to know all works that use two-level models (at least to a significant degree), other works that use this framework include Blake and Adolino (2001), Ertman (1997), Goertz (2003), Jacoby (2000), Kingdon (1984), Linz and Stepan (1996), Marks (1986), Weede (1976), and Wickham-Crowley (1991), see the exercises (described in the appendix to this volume) for more examples. In particular, we have found the literature on states, public policy, and social movements/revolution to be rich in applications of two-level ideas. One of the goals of this chapter is to make explicit explanatory theories that a number of researchers have intuitively found useful. Instead of reinventing two-level models each time, we hope that an explicit awareness of their structure and properties will help increase the theoretical and methodological rigor of future work.

Conclusion

J. S. Mill was absolutely correct to start his discussion of scientific inference and logic with an analysis of names, definitions, and concepts. Over the decades courses on research design and methodology have lost that focus. The various chapters of this volume have stressed the central importance of concepts in theories, case selection, and causal explanation. Much remains to be done to flesh out the characteristics of three-level concepts and how they fit into theories. For example, I have only outlined the prototypical necessary and sufficient condition and family resemblance structures. Clearly, hybrid structures could be built and other modeling techniques chosen (instead of fuzzy logic and set theory). I hope the analysis of concepts such as democracy, welfare state, interstate crisis, corporatism, and social revolution helps students and scholars alike recognize various concept structures in the work they read and helps them produce better and more valid concepts. Without valid concepts, our theories have little value.

* References *

Achen, C., and D. Snidal. 1989. Rational deterrence theory and comparative case studies. *World Politics* 41:143–69.

Adcock, R. 1998. What is a "concept"? Paper presented at the annual meetings of the American Political Science Association.

Adcock, R., and D. Collier. 2001. Measurement validity: A shared standard for qualitative and quantitative research. *American Political Science Review* 95:529–46.

Agresti, A., and B. Finlay. 1997. *Statistical methods for the social sciences,* 3rd edition. Englewood Cliffs, N.J.: Prentice-Hall.

Alvarez, M., et al. 1996. Classifying political regimes. *Studies in Comparative International Development* 31:3–36.

Amenta, E. 2003. Development of social policy. In J. Mahoney and D. Rueschemeyer (eds.) *Comparative historical analysis in the social sciences.* Cambridge: Cambridge University Press.

Amenta, E., B. Carruthers, and Y. Zylan. 1992. A hero for the aged? The Townsend Movement, the political mediation model, and U.S. old-age policy, 1934–1950. *American Journal of Sociology* 98:308–39.

Amenta, E., and J. Poulsen. 1996. Social politics in context: The institutional politics theory and social spending at the end of the New Deal. *Social Forces* 75:33–60.

American Psychiatric Association. 1994. *Diagnostic and statistical manual of mental disorders (DSM-IV),* 4th edition. Washington D.C.: American Psychiatric Association.

Arat, Z. 1991. *Democracy and human rights in developing countries.* Boulder, Colo.: Lynne Rienner.

Babbie, E. 2001. *The practice of social research,* 9th edition. Belmont, N.Y.: Wadsworth.

Bailey, K. 1973. Monothetic and polythetic typologies and their relation to conceptualization, measurement and scaling. *American Sociological Review* 38:18–33.

Banfield, E. 1958. *The moral basis of a backward society.* New York: Free Press.

Barbieri, K. 1996. Economic interdependence: A path to peace or a source of interstate conflict? *Journal of Peace Research* 33:29–49.

———. 2002. *Liberal illusion: Does trade promote peace?* Ann Arbor: University of Michigan Press.

Barbieri, K., and G. Schneider. 1999. Globalization and peace: Assessing new directions in the study of trade and conflict. *Journal of Peace Research* 36:387–404.

Bartels, L. 1996. Pooling disparate observations. *American Journal of Political Science* 40:905–42.

Bates, R. 1988. *Toward a political economy of development: A rational choice perspective.* Berkeley: University of California Press.

Beck, N., J. Katz, and R. Tucker. 1998. Taking time seriously: Time-series–cross-section analysis with a binary dependent variable. *American Journal of Political Science* 42:1260–88.

Beckner, M. 1959. *The biological way of thought.* New York: Columbia University Press.

Bendor, J. 1985. *Parallel systems: Redundancy in government.* Berkeley: University of California Press.

Bendor, J., T. Moe, and K. Shotts. 2001. Recycling the garbage can: An assessment of the research program. *American Political Science Review* 95:169–90.

Bennett, D., and A. Stam. 2000. EUGene: A conceptual manual. *International Interactions* 26:179–204.

Blake, C., and J. Adolino. 2001. The enactment of national health insurance: A Boolean analysis of twenty advanced industrial countries. *Journal of Health Politics, Policy and Law* 26:679–708.

Blalock, H. 1964. *Causal inferences in nonexperimental research.* Chapel Hill: University of North Carolina Press.

———. 1968. The measurement problem: A gap between the languages of theory and research. In H. Blalock and A. Blalock (eds.) *Methodology in social research.* New York: McGraw-Hill.

———. 1979. The Presidential Address: Measurement and conceptualization problems: The major obstacle to integrating theory and research. *American Sociological Review* 44:881–94.

———. 1982. *Conceptualization and measurement in the social sciences.* Beverly Hills, Calif.: Sage Publications.

Bollen, K. 1980. Issues in the comparative measurement of political democracy. *American Sociological Review* 45:370–90.

———. 1989. *Structural equations with latent variables.* New York: John Wiley & Sons.

———. 1991. Political democracy: conceptual and measurement traps. In A. Inkeles (ed.) *On measuring democracy: Its consequences and concomitants.* Bowling Green, Ohio: Transaction Books.

———. 1993. Liberal democracy: Validity and method factors in cross-national measures. *American Journal of Political Science* 37: 1207–30.

———. 2002. Latent variables in psychology and social sciences. *Annual Review of Psychology* 53:605–34.

Bollen, K., and B. Grandjean. 1981. The dimension(s) of democracy: Further issues in the measurement and effects of political democracy. *American Sociological Review* 46:651–59.

Bollen, K., and R. Lennox. 1991. Conventional wisdom on measurement: a structural equation perspective. *Psychological Bulletin* 110:305–14.

Bollen, K., and K. Ting. 2000. A tetrad test for causal indicators. *Psychological Methods* 5:3–22.

Borges, J. 1964. *Other inquisitions, 1937–1952.* Austin: University of Texas Press.

Bowman, K., F. Lehoucq, and J. Mahoney. 2005. Measuring political democracy: Case expertise, data adequacy, and Central America. *Comparative Political Studies* 8:939–70.

Brady, H., and D. Collier (eds.). 2004. *Rethinking social inquiry: Diverse tools, shared standards.* New York: Rowman & Littlefield.

Braumoeller, B. 2003. Causal complexity and the study of politics. *Political Analysis* 11:209–33.

Braumoeller, B., and G. Goertz. 2000. The methodology of necessary conditions. *American Journal of Political Science* 44:844–58.

———. 2002. Watching your posterior: Comment on Seawright. *Political Analysis* 10:198–203.

Brecher, M. 1993. *Crises in world politics: Theory and reality.* New York: Pergamon Press.

Brecher, M., and P. James. 1989. Severity and importance of third world crises: Middle East and Africa. In M. Brecher and J. Wilkenfeld (eds.) *Crisis, conflict and instability.* New York: Pergamon Press.

Brecher, M., and J. Wilkenfeld. 1997. *A study of crisis.* Ann Arbor: University of Michigan Press.

Brecher, M., J. Wilkenfeld, and S. Moser. 1988. *Crises in the twentieth century.* New York: Pergamon Press.

Brecher, M., and J. Wilkenfeld (eds.). 1989. *Crisis, conflict and instability.* New York: Pergamon Press.

Bremer, S. 1992. Dangerous dyads: Interstate war, 1816–1965. *Journal of Conflict Resolution* 36:309–41.

Brown, R. 1965. *Social psychology.* New York: Free Press.

Bueno de Mesquita, B. 1981. *The war trap.* New Haven, Conn.: Yale University Press.

———. 1985. The war trap revisited: A revised expected utility model. *American Political Science Review* 79:156–77.

Burawoy, M. 1989. Two methods in search of science: Skocpol versus Trotsky. *Theory and Society* 18:759–805.

Burger, T. 1987. *Max Weber's theory of concept formation: History, laws, and ideal types.* Durham, N.C.: Duke University Press.

Cameron, D. 1984. Social democracy, corporatism, labor quiescence, and the representation of economic interests in advanced capitalist societies. In J. Goldthorpe (ed.) *Order and conflict in contemporary capitalism.* Oxford: Oxford University Press.

Carment, D., and P. James. 1995. Internal constraints and interstate ethnic conflict: Toward a crisis-based assessment of irredentism. *Journal of Conflict Resolution* 39:82–109.

Carmines, E., and E. Zeller. 1979. *Reliability and validity assessment.* Newbury Park, Calif.: Sage Publications.

Chan, S. 1984. Mirror, mirror on the wall. . . . Are the freer countries more pacific? *Journal of Conflict Resolution* 28:617–48.

Chapin, F. 1939. Definition of definitions of concepts. *Social Forces* 18:153–60.

Cioffi-Revilla, C. 1998. *Politics and uncertainty: Theory, models and applications.* Cambridge: Cambridge University Press.

Cioffi-Revilla, C., and H. Starr. 2003. Opportunity, willingness, and political uncertainty: Theoretical foundations of politics. In G. Goertz and H. Starr (eds.) *Necessary conditions: Theory, methodology, and applications.* New York: Rowman & Littlefield.

Clark, D., and T. Nordstrom. 2003. Risky inference: Unobserved treatment effects in conflict studies. *International Studies Quarterly* 47: 417–29.

Clark, D., and P. Regan. 2003. Opportunities to fight: A statistical technique for modeling unobservable phenomena. *Journal of Conflict Resolution* 47: 94–115.

Clarke, K. 2002. The reverend and the ravens: Comment on Seawright. *Political Analysis* 10:194–97.

Cohen, B. 1989. *Developing sociological knowledge: Theory and method.* Chicago: Nelson-Hall.

Cohen, M., J. March, and J. Olson. 1972. A garbage can model of organizational choice. *Administrative Science Quarterly* 17:1–25.

Cohen, M., and E. Nagel. 1934. *An introduction to logic and scientific method.* New York: Harcourt, Brace.

Cohen, R. 1994. Pacific unions: A reappraisal of the theory that "democracies do not go to war with each other." *British Journal of International Studies* 20:207–23.

Cohen, Y., and F. Pavoncello. 1987. Corporatism and pluralism: A critique of Schmitter's typology. *British Journal of Political Science* 17:117–22.

Colaresi, M., and W. Thompson. 2002. Strategic rivalries, protracted conflict, and crisis escalation. *Journal of Peace Research* 39:263–87.

Collier, D. 1995. Trajectory of a concept: "corporatism" in the study of Latin American politics. In P. Smith (ed.) *Latin America in comparative perspective: New approaches to methods and analysis.* Boulder, Colo.: Westview Press.

Collier, D., and R. Adcock. 1999. Democracy and dichotomies. *Annual Review of Political Science* 2:537–65.

Collier, R., and D. Collier. 1991. *Shaping the political arena: Critical junctures, the labor movement, and regime dynamics in Latin America.* Princeton, N.J.: Princeton University Press.

Collier, D., and S. Levitsky. 1997. Democracy with adjectives: Conceptual innovation in comparative research. *World Politics* 49:430–51.

Collier, D., and J. Mahon. 1993. Conceptual "stretching" revisited: Adapting categories in comparative analysis. *American Political Science Review* 87: 845–55.

Collier, D., and J. Mahoney. 1996. Insights and pitfalls: Selection bias in qualitative research. *World Politics* 49:56–91.

Conybeare, J., J. Murdoch, and T. Sandler. 1994. Alternative collective goods models of military alliances: Theory and empirics. *Economic Inquiry* 33: 525–42.

Copi, I., and C. Cohen. 1990. *Introduction to logic,* 8th edition. London: Macmillan.

Coppedge, M., and W. Reinicke. 1991. Measuring polyarchy. In A. Inkeles (ed.) *On measuring democracy: Its consequences and concomitants.* Bowling Green, Ohio: Transaction Books.

Cornwell, D., and M. Colaresi. 2002. Holy trinities, rivalry termination, and conflict. *International Interactions* 28:325–54.

Cox, E. 1999. *The fuzzy systems handbook: A practioner's guide to building, using, and maintaining fuzzy systems,* 2nd edition. New York: Academic Press.

Cutright, P. 1963. National political development: Measurement and analysis. *American Sociological Review* 28:253–64.

Dahl, R. 1956. *A preface to democratic theory.* Chicago: University of Chicago Press.

———. 1971. *Polyarchy: Participation and opposition.* New Haven: Yale University Press.

———. 1989. *Democracy and its critics.* New Haven, Conn.: Yale University Press.

———. 1998. *On democracy.* New Haven, Conn.: Yale University Press.

Davidson, R., and J. MacKinnon. 1981. Several tests for model specification in the presence of alternative hypotheses. *Econometrica* 49: 781–93.

DeRouen, K. 1995. The indirect link: Politics, the economy, and the use of force. *Journal of Conflict Resolution* 39:671–95.

Diehl, P. 1992. What are they fighting for? The importance of issues in international conflict research. *Journal of Peace Research* 29:333–44.

Diehl, P., and G. Goertz. 2000. *War and peace in international rivalry.* Ann Arbor: University of Michigan Press.

Diehl, P., and P. Hensel. 1994. It takes two to tango: Nonmilitarized response in interstate disputes. *Journal of Conflict Resolution* 38:479–506.

Dion, D. 2003. Evidence and inference in the comparative case study. In G. Goertz and H. Starr (eds.) *Necessary conditions: Theory, methodology, and applications.* New York: Rowman & Littlefield.

273

DiRenzo, G. 1966. Conceptual definition in the behavioral sciences. In G. Di-Renzo (ed.) *Concepts, theory, and explanation in the behavioral sciences.* New York: Random House.

Dixon, W. 1993. Democracy and the management of international conflict. *Journal of Conflict Resolution* 37:42–68.

———. 1994. Democracy and the peaceful settlement of international conflict. *American Political Science Review* 88:14–32.

———. 1998. Dyads, disputes and the democratic peace. In M. Wolfson (ed.) *Political economy of war and peace.* Boston: Kluwer Academic Publishers.

Downing, B. 1992. *The military revolution and political change: Origins of democracy and autocracy in early modern Europe.* Princeton, N.J.: Princeton University Press.

Doyle, M. 1983a. Kant, liberal legacies, and foreign affairs, part I. *Philosophy and Public Affairs* 12:205–35.

———. 1983b. Kant, liberal legacies, and foreign affairs, part II. *Philosophy and Public Affairs* 12:323–53.

———. 1986. Liberalism and world politics. *American Political Science Review* 80:1151–69.

Dumont, R., and W. Wilson. 1967. Aspects of concept formation, explication, and theory construction in sociology. *American Sociological Review* 32:985–95.

Edwards J., and Bagozzi R. 2000. On the nature and direction of relationships between constructs and measures. *Psychological Methods* 5:155–74.

Elkins, Z. 2000. Gradations of democracy? Empirical tests of alternative conceptualizations. *American Journal of Political Science* 44:293–300.

Ertman, T. 1997. *Birth of the leviathan: Building states and regimes in medieval and early modern Europe.* Cambridge: Cambridge University Press.

Esping-Andersen, G. 1990. *The three worlds of welfare capitalism.* Cambridge: Polity Press.

Esping-Andersen, G., and W. Korpi. 1987. From poor relief to institutional welfare states: The development of Scandinavian social policy. In Erikson, R. et al. (eds.) *The Scandinavian model: welfare states and welfare research.* Armonk, N.Y.: M. E. Sharpe.

Fearon, J. 2002. Selection effects and deterrence. *International Interactions* 28:5–31.

Feaver, P., et al. 2000. Correspondence: Brother, can you spare a paradigm? (Or was anybody ever a realist?). *International Security* 25:165–93.

Foran, J. 1997. The comparative-historical sociology of Third World social revolutions: Why a few succeed, why most fail. In J. Foran (ed.) *Theorizing revolution.* London: Routledge.

Fortna, V. 2004. Does peacekeeping keep peace? International intervention and the duration of peace after civil war. *International Studies Quarterly* 48:269–92.

Gärdenfors, P. 2000. *Conceptual spaces: The geometry of thought.* Cambridge: MIT Press.

Gartzke, E., and Q. Li. 2003. Measure for measure: Concept operationalization and the trade independence–conflict debate. *Journal of Peace Research* 40:553–71.

Gastil, R. 1978–. *Freedom in the world.* New York: Freedom House.

Geddes, B. 1990. How the cases you choose affect the answers you get: selection bias in comparative politics. In J. Stimson (ed.) *Political analysis,* vol. 2. Ann Arbor: University of Michigan Press.

———. 2003. *Paradigms and sand castles: Theory building and research design in comparative politics.* Ann Arbor: University of Michigan Press.

Gelpi, C. 1997. Democratic diversions: Governmental structure and the externalization of domestic conflict. *Journal of Conflict Resolution* 41:255–82.

George, A., and A. Bennett. 2005. *Case studies and theory development.* Cambridge: MIT Press.

Gereffi, G., and D. Wyman (eds.). 1990. *Manufacturing miracles: Paths of industrialization in Latin America and East Asia.* Princeton, N.J.: Princeton University Press.

Gerring, J. 1997. Ideology: A definitional analysis. *Political Research Quarterly* 50:957–94.

———. 2001. *Social science methodology: A criterial framework.* Cambridge: Cambridge University Press.

———. 2004. What is a case study and what is it good for? *American Political Science Review* 98:341–54.

Gibler, D. 1999. An extension of the Correlates of War formal alliance data set, 1648–1815. *International Interactions* 25:1–28.

Gibler, D., and M. Sarkees. 2004. Measuring alliances: The Correlates of War formal interstate alliance dataset, 1816–2000. *Journal of Peace Research* 41: 211–22.

Gibler, D., and J. Vasquez. 1998. Uncovering the dangerous alliances, 1495–1980. *International Studies Quarterly* 42:785–807.

Gleditsch, K. 2002. Expanded trade and GDP data. *Journal of Conflict Resolution* 46:712–24.

Gleditsch, K., and M. Ward. 1997. Double take: A reexamination of democracy and autocracy in modern politics. *Journal of Conflict Resolution* 41:361–83.

———. 1999. A revised list of independent states since the Congress of Vienna. *International Interactions* 25:393–413.

Gleditsch, N., and H. Hegre. 1997. Peace and democracy: Three levels of analysis. *Journal of Peace Research* 41:283–310.

Gleditsch, N., C. Metelits, and H. Strand. 2003. Posting your data: Will you be scooped or will you be famous? *International Studies Perspectives* 4:89–97.

Glymour, C. 1997. A review of recent work on the foundations of cause inference. In V. McKim and S. Turner (eds.) *Causality in crisis? Statistical methods and the search for causal knowledge in the social sciences.* Notre Dame: Unversity of Notre Dame Press.

Gochman, C., and Z. Maoz. 1984. Militarized interstate disputes, 1816–1976: Procedures, patterns and insights. *Journal of Conflict Resolution* 28:585–615.

Goertz, G. 2003a. The substantive importance of necessary condition hypotheses. In G. Goertz and H. Starr (eds.) *Necessary conditions: Theory, methodology, and applications.* New York: Rowman & Littlefield.

———. 2003b. *International norms and decision making: A punctuated equilibrium model.* New York: Rowman & Littlefield.

———. 2004. Assessing the importance of necessary or sufficient conditions in fuzzy-set social science. Manuscript. University of Arizona.

———. 2005. Necessary condition hypotheses as deterministic or probabilistic: Does it matter? *Qualitative Methods: Newsletter of the America Political Science Association Organized Section on Qualitative Methods* 3:23–28.

Goertz, G., and P. Diehl. 1986. Measuring military allocations: A comparison of different approaches. *Journal of Conflict Resolution* 30:553–81.

———. 1992. *Territorial change and international conflict.* London: Routledge.

Goertz, G., B. Jones, and P. Diehl. 2005. Maintenance processes in international rivalries. *Journal of Conflict Resolution* 49:742–69.

Goldstone, J. 1990. *Revolution and rebellion in the early modern world.* Berkeley: University of California Press.

Goldstone, J., et al. 2000. State failure task force report: Phase III findings. Manuscript. University of Maryland.

Goodman, N. 1972. Seven strictures on similarity. In *Problems and projects.* Indianapolis: Bobbs Merrill.

Goodwin, J. 2001. *No other way out: States and revolutionary movements, 1945–1991.* Cambridge: Cambridge University Press.

Gornick, J., M. Meyers, and K. Ross. 1997. Supporting the employment of mothers: Policy variation across fourteen welfare states. *Journal of European Social Policy* 7:45–70.

Gowa, J. 1999. *Ballots and bullets: The elusive democratic peace.* Princeton, N.J.: Princeton University Press.

Gunther, R., and L. Diamond. 2003. Species of political parties: A new typology. *Party Politics* 9:167–99.

Gurr, T. 1974. Persistence and change in political systems 1800–1971. *American Political Science Review* 68:1482–504.

Gurr, T., K. Jaggers, and W. Moore. 1990. The transformation of the Western state: The growth of democracy, autocracy, and state power since 1800. *Studies in Comparative International Development* 25:73–108.

Hadenius, A. 1992. *Democracy and development.* Cambridge: Cambridge University Press.

Haggard, S. 1990. *Pathways from the periphery: The politics of growth in the newly industrializing countries.* Ithaca, N.Y.: Cornell University Press.

Hall, P. 2003. Aligning ontology and methodology in comparative research. In J. Mahoney and D. Rueschemeyer (eds.) *Comparative historical analysis in the social sciences.* Cambridge: Cambridge University Press.

Hampton, J. 1995. Testing the prototype theory of concepts. *Journal of Memory and Language* 34:686–708.

Harff, B. 2003. No lessons learned from the Holocaust? Assessing risks of genocide and political mass murder since 1955. *American Political Science Review* 97:57–73.

Harré, R., and E. Madden. 1975. *Causal powers: A theory of natural necessity.* Oxford: Basil Blackwell.

Harvey, F. 2003. Practicing coercion: Revisiting successes and failures using Boolean logic and comparative methods. In G. Goertz and H. Starr (eds.) *Necessary conditions: Theory, methodology, and applications.* New York: Rowman & Littlefield.

Haydu, J. 1998. Making use of the past: Time periods as cases to compare and as sequences of problem solving. *American Journal of Sociology* 104:339–71.

Heckman, S. 1983. *Weber, the ideal type, and contemporary social theory.* Notre Dame: University of Notre Dame Press.

Hegre, H. 2000. Development and the liberal peace: What does it take to be a trading state? *Journal of Peace Research* 37:5–30.

Hempel, C. 1945. Studies in the logic of confirmation I and II. *Mind* 54:1–16, 97–121.

———. 1952. Fundamentals of concept formation in empirical science. In *International encyclopedia of unified science,* vol. 2, no. 7. Chicago: University of Chicago Press.

———. 1965. Typological methods in the natural and social sciences. In *Aspects of scientific explanation.* New York.: Free Press.

———. 1965. *Aspects of scientific explanation.* New York: Free Press.

———. 1966. *Philosophy of natural science.* Englewood Cliffs, N.J.: Prentice-Hall.

Henderson, E. 2002. *Democracy and war: The end of an illusion?* Boulder, Colo.: Lynne Rienner.

Hermann, C. 1969. International crisis as situational variable. In J. Rosenau (ed.) *International politics and foreign policy: A reader in research and theory,* revised edition. New York: Free Press.

Hewitt, J. 2003. Dyadic processes and international crises. *Journal of Conflict Resolution* 47:669–92.

———. 2005. A crisis-density formulation for identifying rivalries. *Journal of Peace Research* 42:183–200.

Hewitt, J., and J. Wilkenfeld. 1996. Democracies in international crisis. *International Interactions* 22:123–42.

———. 1999. One-sided crises in the international system. *Journal of Peace Research* 36:309–23.

Hewitt, J., and G. Young. 2001. Assessing the statistical rarity of wars between democracies. *International Interactions* 27:327–51.

Hicks, A. 1988. National collective action and economic performance: A review article. *International Studies Quarterly* 32:131–53.

———. 1999. *Social democracy & welfare capitalism: A century of income security politics.* Ithaca, N.Y.: Cornell University Press.

Hicks, A., J. Misra, and T. Ng. 1995. The programmatic emergence of the social security state. *American Sociological Review* 60:329–49.

Holsti, K. 1991. *Peace and war: Armed conflicts and international order, 1648–1989.* Cambridge: Cambridge University Press.

Huber, E., and J. Stephens. 2001. *Development and crisis of the welfare state: Parties and policies in global markets.* Chicago: University of Chicago Press.

Huth, P., and T. Allee. 2002. Domestic political accountability and the escalation and settlement of international disputes. *Journal of Conflict Resolution* 46:754–90.

Inkeles, A. (ed.). 1991. *On measuring democracy: Its consequences and concomitants.* Bowling Green, Ohio: Transaction Books.

International Labor Organization. 1949–. *The cost of social security.* Geneva: ILO.

Jackman, R. 1973. On the relation of economic development to democratic performance. *American Journal of Political Science* 17: 611–21.

Jacoby, W. 2000. *Imitation and politics: Redesigning modern Germany.* Ithaca, N.Y.: Cornell University Press.

Jaggers, K., and T. Gurr. 1995. Tracking democracy's third wave with the Polity III data. *Journal of Peace Research* 32:469–82.

Jones, D., S. Bremer, and J. Singer. 1996. Militarized interstate disputes, 1816–1992: Rationale, coding rules, and empirical patterns. *Conflict Management and Peace Science* 15:163–212.

Jungblutt, B., and R. Stoll. 2002. The liberal peace and conflictive interactions: The onset of militarized disputes, 1950–1978. *Journal of Peace Research* 39:527–46.

Karl, T. 1990. Dilemmas of democratization in Latin America. *Comparative Politics* 23:1–21.

Katzenstein, P. 1985. *Small states in world markets: Industrial policy in Europe.* Ithaca, N.Y.: Cornell University Press.

Kegley, C., and R. Skinner. 1976. The case-for-analysis problem. In J. Rosenau (ed.) *In search of global patterns.* New York: Free Press.

Keil, F., and N. Batterman. 1984. A characteristic-to-defining shift in the development of word meaning. *Journal of Verbal Learning and Verbal Behavior* 23:221–36.

King, G., R. Keohane, and S. Verba. 1994. *Designing social inquiry: Scientific inference in qualitative research.* Princeton, N.J.: Princeton University Press.

King, G., and L. Zeng. 2001. Logistic regression in rare events data. *Political Analysis* 9:137–63.

Kingdon, J. 1984. *Agendas, alternatives, and public policies.* Boston: Little, Brown.

Kinsella, D., and B. Russett. 2002. Conflict emergence and escalation in interactive dyads. *Journal of Politics* 64:1045–68.

Kiser, E. 1996. The revival of narrative in sociology: What rational choice theory can contribute. *Politics and Society* 24:249–71.

Kiser, E., K. Drass, and W. Brustein. 1995. Ruler autonomy and war in early modern western Europe. *International Studies Quarterly* 39:109–38.

Kiser, E., and M. Levi. 1996. Using counterfactuals in historical analysis: Theories of revolution. In P. Tetlock and A. Belkin (eds.) *Counterfactual thought experiments in world politics: Logical, methodological, and psychological perspectives.* Princeton, N.J.: Princeton University Press.

Klein, J., G. Goertz, and P. Diehl. 2004. The new rivalry data set: Procedures and patterns. Paper presented at the annual meetings of the Peace Science Society (International).

Kosko, B. 1993. *Fuzzy thinking: The new science of fuzzy logic.* New York: Hyperion.

Kotowski, C. 1984. Revolution. In G. Sartori (ed.) *Social science concepts: A systematic analysis.* Beverly Hills, Calif.: Sage Publications.

Kroeber, A. 1948. *Anthropology: Race, language, culture, psychology, pre-history.* New York: Harcourt, Brace, and Co.

Kugler, J., and D. Lemke (eds.). 1996. *Parity and war: Evaluations and extensions of* The War Ledger. Ann Arbor: University of Michigan Press.

Kurtz, M. 2000. Understanding peasant revolution: From concept to theory and case. *Theory and Society* 29:93–124.

Lai, B., and D. Reiter. 2000. Democracy, political similarity, and international alliances, 1816–1992. *Journal of Conflict Resolution* 44:203–27.

Lakoff, G. 1973. Hedges: A study of meaning criteria and the logic of fuzzy concepts. *Journal of Philosophical Logic* 2:458–508.

———. 1987. *Women, fire and dangerous things: What categories reveal about the mind.* Chicago: University of Chicago Press.

Lakoff, G., and M. Johnson. 1980. *Metaphors we live by.* Chicago: Chicago University Press.

Landau, M. 1969. Redundancy, rationality, and the problem of duplication and overlap. *Public Administration Review* 29:346–58.

———. 1972. *Political theory and political science: Studies in the methodology of political inquiry.* New York: Macmillan.

———. 1973. On the concept of a self-correcting organization. *Public Administration Review* 33:533–42.

Lasswell, H., and A. Kaplan. 1950. *Power and society: A framework for political inquiry.* New Haven, Conn.: Yale University Press.

Lazarsfeld, P. 1966. Concept formation and measurement in the behavioral sciences: Some historical observations. In G. DiRenzo (ed.) *Concepts, theory, and explanation in the behavioral sciences.* New York: Random House.

———. 1972. *Qualitative analysis: Historical and critical essays.* Boston: Allyn and Bacon.

Lazarsfeld, P., and A. Barton. 1951. Qualitative measurement in the social sciences: Classification, typologies, and indices. In D. Lerner and H. Lasswell (eds.) *The policy sciences: Recent developments in scope and method.* Stanford: Stanford University Press.

Leeds, B. 1999. Domestic political institutions, credible commitments, and international cooperation. *American Journal of Political Science* 43: 979–1002.

Legro, J., and A. Moravcsik. 1999. Is anybody still a realist? *International Security* 24:5–55.

Lehmbruch, G. 1977. Liberal corporatism and party government. *Comparative Political Studies* 10:91–126.

Lemke, D. 1995. The tyranny of distance: Redefining relevant dyads. *International Interactions* 21:23–38.

Lemke, D., and W. Reed. 1996. Regime types and status quo evaluations: Power transition theory and the democractic peace. *International Interactions* 22:143–64.

———. 2001. The relevance of politically relevant dyads. *Journal of Conflict Resolution* 45:126–45.

———. 2001. War and rivalry among great powers. *American Journal of Political Science* 45:457–69.

Leng, R. 1983. When will they ever learn? Coercive bargaining in recurrent crises. *Journal of Conflict Resolution* 27:379–419.

Lichbach, M. 1995. *The rebel's dilemma.* Ann Arbor: University of Michigan Press.

Linz, J., and A. Stepan. 1996. *Problems of democratic transition and consolidation: Southern Europe, South America, and post-communist Europe.* Baltimore: Johns Hopkins University Press.

Lipset, S. 1960. *Political man: The social bases of politics.* New York: Doubleday.

———. 1977. Why no socialism in the United States? In S. Bialer and S. Sluzar (eds.) *Radicalism in the contemporary age.* Boulder, Colo.: Westview Press.

Locke, J. 1959 (1690). *An essay concerning human understanding.* New York: Dover.

Locke, R., and K. Thelen. 1995. Apples and oranges revisited: Contextualized comparisons and the study of comparative labor politics. *Politics and Society* 23:337–67.

Luebbert, G. 1987. Social foundations of political order in interwar period. *World Politics* 39:449–78.

Magagna, V. 1991. *Communities of grain: Rural rebellion in comparative perspective.* Ithaca, N.Y.: Cornell University Press.

Mahoney, J. 1999. Nominal, ordinal, and narrative appraisal in macrocausal analysis. *American Journal of Sociology* 104:1154–96.

Mahoney, J., and D. Rueschemeyer (eds.). 2003. *Comparative historical analysis in the social sciences.* Cambridge: Cambridge University Press.

Mainwaring, S., D. Brinks, and A. Pérez-Liñán. 2001. Classifying political regimes in Latin America, 1945–1999. *Studies in Comparative International Development* 36:37–65.

Mansbach, R., and J. Vasquez. 1981. *In search of theory: A new paradigm for global politics.* New York: Columbia University Press.

Mansfield, E., and J. Pevehouse. 2000. Trade blocs, trade flows, and international conflict. *International Organization* 54:775–808.

Mansfield, E., and B. Pollins (eds.). 2003. *Economic interdependence and international conflict: New perspectives on an enduring debate.* Ann Arbor: University of Michigan Press.

Maoz, Z. 1996. *Domestic sources of global change.* Ann Arbor: University of Michigan Press.

Maoz, Z., and B. Russett. 1993. Normative and structural causes of democratic peace, 1946–1986. *American Political Science Review* 87:624–38.

Marks, G. 1986. Neocorporatism, and incomes policy in Western Europe and North America. *Comparative Politics* 18:253–77.

Marshall, M., and K. Jaggers. 2002. Polity IV Project: Political regime characteristics and transitions, 1800–1999: dataset users manual. Manuscript. University of Maryland.

Mazur, A., and D. Stetson. 2003. Quantifying complex concepts: The case of the *women's movement* in the RNGS project. *APSA-CP: Newsletter of the APSA Comparative Politics Section* 14:11–14.

McMillan, S. 1997. Interdependence and conflict. *Mershon International Studies Review* 41:33–58.

Meehan, E. 1971. *The foundations of political analysis: Empirical and normative.* Homewood, Ala.: Dorsey Press.

Miller, G., and P. Johnson-Laird. 1976. *Language and perception.* Cambridge: Harvard University Press.

Moore, B. 1966. *The social origins of dictatorship and democracy: Lord and peasant in the making of the modern world.* Boston: Beacon Press.

Morrow, J. 1989. Capabilities, uncertainty, and resolve: A limited information model of crisis bargaining. *American Journal of Political Science* 32:941–72.

Most, B., and H. Starr. 1984. International relations theory, foreign policy substitutability, and "nice" laws. *World Politics* 36:383–406.

———. 1989. *Inquiry, logic, and international politics*. Columbia: University of South Carolina Press.

Mousseau, M. 1997. Democracy and militarized interstate collaboration. *Journal of Peace Research* 34:73–87.

———. 2000. Market prosperity, democratic consolidation, and democratic peace. *Journal of Conflict Resolution* 44:472–507.

Munck, G., and J. Verkuilen. 2002. Conceptualizing and measuring democracy: evaluating alternative indices. *Comparative Political Studies* 35:5–34.

———. 2003. Bringing measurement back in: Methodological foundations of the Electoral Democracy Index. Paper presented at the annual meetings of the American Political Science Association.

Murphy, G. 2002. *The big book of concepts*. Cambridge: MIT Press.

Nussbaum, M. 1992. Human functioning and social justice: In defense of Aristotelian essentialism. *Political Theory* 20:202–46.

O'Connor, J., A. Orloff, and S. Shaver. 1999. *States, markets, families: Gender, liberalism, and social policy in Australia, Canada, Great Britain, and the United States*. Cambridge: Cambridge University Press.

Oneal, J. 2003. Measuring interdependence and its pacific benefits: A reply to Gartzke & Li. *Journal of Peace Research* 40:721–25.

Oneal, J., and B. Russett. 1997. The classical liberals were right: Democracy, interdependence, and conflict, 1950–1985. *International Studies Quarterly* 41:267–93.

———. 1999. Assessing the liberal peace with alternative specifications: Trade still reduces conflict. *Journal of Peace Research* 36:423–42.

———. 1999. Is the liberal peace just an artifact of Cold War interests? Assessing recent critiques. *International Interactions* 25:213–42.

Organski, A., and J. Kugler. 1980. *The war ledger*. Chicago: University of Chicago Press.

Orloff, A. 1993. Gender and the social rights of citizenship: the comparative analysis of gender relations and welfare states. *American Sociological Review* 58:303–28.

———. 1996. Gender in the welfare state. *Annual Review of Sociology* 22:51–78.

Osherson, D., and E. Smith. 1981. On the adequacy of prototype theory as a theory of concepts. *Cognition* 9:35–58.

———. 1982. Gradedness and conceptual conjunction. *Cognition* 12:299–318.

Ostrom, E. 1991. *Governing the commons: The evolution of institutions for collective action*. Cambridge: Cambridge University Press.

———. 1998. A behavioral approach to the rational choice theory of collective action. *American Political Science Review* 92:1–22.

Paige, J. 1975. *Agrarian revolution: Social movements and export agriculture in the underdeveloped world*. New York: Free Press.

Palmer, G., and A. Bhandari. 2000. The investigation of substitutability in foreign policy. *Journal of Conflict Resolution* 44:3–10.

Panitch, L. 1980. Recent theorizations of corporatism: Reflections on a growth industry. *British Journal of Sociology* 31:159–87.

Papineau, D. 1976. Ideal types and empirical theories. *The British Journal for the Philosophy of Science* 27:137–46.

Pawson, R. 1989. *A measure for measures: A manifesto for empirical sociology.* London: Routledge.

Pevehouse, J. 2002. Democracy from the outside-in? International organization and democratization. *International Organization* 56: 515–49.

———. 2004. Interdependence theory and the measurement of international conflict. *Journal of Politics* 66:247–66.

Pierson, P. 2000. Three worlds of welfare state research. *Comparative Political Studies* 33:791–821.

Popkin, S. 1979. *The rational peasant: The political economy of rural society in Vietnam.* Berkeley: University of California Press.

Przeworski, A., et al. 2000. *Democracy and development: Political institutions and well-being in the world, 1950–1990.* Cambridge: Cambridge University Press.

Przeworski, A., and H. Tuene. 1970. *The logic of comparative social inquiry.* New York: John Wiley and Sons.

Ragin, C. 1987. *The comparative method: Moving beyond qualitative and quantitative strategies.* Berkeley: University of California Press.

———. 2000. *Fuzzy-set social science.* Chicago: University of Chicago Press.

Ray, J. 1993. Wars between democracies: Rare or nonexistent? *International Interactions* 18:251–76.

Redfield, R. 1960. *The little community, and peasant society and culture.* Chicago: University of Chicago Press.

Reed, W. 2000. A unified statistical model of conflict onset and escalation. *American Journal of Political Science* 44:84–93.

Reed, W. (ed.). 2002. Managing selection effects on research in world politics. *International Interactions* 28:1–115.

Reiter, D., and A. Stam. 1998. Democracy, war initiation, and victory. *American Political Science Review* 92:377–89.

Rioux, J.-S. 1998. A crisis-based evaluation of the democratic peace proposition. *Canadian Journal of Political Science* 31:263–83.

Robinson, R. 1950. *Definition.* Oxford: Oxford University Press.

Rosch, E., et al. 1976. Basic objects in natural categories. *Cognitive Psychology* 8:382–439.

Rousseau, D., C. Gelpi, D. Reiter, and P. Huth. 1996. Assessing the dyadic nature of the democratic peace, 1918–88. *American Political Science Review* 90: 512–33.

Rummel, R. 1985. Libertarian propositions on violence within and between nations: A test against published research results. *Journal of Conflict Resolution* 29:449–55.

Russett, B. 1995. The democratic peace: "and yet it moves." *International Security* 19:164–75.

Russett, B., and J. Oneal. 2001. *Triangulating peace: Democracy, interdependence, and international organizations.* New York: W. W. Norton.

Sambanis, N. 2004. What is civil war? Conceptual and empirical complexities of an operational definition. *Journal of Conflict Resolution* 48:814–58.

Sample, S. 2002. The outcomes of military buildups: Minor states vs. major powers. *Journal of Peace Research* 39:669–91.

Sartori, G. 1970. Concept misformation in comparative politics. *American Political Science Review* 64:1033–53.

———. 1984. Guidelines for concept analysis. In G. Sartori (ed.) *Social science concepts: A systematic analysis.* Beverly Hills, Calif.: Sage Publications.

Sartori, G., F. Riggs, and H. Teune. 1975. *The tower of Babel: On the definition and analysis of concepts in the social sciences.* Pittsburgh: International Studies Association.

Schmitter, P. 1979. Still the century of corporatism? In P. Schmitter and G. Lehmbruch (eds.) *Trends toward corporatist intermediation.* Newbury Park, Calif.: Sage Publications.

———. 1982. Reflections on where the theory of neo-corporatism has gone and where the praxis of neo-corporitism may be going. In G. Lehmbruch and P. Schmitter (eds.) *Patterns in corporatist policy- making.* Newbury Park, Calif.: Sage Publications.

Schmitter, P., and T. Karl. 1991. What democracy is ... and is not. *Journal of Democracy* 2:75–88.

Scott, J. 1976. *The moral economy of the peasant: Rebellion and subsistance in Southeast Asia.* New Haven: Yale University Press.

Seawright, J. 2002a. Testing for necessary and/or sufficient causation: Which cases are relevant? *Political Analysis* 10:178–193.

———. 2002b. What counts as evidence? Reply. *Political Analysis* 20:204–7.

Sekhon, J. 2004. Quality meets quantity: Case studies, conditional probability, and counterfactuals. *Perspectives on Politics* 2:281–93.

Selbin, E. 1993. *Modern Latin American revolutions.* Boulder, Colo.: Westview Press.

Sen, A. 1985. Well-being, agency and freedom: The Dewey Lectures 1984. *Journal of Philosophy* 82:169–221.

———. 1999. *Development as freedom.* New York: Anchor Books.

Senese, P. 1997. Between dispute and war: The effect of joint democracy on interstate conflict escalation. *Journal of Conflict Resolution* 59:1–27.

Senese, P., and J. Vasquez. 2003. A unified explanation of territorial conflict: Testing the impact of sampling bias, 1919–1992. *International Studies Quarterly* 47:275–98.

Shanin, T. 1971. Peasantry: Delineation of a sociological concept and a field of study. *Archives Européennes de Sociologie* 12:289–300.

Sherman, R. 2001. Democracy and trade conflict. *International Interactions* 27:1–28.

Siaroff, A. 1999. Corporatism in 24 industrial countries: Meaning and measurement. *European Journal of Political Research* 36:175–205.

Signorino, C. 1998. Strategic interaction and the statistical analysis of international conflict. *American Political Science Review* 93:279–97.

Signorino, C., and J. Ritter. 1999. Tau-b or not tau-b: Measuring the similarity of foreign policy positions. *International Studies Quarterly* 43:115–44.

Singer, J., and M. Small. 1972. *The wages of war, 1816–1965: A statistical handbook.* New York: John Wiley and Sons.

Skocpol, T. 1979. *States and social revolutions: A comparative analysis of France, Russia, and China.* Cambridge: Cambridge University Press.

———. 1984. Emerging agendas and recurrent strategies in historical sociology. In T. Skocpol (ed.) *Vision and method in historical sociology.* Cambridge: Cambridge University Press.

———. 1992. *Protecting soldiers and mothers: The political origins of social policy in the United States.* Cambridge: Harvard University Press.

Small, M., and J. D. Singer. 1969. Formal alliances, 1816–1965: An extension of the basic data. *Journal of Peace Research* 6:257–82.

———. 1982. *Resort to arms: International and civil wars, 1816–1980,* 2nd edition. Beverly Hills, Calif.: Sage Publications.

Smith, A. 1998. A summary of political selection: The effect of strategic choice of the escalation of international crises. *American Political Science Review* 42:698–701.

Smith, E., and D. Osherson. 1984. Conceptual combination with prototype concepts. *Cognitive Science* 8:337–61.

Smith, E., A. Patalano, and J. Jonides. 1998. Alternative strategies of categorization. *Cognition* 65:167–96.

Smithson, M. 1987. *Fuzzy set analysis for behavioral and social sciences.* New York: Springer Verlag.

Snow, D., and D. Cress. 2000. The outcomes of homeless mobilization: The influence of organization, disruption, political mediation, and framing. *American Journal of Sociology* 105:1063–1104.

Sobek, D. 2003. Regime type, preferences, and war in renaissance Italy. *Journal of Conflict Resolution* 47:204–25.

Stepan, A., and C. Skach. 1993. Constitutional frameworks and democratic consolidation: Parliamentarism versus presidentialism. *World Politics* 46:1–22.

Stinchcombe, A. 1968. *Constructing social theories.* New York: Harcourt, Brace & World.

———. 1978. *Theoretical methods in social history.* New York: Academic Press.

Stokke, O. 2004. Boolean analysis, mechanisms, and the effectiveness of international regimes. In A. Underdal and O. Young (eds.) *Regime consequences: Methodological challenges and research strategies.* Boston: Kluwer Academic Publishers.

Taylor, M. 1989. Structure, culture and action in the explanation of social change. *Politics and Society* 17:115–62.

Thompson, W. 1995. Principal rivalries. *Journal of Conflict Resolution* 39:195–223.

———. 2001. Identifying rivals and rivalries in world politics. *International Studies Quarterly* 45:557–86.

Thurston, L. 1935. *The vectors of mind; Multiple-factor analysis for the isolation of primary traits.* Chicago: University of Chicago Press.

Tsebelis, G. 1999. Veto players and law production in parliamentary democracies: an empirical analysis. *American Political Science Review* 93:591–608.

Tures, J., and P. Hensel. 2000. Measuring opportunity and willingness for conflict: A preliminary application to Central America and the Caribbean. Paper presented at the annual meetings of the American Political Science Association.

Tversky, A. 1977. Features of similarity. *Psychological Review* 84:327–52.

Vanhanen, T. 1990. *The process of democratization: A comparative study of 147 states 1980–88.* New York: Crane Russak.

Vasquez, J. 1993. *The war puzzle.* Cambridge: Cambridge University Press.

———. 2004. The probability of war, 1816–1992. *International Studies Quarterly* 48:1–27.

Velicer, W., and D. Jackson. 1990. Component analysis versus common factor analysis: Some issues in selecting an appropriate procedure. *Multivariate Behavioral Research* 25:1–28.

Waldner, D. 1999. *State building and late development.* Ithaca, N.Y.: Cornell University Press.

Walker, H., and B. Cohen. 1985. Scope statements: Imperatives for evaluating theories. *American Sociological Review* 50:288–301.

Wang, K. 1996. Presidential responses to foreign policy crises: Rational choice and domestic politics. *Journal of Conflict Resolution* 40:68–97.

Weart, S. 1998. *Never at war: Why democracies will not fight one another.* New Haven, Conn.: Yale University Press.

Weber, M. 1949. *Max Weber on the methodology of the social sciences.* New York: Free Press.

Weede, E. 1976. Overwhelming preponderance as a pacifying condition among contiguous Asian dyads, 1950–1969. *Journal of Conflict Resolution* 20:395–411.

———. 1989. Extended deterrence, superpower control, and militarized interstate disputes, 1962–76. *Journal of Peace Research* 26:7–17.

Wendt, A. 1998. On constitution and causation in international relations. *Review of International Studies* 24:101–17.

———. 1999. *Social theory of international politics.* Cambridge: Cambridge University Press.

White, H. 1980. A heteroskedasticity-consistent covariance matrix estimator and a direct test for heteroskedasticity. *Econometrica* 48: 817–38.

Wickham-Crowley, T. 1991. *Guerrillas and revolution in Latin America: A comparative study of insurgents and regimes since 1956.* Princeton, N.J.: Princeton University Press.

Wilkenfeld, J. 1991. Trigger-response transitions in foreign policy crises, 1929–1985. *Journal of Conflict Resolution* 35:143–69.

Williamson, P. 1989. *Corporatism in perspective: An introductory guide to corporatist theory.* Newbury Park, Calif.: Sage Publications.

Wittgenstein, L. 1953. *Philosophical investigations.* London: Macmillan.

Wolf, E. 1969. *Peasant wars of the twentieth century.* New York: Harper & Row.

Zannoni, P. 1978. The concept of elite. *European Journal of Political Research* 6:1–30.

Zelditch, M. 1971. Intelligible comparisons. In I. Vallier (ed.) *Comparative methods in sociology: Essays on trends and applications.* Berkeley: University of California Press.

✻ *Exercises and Web Site* ✻

A Web site accompanies this volume:

http://pup.princeton.edu/titles/8089.html

The main purpose of the site is to provide exercises related to the material covered in this book. These range from relatively simple exercises in the logic of necessary and sufficient conditions to suggestions for large-N data analyses. All the exercises draw on existing work and most cover topics of comparative politics and international relations that form the substance of the examples discussed in the chapters above. However, many exercises extend the examples discussed in the text and some deal with concepts and substantive areas that do not appear in the text. For purposes of length and readability I made a conscious decision to restrict the examples in the text; hence the exercises are the place to find other substantive illustrations and issues.

The web site also provides replication data sets for the various large-N analyses in various chapters. Since data sets are in relatively constant flux, these data sets should be used for replication and exercise purposes only. Check the relevant web sites for current versions of the data sets used.

These exercises are a continuation and extension of the text itself. Material that might have appeared in a paragraph or a footnote has often been changed into an exercise. Particularly, commentary on relevant parts of various literatures appears in this form.

Often the best way to learn is by doing. These exercises provide instructors, students, and readers with an occasion to test their (and my) comprehension of the issues involved in constructing concepts. For example, the exercise of drawing figures corresponding to three-level concepts or two-level theories often reveals important ambiguities in the concept or theory.

These exercises provide readers and instructors with ideas about using other data sets or concepts as a means of reinforcing or extending the various analyses presented in this book. If possible, links to the data sets themselves are provided. In addition, many of the exercises refer to existing work. When possible I have chosen articles that are available electronically, normally via library subscriptions.

Answers to the exercises are available from me via email request. Normally, these will be given only to instructors; exceptions under reasonable circumstances will be made.

These exercises are a work in progress, an experiment. While web sites and exercises are normal for textbooks, they are rare to nonexistent for books that present novel ideas and methodologies. In particular, the use of exercises is rare in qualitative methods books of any sort. I welcome feedback on the whole enterprise.

Finally, I welcome suggestions for new exercises or variations on existing ones. If you would like to be kept informed of changes to the exercises (i.e., additions or corrections), please email me (ggoertz@u.arizona.edu) and I will put you on the emailing list.